'*Teaching Freud Now: Time Traveling Dialogues* is an outstanding book, which should be read by everyone teaching psychoanalytic concepts and practice. With a focus on Freud's papers, Dr. Roussel invites his students to join him in imagining Freud's search for greater understanding of his patients, a search reflected in the changes in Freud's thinking from one paper to another. One senses in the transcript of the classes, the excitement generated as the students see the similarities between their struggles and Freud's. Dr. Roussel's style of teaching leads not to an idealized theory (which for too many analyses results in a therapeutic impasse) but to an experience that increases the students' comfort in closely examining their own work. Essentially, the consideration of Freud's struggles to find useful ways to help his patients encourages students, candidates and graduates alike, to sharpen their own thinking about their patients and themselves.

Practicing psychoanalysis is difficult; one is constantly dealing with uncertainty. Dr. Roussel's willingness to explore his own analytic work without any defensiveness or attempt to appear invulnerable leads to the students' increasing ability to do the same. As he says "I tried to convey that struggle, tension and uncertainty are inherent to the process of learning psychoanalysis…" This book is a superb guide for all forms of teaching…not just for teaching Freud or psychoanalysis.'

Judith Fingert Chused, MD, *Emeritus Training and Supervising Psychoanalyst, Washington Baltimore Center for Psychoanalysis, Emeritus Supervising Psychoanalyst, Denver, Cleveland, and Seattle Institutes. Emeritus Clinical Professor of Behavioral Sciences and of Pediatrics, George Washington School of Medicine.*

'Dr. Louis Roussel beautifully demonstrates his innovative ideas about teaching and engaging a class to facilitate learning. He outlines his core teaching principles, then provides us with a fascinating casebook of classes teaching various texts of Freud's (three clinical papers and three theoretical ones) illustrating with each the dialogue between all class members, which includes the instructor. The class is asked to engage with Freud, pose questions and imagine Freud's responses; to share their own reactions and associations to the text, and to listen to other's responses as the class plays with not only Freud's ideas, but their own; and as they consider what Freud is struggling with in the paper, to relate this to their own struggles both clinically and personally. As a result, candidates experience the class as without outside authority where ideas are seen with fresh eyes, where they and their reactions and associations to the text, to each other, and to ideas are taken seriously, and their encounter with these ideas comes alive in the 21st century. Whether your interest is in Freud or an ingenious, original method of teaching, I highly recommend Dr. Roussel's book.'

Jill M. Miller, PhD, *FABP, Co-Editor-In-Chief, The Psychoanalytic Study of the Child Faculty, Training Analyst and Supervisor, The Washington Baltimore Psychoanalytic Institute; and a Child and Adolescent Supervisor*

'"Try to let yourself be a tourist in a strange land," Dr. Louis Roussel tells his students as they encounter Freud's writings, sensibility, and struggles. What a journey it is, and what a guide we have! We drop in on Roussel's classes on key Freudian texts – those that nearly every psychoanalytic candidate must grapple with – as if we are reading a diary of the most personal and intimate kind … which, in essence, we are. In *Teaching Freud Now*, we learn so much new about Freudian concepts, the problems they were – and still are – meant to address, and the nature of teaching, clinical work, and ourselves. This book is truly unique – the definitive must-read. Dr. Roussel has given psychoanalysis a precious gift.'

Mitchell Wilson, MD, *Editor-in-Chief Emeritus* Journal of the American Psychoanalytic Association

'This is a deeply human book of far broader relevance than the title— *Teaching Freud Now: Time Traveling Dialogues*—might suggest to readers beyond the world of psychoanalysis. While Freud's writings are the landscape on which the pedagogical, transtemporal conversations take place, author Louis Roussel and his students collaboratively grapple with the significance of Freud's writings and method not only for their own practices of psychoanalysis, but also for their personal lives of growth, self-understanding, and collegiality. In this way, the presentation is akin to Freud's empirical and adaptive process of theory development for the sake of healing and wholeness, and is eminently transferable to other caregiving practices, especially those of teaching all kinds of listening arts.

Drawing from deep wells of knowledge from study and practice, as well as his commitment to benefit his students and through them their patients, Roussel brings transparency and a fresh spirit to psychoanalytic training. Taking the time to sit with these dialogues of reflective andragogy will enhance the experience of all teachers. Indeed, it just may lead to "incarnating a love of discovery in pursuit of the unknown" (Roussel's words).'

Susan S. Phillips, PhD, *sociologist and professor of spirituality, has for many years trained psychotherapists and spiritual directors.*

Teaching Freud Now

This book offers practitioners involved in teaching and learning about Freud a new way to access and understand his ideas, blending the author's teaching experiences with feedback and insights from students.

Each chapter is an exploration of the author's experience of teaching a different part of Freud's work. Students are invited to relate to the unique and overlapping struggles of the work by personalizing their efforts through examples from their own lives and clinical experiences. By means of these dialogues taking place between the teacher and the students across years, the reader learns what the key features of Freud's ideas are, what aspects students may struggle with, and how Freud's ideas may be understood and have resonance in contemporary psychoanalysis and psychotherapy, as well as beyond.

With an innovative approach to teaching and learning, this book will be key reading for psychoanalysts and psychotherapists involved in teaching Freud's ideas, students of Freud, as well as anyone interested in understanding Freud's ideas better in a contemporary context.

Louis Roussel is a Child and Adult Psychoanalyst and a Training and Supervising Analyst at the San Francisco Center for Psychoanalysis. He has been teaching psychoanalytic courses for the past 25 years in diverse programs. He was a core faculty member at New College of California. He has supervised many analysts in training at the San Francisco Center for Psychoanalysis and other psychoanalytic centers. He is in full-time private practice in San Francisco, working with children, adolescents, and adults in psychoanalysis.

Teaching Freud Now
Time Traveling Dialogues

Louis Roussel

Routledge
Taylor & Francis Group

LONDON AND NEW YORK

Designed cover image: "Finding Freud" by Lee Grossman

Mary Evans / Sueddeutsche Zeitung Photo

First published 2026
by Routledge
4 Park Square, Milton Park, Abingdon, Oxon OX14 4RN

and by Routledge
605 Third Avenue, New York, NY 10158

Routledge is an imprint of the Taylor & Francis Group, an informa business

For Product Safety Concerns and Information please contact our EU representative GPSR@taylorandfrancis.com. Taylor & Francis Verlag GmbH, Kaufingerstraße 24, 80331 München, Germany.

British Library Cataloguing-in-Publication Data
A catalogue record for this book is available from the British Library

ISBN: 9781041006510 (hbk)
ISBN: 9781003864219 (pbk)
ISBN: 9781003610977 (ebk)

DOI: 10.4324/9781003610977

Typeset in Optima
by codeMantra

Contents

Acknowledgments

Teaching Freud Now developed over many years in a gradual, quiet way, outside of my conscious awareness. The terrain from which it emerged consisted of many years of collaborative struggles in teaching and learning Freud with graduate students and psychoanalytic candidates. I am grateful to the students I have learned with across time for their trust and courage in sharing their ideas, feelings, and vulnerabilities openly. They have taught me so much about teaching. I also thank my patients for teaching me in ways that have helped me grow along with them.

The inception of my encounter with learning about Freud and psychoanalysis came from my first psychology instructor in college, Professor Gary S. Goldstein at the University of New Hampshire. He brought Freud and other psychoanalytic theorists to life in his teachings. He also embodied a playfulness and humor in his teaching that gave me hope for a future life worth living.

I am grateful to my first analyst, Erik Gann, for helping me see so many possibilities that I was so blind to.

My first psychoanalytic study group, beginning with reading all of Freud's texts, was with Lee Grossman and Janis Baeuerlen. The group continues to keep my mind stretching into enlightening areas of thought. I am grateful to them both for our dialogues on many texts we've read and explored together over the years and the sparks of novel ideas that have emerged from our process.

I had the great fortune of working with Lee Grossman in many capacities and I owe him a great deal on a number of levels. Lee was my clinical supervisor for many years, supervising two of my analytic cases. We also co-taught psychoanalytic courses together for many years. Lee has been incredibly generous in his encouragement and helping me with this book, reading multiple drafts of the manuscript and suggesting needed revisions, while being ever respectful of my own ideas, writing style, and final decisions. I am also thankful for his foreword to this book and for the wonderful photograph on this book cover that he took and re-created. I have learned more from Lee about psychoanalysis than from any other instructor I have worked with.

I thank my wife, Bronwen Lemmon, for her love, steadfast encouragement, support, and helpful criticism of particular parts of the text in ways that have greatly enhanced its clarity and accessibility for the reader.

I would like to thank Kate Hawes, Aakriti Aggarwal, Muhilan Selvaraj, and the team at Routledge for all of their hard work in guiding me through the process of giving shape to this book.

Gina Atkinson edited a chapter that I struggled with and she was able to organize this section in a way that emphasized the central ideas very well. Celeste Schneider and Philippe Gendrault read the entire manuscript and offered valuable comments.

Mitchell Wilson offered a helpful idea for re-organizing the beginning of my introduction, as did Agnes Consolacion and Michael Rottmayer. To all these fine people, I thank you for your help.

Foreword

A Student among Students

Louis Roussel is a supremely gifted and sought-after analyst, supervisor, and teacher. I have had the privilege of knowing him and his work well, going back twenty-something years to the beginning of his analytic training. I have taught him and taught with him, and I have read the evaluations by his students with more than a little envy. Along with the global signifiers great, amazing, fabulous, and fantastic, the words that recur in their reports include rigorous, thoughtful, deep, and well-informed. But to me, the most impressive responses are generous, kind, warm, playful, curious, approachable, actively sharing himself, respectful, engaged, and engaging. Here are a few samples, all from his classes on Freud:

"[T]he most playful, generative, and stimulating group experience I have had in my training."

"Louis is… a model teacher…. [He] is very engaged with every member of the class at all times…. He is able to… respond creatively and curiously to where we are."

"I appreciated his respect for us. This should go without saying, but he treated us as if we knew something and/or had some intelligence and his assumptions that we may possibly have read other analytic writings were … flattering, sweet, and often humorous…. This stands in stark contrast to various other teachers we have had that outright… insulted our level of knowledge and/or perceived naivete relative to the material."

"Louis is a great teacher- well -informed, thoughtful and approachable. His affable nature made it easier to discuss delicate topics and I particularly appreciated his case examples."

So why does he insist on calling himself a "student among students" (p. 24_). Roussel is very modest, but I don't believe the phrase comes from modesty, real or false. Citing Paolo Freire, the author of *Pedagogy of the Oppressed*, he sees teaching and learning as dialectical mutuality. He relates this to the "Zen mind/beginner's mind" interaction.

In Zen and in analysis, the goal is to regain the capacity to see the world with fresh eyes, unencumbered by false assumptions about oneself in the world. To accomplish either form of liberation, one of the tasks of the master is to deconstruct her master status. The teacher must help provide the aspirant with an experience that shows that there is no outside authority on the subject's life and that the student has only to regain the childhood freedom to see things as new. Roussel does that by taking his students seriously when they react to the Freud text. By respecting their associations to the text, and to the discussion, he lets Freud's ideas come to life in the 21st century. This is the time machine of his title. Roussel becomes, as he tells us, one of the students. As one of them wrote about him,

> He...seems to democratically situation himself as a member of the group and a fellow-learner, which created an atmosphere that felt very safe to ask questions and think and speak freely within. This approach is infectious and created a lovely group experience. He was also able to strike a great balance between active teaching and case presentations (generously of his own clinical material that were fantastic when paired with the assigned texts)...allowing for a free flow of ideas from the class members.

Roussel's students do not experience him as authoritarian, although they certainly recognize that he is an authority on Freud. Rather, they see him as someone who provides a context of safety in which to explore. One of his students understood how he did that as follows:

Louis's approach, in addition to satisfying our intellectual needs, felt deeply personal and vulnerable. It opened the space for us to reach deep inside ourselves and explore the resonances of the material in us and our work. I was very grateful for his authentic, non-defensive presence.

This is how a gifted analyst works with a patient.

One might assume that anyone competent to do analysis would be able to apply analytic principles to teaching Freud; but that turns out not to be the case. Although there are certainly talented teachers among analysts, many teachers fall into one of two problematic approaches. One, which I think of as pseudo-analytic, is the "what did you think of the readings" type, in which that invariable opening question is followed by maddening passivity or silence. The other, which I think of as anti-analytic, is the lecturer from on high, who intentionally or inadvertently discourages any interaction. The latter, although trained to listen, seems to forget how in the context of teaching.

Roussel, on the other hand, knows how to listen. As he puts it,

> We can... listen to Freud not only for what he says, but also for hints of what he seemed to be leaning toward, but wasn't quite able to fully say. I think that's not a bad way to listen to each other, to our patients, and to ourselves, wherein we try to listen for the seeds of potentiality, the possibility for more within what we and others are trying to say
>
> (p. 362).

Warren Poland (personal communication) once joked that he became an analyst because he wanted to help people, and because they do not come in groups smaller than one. His joke may suggest another reason why many talented analysts are not great classroom teachers. The development of intimacy in analysis requires privacy without which both participants will feel inhibited. The safety of the consulting room is not portable; it does not automatically transfer to the classroom. Roussel's students frequently comment on his remarkable ability to create a safe place, often citing his being "vulnerable," which I would understand as his being nondefensively open to his students' ideas and to sharing his own experiences. It is not, for Roussel, a vulnerability because Roussel does not feel threatened by participating in the group's shared task as a student among students.

But many analysts would indeed feel threatened. I recall the analyst Sol Grossman (personal communication) saying he would never work with groups because he could never manage all the transferences. Putting aside the question of what "managing" the transferences in a group might mean, I bring this up because Grossman was teaching at the Michigan Psychoanalytic Institute at the time. He clearly did not make the connection between teaching and "working with groups," or (I would infer) he would have despaired of all the transferences requiring "management." Among the appeals of analysis as a profession is the fact that one deals with people one at a time. For many analysts, working with groups -classes included – takes them out of their comfortable routine. Many then handle their anxiety by inappropriately imposing a pseudoanalytic model of silently collecting associations, or an antianalytic model in which they ignore what they know about people and their sensitivities.

Roussel tells us how he handled his initial anxiety about teaching Freud (see introduction): he reminded himself that he was a student among students. I think there are two related traits that help make great analytic work possible, which can and should be carried over to teaching. One, which can be mistaken for modesty, is genuine humility; that is to say, a solid grasp of the truth that analysts cannot know anything about their patients in advance. As Poland (2018) put it, the patient is understandable – not already understood. Every analysis starts at zero. Whether one believes everything stems from the Oedipus complex, or that every interaction is rooted in projective identification, or that everyone harbors a false self – those sorts of preconceptions do not help a good clinician start an analysis, because in each case, they must be discovered in context.

In other words, the analyst has to approach each analytic hour with a beginner's mind, a state of wonder at what is uncovered and an openness to being surprised. Every analyst, even when conducting an analysis, is therefore a student among students. Among Roussel's profound insights is to approach Freud's text as a living thing, as one might approach a patient: what must be discovered anew with each reading and each reader is not what is between the book covers, but what happens in the engagement with the text.

I said there were two traits. Several students commented on Roussel's playfulness. I think the proper attitude toward analysis – and as Roussel shows in this book, toward teaching – is to approach it as creative play. As Freud (1908) pointed out, the opposite of play is not what is serious, but what is real. Anyone who has raised a child knows how serious play can be. Play is children's work; it helps form (and reform) our notions of reality. Toys lay the foundation for reasons, as Erikson (1977) told us. Freud's earliest model of analysis, once he abandoned hypnosis, involved inviting the patient to "free associate," i.e., to daydream out loud. Although this approach is still prevalent, it has been modified by the increasing awareness of the analyst's constant and largely unwitting participation in the process. Daydreaming is usually solitary play; daydreaming in the presence of others is a form of engagement.

There is a small and very recent psychoanalytic literature about teaching (and a larger one in the field of literary criticism, about the dialectical engagement with a text). What Roussel offers in this volume is a set of demonstrations of his ideas in action – a casebook, to use his word, of classes on various Freudian texts. As far as I know, no other such collection exists. In the classroom situation as Roussel structures it, a group of people share associations to Freud's text, with the context of their own cases and personal analyses in the background. The tone that Roussel sets by example invites people to add to what has been said, but not to subtract from it. In improvisational theatre, an actor may say "yes, and…" but not "no" (imagine an analyst inviting associations, and then saying "wrong!"). They play freely with the ideas that come up. Roussel creates this same ethos in his classes (note the word "generative" in the review comment above).

Just as analysis evolved, via Freud's technique papers, from analyzing the patient's associations to analyzing the enacted relationship, Roussel has moved teaching Freud from analyzing the published text to exploring the group members' interaction with Freud's ideas – to illuminate Freud's thought in today's context, not to analyze the students. The result is that Freud's ideas achieve an incomparable fullness, a richness appropriate to the study of human nature. Time and again, the participants in his seminars, relative beginners in studying Freud, generate torrents of subtle, sophisticated ideas that emerge from, say, 1914 Freud but come to life in the 21st century.

Consider, for example, how the discussion of "Remembering, repeating and working through" yields the following completely modern ideas about the nature of interpretation, all consistent with, but none explicitly stated in, Freud's text: An interpretation can organize an experience of confusion, make sense of suffering, provide a way to think the unthinkable, stimulate further thought, provide that stimulus even if it is incorrect, undo a fixed idea and upset a pathological equilibrium (p. 106). Or note how the classroom discussion gives rise to a student's hypothesis that the transference neurosis is the point of intersection between the patient's and the analyst's transferences to each other (p. 59). I want to underscore that these ideas did not come from the instructor but from the students who, thanks to Roussel's approach, seemed to have uncommon license to think freely.

I imagine that most practicing analysts return to Freud's text repeatedly throughout their careers. Everyone who does so says they find something new each time they read. That is because Freud's work, much like Shakespeare's, describes living people – including Freud himself. Each reading is a new inter-action, something akin to a reanalysis of a returning patient in which both analyst and patient have grown and the social context has changed. Win-nicott once said there was no such thing as a baby; rereading Freud reminds us that there is no such thing as a text. In both cases, the interaction with the mother-reader-analyst-patient is new and expanded. Roussel approaches teaching Freud to analytic candidates as if he were introducing a favorite wine to a group of friends. He knows the wine, but he and it have matured since his last taste, and he knows each friend will find something new in the experience – as will he.

The "casebook" aspect of Roussel's contribution deserves another reminder. The classroom sessions reported here are not verbatim transcripts, but they capture the feel of extemporaneous speech, with its unpolished, occasionally repetitive, sometimes awkward nature.

I would like to close with another quote from one of Roussel's students: "Please consider asking Louis to lead a workshop for other instructors about how to best engage a class group to facilitate learning." If you want to arrange such a workshop, and you can't get Roussel in person, the book you are hold-ing in your hand is a great place to start. With the same humility and respect that pervades his teaching, he shows you what he does and how it comes to life.

Lee Grossman, MD
Oakland, California 2025

References

Erikson, E.H. (1977). *Toys and Reasons. Stages in the Ritualization of Experience*. W.W. Norton.
Freud, S. (1908). Creative Writers and Day-Dreaming. SE 9: 143–153.
Poland, W.S. (2018). *Intimacy and Separateness in Psychoanalysis*. Routledge.

Introduction

When I first began teaching Freud, I had just finished graduate training myself. When an opportunity to teach presented itself, it felt like a precious gift, my chance to fulfill a long-held dream. Then a few days before I was to teach that first class, a practicum student at my post-doctoral internship informed me that he was a student in the class I would be teaching. He warned me that his class cohort had a reputation for destroying instructors. When I tried to learn more about what he meant, he said he preferred not to say anything else about it. I was frightened.

When I got to the classroom, I immediately noticed that many of the students were older than I was and appeared to have much more life experience than I did. I wondered how on earth I would be able to survive this experience. I searched my mind for a way to find my bearings, filled with doubts, and insecurities.

In those anxious first moments of teaching, it hit me like a flash that I was literally still a student of the subject that I was going to teach. I was able to access memories of being a student offering ideas to the class dialogue that were welcomed and appreciated by my fellow students. That image eased my fears and brought my excitement back. This insight continues to be central to the way I teach and learn. This positioning myself as a student among students is the heart of the way I teach, and learn. It was and continues to be a true realization that gives me a sense of liberation.

Teaching, like psychoanalysis, is a kind of trial by fire. We learn to think in the heat of interactions that we cannot predict. There is fear and excitement in the experience of not knowing what will happen next.

In this book, I will focus on illustrating an approach to teaching Freud through spontaneous dialogue with his core concepts and what it can look and feel like in action. In this sense, it is a casebook for teaching Freud.

Each chapter will explore my experience of teaching different parts of Freud's work, each representing unique and overlapping struggles that emerged. Freud faced a particular problem in every one of the writings that we explored. I invited students to relate the problem Freud was grappling with to their own struggles in their clinical work and personal lives. In this way, they actively struggle with these matters side by side with Freud by personalizing their efforts with examples from their own lives and clinical experiences.

I will share the inferences that I have made from these interactions to demonstrate the kinds of attitudes and techniques that have contributed to this kind of teaching process. I will outline an approach to teaching that demonstrates how to teach Freud's text with an open mind through a dialectical method, one that is similar to the dialectical relationship we encounter in the actual practice of psychoanalysis. I will articulate what I consider to be core psychoanalytic principles for teaching Freud.

What I have learned about teaching has grown out of my own experiences with learning and teaching, good, bad, and mixed. As a young clinician, I looked forward with a great sense of eagerness toward immersing myself in studying Freud. Early on, I noticed that some of my instructors would reference sections of the readings and quickly describe what they thought Freud meant. There was very little room for uncertainty. Students' ideas and reactions to the readings were seldom taken up in a serious way. We were rarely asked what we made of it, what it led us to think about from our own lives, nor did there appear to be any expectation of learning something new from us. Other instructors asked us what we thought of the readings, but rarely responded to anything we said.

It also struck me that, for the most part, instructors were the only ones referencing prior knowledge relevant to what Freud was writing about. Students never did so, and yet, I knew that it could not be the case that we did not have prior knowledge to contribute. I also noticed that we tended to speak directly to the instructors, asking questions about Freud's concepts without first trying to think about it for ourselves. We rarely turned to one another with any expectation of collaborative dialogue. In fact, we tended to not even look at each other in class. There was an implicit contract that instructors would be the ones to disseminate their knowledge and we, the students, would remain empty vessels passively receiving their wisdom. This notion spread to how we were treating one another, with the assumption that we didn't have our own thoughts and feelings to offer. These experiences left me disappointed, and at times deadened.

I have also, over the years, heard similar complaints from both graduate students and psychoanalysts in training. Students have said that they felt that there was no space for them to find their own way with Freud, that instructors tended to give the official verdict on what Freud meant in ways that foreclosed dialogue, exploration, and discovery of something new. Some described feeling that their own thoughts didn't matter to the instructor, leaving them thinking that their minds were of no value within the teaching/learning context. Many were left wondering if Freud was even relevant to their lives and their work.

This form of "learning" was greatly troubling to me and left me with a strong drive to create something different in my own teaching. These experiences were such a stark contrast to what I felt in my undergraduate studies of Freud. In those classes, I felt a spirit of adventure, discovery, and excited anticipation for our dialogues on Freud's ideas. After class, I would often sit for hours contemplating the ideas that had come up in class, sometimes going to a nearby river to stare at the current, waiting for the flow of ideas that would inevitably arise, feeling the depth and vastness of what we were studying. There were moments when so many thoughts would suddenly, effortlessly coalesce in the form of a richer perspective, a burst of insight. These were numinous experiences for me within which I felt like there was no other place I wanted to be.

I was fortunate to have had a number of teachers, two stand out to me, who taught in ways that inspired. In my undergraduate years, for example, the first class I had on Freud was taught by a professor who listened to us in a way I had never been listened to before. The way he listened sparked a feeling in me of having something important to say. In my psychoanalytic training, as a candidate, there was an instructor who became my most valued supervisor and teacher of clinical psychoanalysis. He could hear things in the text and in what we were saying, as well as in what our patients were saying that no one else seemed to hear. What was even more remarkable and immensely generous about him was that he would show us/teach us how to listen in this way. He was like a master magician sharing the method behind his magic.

In the past decade, I have witnessed a shift in many training programs across the country toward a greater emphasis on contemporary psychoanalytic theories, and a watering down of courses on Freud with the unfortunate result being that many psychoanalysts are graduating from their training without a sufficient grasp of Freud's concepts, and even worse, without an appreciation for how valuable and exciting these ideas can be in their work and in their lives, particularly when held flexibly, as Freud himself intended. I have also witnessed a hunger in students and candidates themselves to learn more about Freud, especially when they can be more actively involved in that process.

The teaching approach that I will demonstrate in this book is one that I have found to involve students in ways that bring out their own personal engagement with Freud's ideas. It is less about getting Freud into them and more about getting Freud out of them, i.e., giving them space to reach down deeply inside of themselves to explore the resonances of Freud's ideas within them. I try to provide a bridge for them to pursue their own passionate interests in Freud and facilitate what I hope will be a lifelong relationship with Freud.

In the past few decades, I have seen in some of the psychoanalytic literature that there have been noble efforts to struggle with a number of these problems, aiming to innovate the approach to teaching Freud, such as attempts to find ways to help students to become more engaged, connecting with the students' language, and making their learning experience more personal and relevant, Burstein & Gillian (1997), Auchincloss & Kravis

(2000), Blass (2001), Jonte-Pace (Ed.) (2003), Stuart (2018), Blum (2018), Reynoso (2022), Jacobs (2024). Importantly, these writings have taken us some distance toward more experiential, interactional, and humanistic ways of teaching Freud, each making significant contributions to adding their own techniques toward those ends.

I see this book as adding to that project. In contrast to the other writings on teaching Freud, I will demonstrate an approach that, while focusing on treating the text as a living presence, analogous to the process of psychoanalytic clinical work itself, does so in a way that illustrates the nature of teacher/student dialogue that I have experienced over the years. What is most meaningful and alive about Freud's ideas must be discovered anew within the students' active engagement with the text. The life of the text is manifest in the living dialogue that ensues in the interaction with Freud's ideas.

This book represents an amalgam of my experiences teaching Freud leading to a framework that I have found quite generative. For the purpose of illustrating a fuller living portrait and clear demonstration of the central themes of my experience teaching Freud, I have abridged, condensed, and, at times, elaborated on these classroom conversations in a manner that is consistent with how I engaged with students in our classes. I will show how these experiences have culminated into a teaching frame, derived from my own experiences, composed of psychoanalytic principles for teaching Freud.

In the process of writing of this book, I engaged in a kind of time traveling expedition, making use of my lecture notes, notes on my dialogues with students, private journals chronicling my teaching experiences which I kept while teaching, student response papers as well as my responses to their papers, comments from students in my teaching evaluations, and memories from many classroom experiences over the course of many years to reconstruct a condensation of my experience teaching Freud, one that illustrates core themes that have emerged in our dialogues.

I make use of these techniques to help readers journey to those times as well, and to be able to engage with these recounted experiences in a way wherein they can feel themselves to be there. Teaching lives in the space of actual dialogue. This representation is the closest approximation to my teaching experience that I have been able to capture in written form. I make use of these experiences to demonstrate an approach to teaching and learning Freud with an open mind.

To give the reader a vicarious feeling of being in the classroom, the depictions aim to stay true to the nature of the dialogue, core discussion themes, conversational rhythms and tempo. I have created fictional character names for each student in the dialogue and disguised their comments in ways that are condensed with many student comments I have heard over the years, including the teaching of graduate students and extending into teaching psychoanalytic candidates. In the interest of providing clarity on the kinds of dialogue I have experienced over the years, I have taken some liberties in my reconstruction of these conversations. These are not verbatim accounts of student dialogue. The confidentiality and privacy rights of students and patients have been protected in that identifying information has been removed and some details of their statements have also been altered.

References

Auchincloss, E. & Kravis, N. (2000). Teaching Freud to Undergraduates: A Case Report. *International Journal of Psychoanalysis*, 81, 753–770.

Blass, R. (2001). The Teaching of the Oedipus Complex: On Making Freud Meaningful to University Students by Unveiling his Essential Ideas on the Human Condition. *International Journal of Psychoanalysis*, 82, 1105–1121.

Blum, L. (2018). Teaching Freud, Teaching Psychoanalysis: From College Students to Professionals. *American Imago*, 75 (2), 307–317.

Burstein, A. & Gillian, J. (1997). Teaching Freud: A Lesson. *Psychoanalytic Psychology*, 14 (4), 457–473.

Jacobs, D. (2024). Teaching Freud: Challenges and Opportunities. *Psychoanalytic Inquiry*, 44 (2), 210–217.

Jonte-Pace, D. (2003). *Teaching Freud*. Oxford University Press.

Reynoso, J. (2022). The Celebrity as a Teaching Object: Using Kanye West and Kim Kardashian to Explain Freud. *International Journal of Applied Psychoanalytic Studies*, 19, 341–351.

Stuart, J. (2018). Teaching Freud: A Symposium. *American Imago*, 75 (2), 287–323.

Part I

Teaching Freud's Clinical Writing

In Part I, Teaching Freud's Clinical Writings, we will take a deeper look into Freud's texts for their clinical implications. We will read and discuss Freud's technique papers which bear directly on the practice of clinical psychoanalysis. We will also look at clinical material to illustrate some of the key concepts outlined in Freud's written work.

Freud's fundamental clinical concepts were created to deal with specific clinical tensions and struggles in his efforts to treat neurotic patients. These concepts evolved over time from his clinical experiences. He was continuously raising questions and interrogating accepted images of our intra-psychic processes. In carefully reading his work and making links to our own similar experiences, we can obtain a more personal, visceral sense of the kinds of pressures which led Freud to these ideas and appreciate psychoanalytic thinking as an alive, ever-moving, unfixed process.

Lawrence Friedman (2019) argued that Freud's technique papers, the book that comprises them, stand in contrast to his other writings. His contention is that the technique book is not an application of theory, but rather a representation of Freud's own struggles and challenges as he encountered problems in his effort to practice psychoanalysis.

This viewpoint really underscores the idea that it is only by an appreciation of the personal struggles and difficulties that Freud was contending with in his efforts to practice psychoanalysis that we can fully grasp the principles behind these concepts and the specific tensions that gave rise to these ideas, the clinical fires out of which they were born.

The clinical hours that I will present are meant to link Freud's concepts to the kinds of clinical experiences that gave rise to these ideas. These hours are intended to provide a vivid picture for us to embody these hypotheses, one that will also allow us to grasp Freud's concepts from multiple angles and modalities, e.g., through visualization of the clinical scene with its interpersonal interactions, the auditory experience of hearing the words spoken within the hour, and the feelings that are conjured up in listening to the material. They are also intended to show the kinds of struggles and difficulties

DOI : 10.4324/9781003610977-1

that I encountered in my own work. To protect the privacy of patients, I have disguised the clinical vignettes.

Thinking about the experiences out of which these concepts appeared will be a central guiding light in our reflections. We will think together about the problems that Freud encountered in his attempts to bring about the psychoanalytic phenomenon. We will consider the concepts embedded within these technique papers in the context of the problems they were meant to deal with. We will reflect on these issues in a way that involves our own current, personal struggles and tensions in our individual and collective efforts to practice psychoanalysis and facilitate a psychoanalytic process.

One way that I think about teaching is that it is a collaborative process. Some of the views of Paolo Freire (1970), a Brazilian educator, social theorist, and revolutionary activist, are consistent with what I have learned from my own teaching experiences. According to Freire, the teacher is not merely the one who teaches, but also one who is taught by students in mutual dialogue.

The number of concepts we will be exploring is extensive. What I am envisioning is that these ideas will most likely come up in our discussions of the papers. I am holding this list in a flexible way and recognize that the spontaneous flow of our conversation may very well leave some of these ideas out of the mix. That is fine with me.

What's more important, to my mind, in reading Freud, is that we take an open hearted look at Freud's clinical writings, temporarily suspend a strong tendency to dismiss his ideas within our contemporary ethos long enough to really get a feel for his struggles, to engage his work in a more personal way, to see for ourselves the value of many of his ideas for our own lives and work.

I am hoping that we can try to put ourselves in his shoes and think about our own similar and very unique struggles in trying to practice psychoanalysis. I would like to suggest that we strive to maintain a particular attitude as we approach these concepts. I think it's a sensibility best captured by a quote that Noam Chomsky (2013) cites from Victor Weisskopf, an American-Austrian theoretical physicist, "It doesn't matter what we cover. It matters what you discover" (Chomsky, p. 279).

References

Chomsky, N. (2013). *Power Systems: Conversations on Global Democratic Uprisings and the New Challenges to U.S.* Empire. Metropolitan Books.
Freire, P. (1970). *Pedagogy of the Oppressed*. Continuum.
Friedman, L. (2019). *Freud's Papers on Technique and Contemporary Clinical Practice*. Routledge.

1 Transference

A Note on My Intentions

Since this was the first meeting of the class, I planned to spend a good deal of time discussing my approach to teaching Freud's ideas as a living presence, and to encourage and attain as much openness as possible about our struggles with Freud's ideas. Turning to the reading, "The Dynamics of Transference" (1912), I wanted to explore the transference impact on the interaction between patient and analyst, the notion of re-enactment of earlier repressed scenes, and the inevitable frustrations and setbacks one encounters in the practice of psychoanalysis.

Instructor: I think it will be useful to try to engage these writings as a dialogue with Freud, to imagine that we are actively engaging with Freud, posing questions, sharing reactions, and imagining responses, as we read. We can also do that in our discussions of the text and see what comes of it. The more fixed these ideas are in our minds, the less alive they are, in the sense that the fixity of ideas puts a stop to our own internal and external dialogue, to the movement of our own thinking.

   I want to try to be transparent with you in how I approach teaching Freud so that you have a sense of what it is I am aiming for and what it is that I would like you to try to do as well. Although I have spent years teaching Freud, I attempt to forget what I know about Freud and imagine myself to be a fellow student taking this class with you, engaging in a shared exploration of the text. I say, I imagine it, but, on a deeper level, it's actually a realization.

   This is very relevant to our practice of psychoanalysis. We can acquire much knowledge from our readings and yet clinical experience has shown us that it's necessary to strive to approach our patients with an open mind and learn, as well as re-learn everything within the context of the interactions that unfold within each particular treatment. I would suggest that we attempt to

DOI : 10.4324/9781003610977-2

do that in our approach to Freud. Even if you have read Freud before, try to let yourself be like tourist in a strange land, with an openness to discovery.

I am primarily interested in looking at our interaction with Freud's ideas as a way of learning Freud that engages his thinking as one would in a dialogue with a living being. We can pose questions for Freud and try to think of his ideas, as he did, as an unfinished and unsettled dialogue that we can make meaningful contributions to. Also, another way, in addition to our in-class discussions, that I think will facilitate that is for you to write a short paper every week in reaction to the reading of that week. Try to allow yourselves to write as freely as you can about whatever moves you, what it is that you find yourself resonating with or anything you are interested in exploring further. Your writings will also allow me to have your interests in the back of my mind, held loosely, as we discuss the text. Our in-class dialogue will be our primary focus.

I would like for you to try to allow yourselves to associate as freely and spontaneously as you can in our discussions of Freud's writings. Keeping in mind that Freud created his ideas from his own clinical struggles, I think it would be useful for us to try to associate to the readings and to our dialogue with resonances to our own clinical experiences, both as therapists and as patients in analysis. This I see as a form of play, a kind of improvisation in the sense of letting yourselves say what comes to mind initially with no concern for whether it's right or not. We will, as a group, over time, reflect on our discussions in ways that attend to tensions, potential problems, and parts left out. In that sense, analogous to psychoanalysis itself, we will have an oscillation between freely associating to the material and stepping back to reflect more critically on our evolving ideas.

Also, I would suggest that we try to listen to one another with an attitude that I think Freud himself lived by, namely, that nothing human is alien to us. That sensibility was described by a dramatist of the Roman Republic in 163 BC named Publius Terentius (1880), sometimes referred to as Terrence. He said, "I am a man: I consider nothing pertaining to man foreign to myself" (p. 9). Freud had read and was quite familiar with his work. Try to listen to one another with the assumption that there is something potentially important and useful to you in what is being said. Try to listen from a place of aiming to see what speaks to you in what you hear. Listen from a place of trying to hear the potential in the ideas expressed, e.g., where might these ideas be trying to go? I hope that we can create an atmosphere together here where we can play with these ideas.

It will be important to try to think of the kinds of things that Freud was struggling with when he wrote these papers and to keep your own clinical struggles in mind. We will be struggling alongside of Freud, embarking on a process similar to his. Try to be as open as you can about the aspects of your clinical work that you find most difficult. I will do the same when I present some of my own clinical work. The work we do is emotionally very demanding. At times it can feel quite impossibly difficult. I hope that we can strive to cultivate a shared acceptance and empathy for ourselves and each other around these matters and to be able to talk about it when we're having trouble doing that.

You might see that the suggestions that I have made for how to approach Freud have relevance for how we practice psychoanalysis. It has been my experience that the effort to engage and interact with Freud is one that has many parallels to the dialectical relationship that we find in clinical psychoanalysis. Reading and studying Freud is a process that will inherently bring up tensions and difficult feelings. I want us to work together to create a space for expressing these experiences openly and with curiosity.

This list of aims that I presented to you for this class is also similar to the practice of analysis in that there too we have ideas about what it is we are striving for. In both cases, in the clinical realm and in this class, what we aim for and what actually happens will not be identical. That is part of what is so exciting about both endeavors. We cannot know how our dialogue will play out and what we will find. I think it's particularly exciting when we don't know what will be said next.

As a starting point today, I wonder if you could each try to speak to what you find most challenging and difficult in your efforts to learn Freud's concepts as well as psychoanalysis overall. Try to speak as honestly as you can about what it feels like for you.

Eli: I feel tension between trying to hold psychoanalytic ideas flexibly and trying to have them solidly pinned down. I have a hard time holding onto Freud's ideas.

Reyna: For me, it's been difficult to feel the freedom to play with these ideas in the face of a pressure to prove that I understand them. I also feel like it's been difficult to experience mastery of Freud's ideas.

Bethany: I feel ashamed talking about Freud when I am not sure I really understand what I am talking about. It's been difficult to get Freud in a deep way in previous classes I have had in college, graduate school, and now in analytic training.

Ernest: I feel frustrated when I get bogged down in confusion about what Freud means to say. I often have the experience of feeling

	like I'm starting to get it and then Freud moves into a completely different way of thinking and I'm totally confused all over again.
Natalie:	I can relate with the feelings everyone is expressing, but for me, my own distress is centered more around this feeling of pressure to prove that I am developing as an analyst.
Bethany:	I appreciate the idea of approaching Freud as if we have not read anything of his writings in the past. Something about that makes me feel more open about what I think. I felt I was a lot more open about my reactions to Freud's writings when I was just starting my training. Now I feel more careful as if I have been here long enough and should just know it.
Instructor:	I want to emphasize some tensions that I hear in what you're saying. There are tensions related to the learning process itself, namely the way we can feel unmoored by Freud's writings, the complexity and the continuous movement and change of his ideas. We start to feel that we have grasped something and then Freud turns it on its head and we are back to a scrambled state of trying to understand all over again. These kinds of challenges are inherent to the learning process, especially with Freud and psychoanalysis, and yet I can hear in your comments that it can feel quite discouraging at times, as if the effort involved represents some kind of failure.
	You've also spoken on the issue of tensions involved in training and how the experience of being evaluated can paradoxically interfere with the state of mind conducive to learning about psychoanalysis. I wonder if you have any other thoughts about that?
Ernest:	Sometimes I feel self-conscious, feeling like I have to prove that I understand these concepts. It leads me to lose my feelings of fascination which I originally felt about these ideas. I hear analysts sometimes angrily talk about the need for more rigor in training and yet they seem quite dogmatic and rigid in their attitude. Frankly, they seem joyless to me, which I find off-putting.
Reyna:	I do feel a sense of competition sometimes in classes and that can turn me off from participating.
Ezra:	Sometimes it feels like comments we make are more about an effort to sound impressive and less about truly exploring, less about curiosity and discovery.
Midge:	For me, when people talk about Freud with a sense of certainty, I feel really put off, like there's no room to speculate freely. It can be overbearing.
Bethany:	The classes on Freud that I have had so far have felt rigid to me, many times the application to clinical experience feels like a forced fit.
Eli:	I think that our own narcissism can create problems for us.
Instructor:	How do you see narcissism playing out here?

Eli: I was thinking about how we might misinterpret feelings of confusion that are part of the process of learning in ways that lead us to experience a narcissistic injury, a blow to our sense of having to know everything and be clear all the time.

Instructor: One suggestion in these remarks has to do with the capacity to tolerate uncertainty, states of confusion, the continuous movement of ideas, and humility in the learning process. These capacities are also vitally important in our clinical work. Something for us to think about together over time has to do with the obstacles to these capacities. Midge and Bethany's points are also very important to pay attention to. Certainty and rigidity in the practice of psychoanalysis can lead to harmful effects for our patients. The idea of force- fitting our preconceptions on our patients is crucially important to listen for. Let's try to listen for that and speak to it when we notice it coming up, whether in what I'm saying or in what we hear in our dialogue. I also invite us all to listen very carefully for these tendencies when I present my clinical material.

Natalie: Related to what Midge and Bethany were saying, I also think that Freud tends to be idealized, even worshiped in ways that inhibit us from feeling free to be critical of anything he says.

Instructor: I'm really glad that you said that Natalie. I am familiar with the tendency you're describing and it does a grave disservice to Freud's work. It is so important for us to feel free to openly express our criticism, as well as any struggle we're having with our experience of reading Freud. That brings the dynamics embedded in these ideas to life for us. I think we should all bear this in mind and draw attention to this phenomenon if we notice it, so that we can explore it together and learn more about it.

     In terms of this paper, one question that I would like us to begin to think about is why Freud felt concerned about patients knowing too much about analytic technique.

Midge: I wonder if it could lead patients to try to comply with what they imagine the analyst might expect of them, like try to be what they read the analyst wanting them to be.

Eli: This reminds me of my work with a patient who is quite knowledgeable about psychoanalysis and who seems to intentionally try to speak about their feelings about me in ways that feel forced and unconvincing, making use of a lot of psychoanalytic jargon. It's like he's simulating the kinds of reactions to me that he thinks he should be having based on what he's read.

Natalie: It's sort of a counterphobic approach. If the analyst is scared of the transference, he might do the same thing though. The things we read become a kind of expectation for what analytic work should look like.

Instructor: Interesting. What do you have in mind here?

Natalie: I have done this myself. I have made continuous comments about the patient feeling something about me in ways that felt forced, almost as if I am trying to imitate interpreting transference in a way that approaches what I have read about it.

Instructor: You're recognizing and speaking to something that does not receive enough attention among analysts, namely that it is a regular part of our work as analysts to struggle with our own resistances, in this case it's maybe a resistance to engaging the unknown. When I first started supervising candidates, I had an experience working with someone whose work at first felt quite stilted at times. It hit my one day that her patient was trying to act like a person in psychoanalysis, the candidate was trying to act like an analyst, and I was trying to act like a supervisor.

Bethany: That is similar to an experience I had in supervision. I was feeling very self-conscious about my work, preoccupied with how it might sound to my supervisor when I presented the hour. I ended up trying to sound like an analyst when I was talking to the patient. It felt very unnatural and stiff. I'm still trying to give that up.

Ernest: I can appreciate that but I also feel a kind of analytic superego watcher in the room with me, leading me to feel self-conscious about what I'm doing. I focus a lot on trying to get it right.

Instructor: From our dialogue so far, it is clear that you are not alone in that experience. What you describe there is something that is particularly heightened in our early years of training, although it can present itself at times even later down the road, when we've acquired more experience. We can wonder together what various roles this watcher plays for us. I remember a patient I saw as a candidate responding to something I interpreted with, "Oh yes, it's Wednesday. You met with your supervisor today. That wasn't you talking just now." She was absolutely right in that I was parroting something my supervisor said, but, more startling to me was that she figured out the exact day that I was meeting with my supervisor.

    I do want to pose a question for us to think about together. Do you think it is possible for a patient to experience transference to the analyst without it resulting in an actual change in how the analyst is with them? This is a question about how the patient's transference impacts and alters the analyst.

Midge: I think that for the patient, when they experience the analyst in the transference, unconsciously within a particular frame or scene, that has to affect the way the patient is engaging with the analyst.

Instructor: Do you think that engagement will impact the analyst's response?

Midge: I do think that it would inevitably affect the analyst's response in some way. I know that I respond differently to different patients. That response itself may not be verbal, but most likely experienced by the patient, maybe not consciously.

Instructor:	How do you think this process of the patient's transference impacting the analyst works?
Ezra:	I remember reading an article in social psychology, looking at the way stereotypes held in mind affect one's interlocutor. Holding an image or stereotype in mind about another person you're interacting with leads to that other person being subtly shaped to respond in ways that confirm the stereotype.
Instructor:	This is a fascinating idea, that these transference fantasies become part of the interaction and may bring about responses in the analyst that approximate the transference fantasy, in a sense creating the analyst that will embody their underlying unconscious imago.
Bethany:	This way of talking about transference complicates our sense of reality. It isn't so easy to just think of the transference as the patient's distortion if it results in an actualization of these prototypical interactions. It actually may alter reality, at least interpersonally.
Ernest:	How would we even know if that had happened?
Instructor:	That is a very useful question. The analyst might not be conscious of this initially or even for quite some time.
Eli:	What kinds of things would the analyst have to notice about himself to begin to suspect that they've come to personify something approximating the patient's transference fantasy?
Natalie:	That reminds me of a time when I felt a well of rage toward a patient without having a clear sense of what it was about, only later to learn that the patient experienced her mother as often enraged at her for no apparent reason.
Instructor:	So Natalie here is showing us a good illustration of the way an analyst might come to incarnate a reaction that approximates the patient's transference fantasy. We might imagine ways that an analyst could come to know that this is happening. For example, when Natalie felt this rage, she might have asked herself who was enraged with the patient, who had Natalie become for the patient, wondering about the possibility that the patient may have an unconscious transference to such an object. It is orienting to regularly ask ourselves who we are for the patient as we listen, for example, or what kind of person does it sound like the patient is speaking to, or what kind of person do we sound like as we listen to ourselves talking to the patient.
Ezra:	This is making me think about my work with a child case. After meeting with the mother of this patient, I was disturbed by how much I had come to sound much like this mother in my comments to the patient. I realized that I was nagging the patient in a way that bore a striking resemblance to even the mother's tone of voice. It was very strange. I could actually hear that I sounded just like her when I was with this patient and I don't sound like that anywhere else.

Instructor: What did you make of it?

Ezra: I was confused by it, but right now I'm thinking about it in the context of our discussion, as the effect of the patient's transference-based interaction with me, how it seemed to groom me into a way of relating with the patient that was just like the patient's experience of this internal maternal object.

Instructor: We have been talking about how the patient's transference can change the analyst. I wonder how we might think of the analyst's transference in this type of case? What role does the analyst's transference play in the process we have been exploring? And, relatedly, what do we think about Ezra's interesting use of the word grooming in this context?

Midge: I wonder if the patient's grooming, as Ezra put it, might be too one sided. I think that for such an impact to be possible, it has to hook into something in the analyst's transference.

Instructor: Could you think of an example to flesh that out a little more, give us a sense of how you see that playing out?

Midge: There have been times when I felt angry and competitive with a patient who tends to try to outdo me. While I can see how the patient's interpreting me as someone out to get one over on her led to the patient, in a way, grooming me to take on the shape of such an object, that process hooked into my own transference involving my mother who rarely affirmed me.

Instructor: Midge's example provides us with an important picture of how the patient's transference will often intersect with our own transference in ways that will lead to complex and unique interacting effects. I think that one implication of what Midge is showing us here is that we need to work on being mindful of and familiar with our own transference reactions to the patient's transference in order to make distinctions and take into account our own role in the interaction, alongside of the patient's role.

　　Also the point that Ezra brought out is that we will often subjectively experience this interaction in a more one-sided way, namely as something being done to us. That's often the first level at which we will notice the transference, before we are able to tune into the more complex field of the interaction.

　　These roles, like the example given, are related. Another example of that is how Midge's transference was connected to a parental figure who interacted with her in ways that were similar to how the patient interacted with her. The more acquainted we can be with the nuances of our own transference reactions, the more likely we are to be able to interpret the patient's transference from a more holistic perspective, with empathic understanding for the patient's experience within that broader interpersonal context.

Freud wrote about how everyone has their own idiosyncratic way of loving. I think that Freud is talking about the way our libido or desire, often manifesting as absorption or engrossment, can, in childhood become attached to certain persons, like our parents, siblings, others we are close to and their internal representations, the types of relationships we have experienced with them, the aims of satisfaction we tend to adhere to. These early experiences and their related fantasies leave traces in our psyches and we retain a kind of passionate adhesive tie to them unconsciously.

Midge: What is libido? We've heard that term many times and yet there is something about it that feels elusive to me. Can we flesh out what it would be like to encounter subjectively? I feel a longing for a language for talking about it that might feel relatable in terms of my own experience, like how might we use the word libido in a relationship?

Instructor: This is exactly the kind of question that we need to be asking ourselves continuously in our efforts to bring Freud's ideas to life for us. Freud talked about libido as a dynamic energy involved in the morphing of the various manifestations of the sexual drive that we see occurring from one phase of development to the next. We can see displacements of this postulated intensity and energy from various bodily zones, objects and aims across child development. We also can see the displacement of this tendency in the form of our most passionate wishes and desires attaching to different relationships through the transference.

Freud gave an example from his own life, when he spoke about an early childhood relationship with his nephew, John, who was one year older than Freud. He had a very competitive relationship with him marked by intense emotional oscillations of passionate love and hate. Freud said that he subsequently felt compelled to repeatedly replace this relationship dynamic well throughout his adulthood. Often, he felt he needed someone in his life that he could love intensely and also someone to hate just as intensely. Sometimes he was able to embody these affective poles in one person.

Freud said of this relationship, "We had loved each other and fought each other; and this childhood relationship…had a determining influence on all my subsequent relationships with contemporaries" (Roazen, 1971, p. 31). He also said, "All my friends have in a certain sense been reincarnations of this first figure…" (Roazen, 1971, p. 31).

Eli: What Freud described in that personal example was the interaction in the relationship and that became an interaction that Freud felt compelled to repeat, something he must have internalized.

Bethany: As Freud described, we seem to bring unconscious prototypes for particular kinds of interactions into our current relationships and those ways of interacting then have an impact on the other person.

Midge: The impact on the other person will be different depending on the particular transference tendencies or leanings of that person. For example, some things are going to hook into my stuff that won't hook into Ezra's stuff.

Instructor: Well put. You are describing some very important ways of framing what Freud has referred to as libido. The hypothesized energy associated with its unconscious prototypes, as you put it, can have real interpersonal impact and lead to reactions that then move into more complex back and forth processes between the involved parties.

              Freud said that the fixation can be described as a "stereotyped plate" that keeps getting replayed or re-pasted over and over again in our relationships (Freud, 1912, p. 100).

              Does this way of thinking about transference resonate with your experience?

Ernest: I do have a feeling of aversion to the use of the image of a stereotyped plate to describe psychic phenomena.

Instructor: What is it about this image that evokes the feeling of aversion?

Ernest: I think it's the one way quality of that, as if it has nothing to do with how the object received and reacted to this pressure coming from the patient.

Reyna: I agree. There is something about it that feels less alive and less related.

Bethany: It doesn't touch on the way transference is something that plays out between the analyst and patient, how there are mutual inter-shaping or inter-grooming processes leading to a unique interactive hybrid formation, almost like a kind of unconscious negotiation between patient and analyst about what shape the interaction is to take.

Instructor: Wow, I really love the way you put that. I want us to notice how you are working with Freud's ideas here. You are taking in Freud's concepts, in interaction with your own present analytic experiences in ways that are leading to increased complexity, depth, and movement.

Bethany: It feels alienating to me how Freud talks about fixation and energies at times in ways that are split off from the human relationships within which these dynamics play out. The story you shared of Freud's fixation within the context of his relationship with his nephew, for example, provided an image that was full of emotions and sensations we are all familiar with in relationships and I can really feel it, but it's harder to feel the poignancy of these dynamics when they are not part of a more personal, human story that we can find our way into.

Instructor: That's an excellent point and it also provides us with some ideas for our readings. One implication here is that we need to flesh out our readings, as we are already doing, with our own imaginings of actual relationship scenarios where we can see and feel these dynamics playing out in living color, to bring these concepts into relation with our experiences in ways that do justice to the fluidity with which Freud held them. We can do that with clinical cases, which we are doing, as well as the stories and scenes from our own lives.

I wonder what you made of Freud's approach to dealing with setbacks, when his aims were frustrated?

Eli: This seems to be an important way in which Freud operated. Freud would bump into obstacles but always appeared to make new discoveries in the process.

Instructor: Yes. Freud would be trying to achieve a particular aim, such as uncovering repressed material, encounter an obstacle to that, when faced with the transference, and then discover that the obstacle held within it important secrets to be revealed. These observations alert us, as Eli drew our attention to, something about the way Freud worked, one of the methods he used in thinking through problems.

Midge: It also seemed potentially useful, not only conceptually but as a clinical approach.

Instructor: How do you see it as useful in terms of your own clinical work?

Midge: It's a very adaptive way of dealing with impediments to what the analyst is trying to achieve. Sometimes I feel frustrated with patients when they're resistant to taking in an interpretation that I feel is important for them to face. I see the shift to being curious about the resistance itself, as serving important functions, as a meaningful source of insight in itself. It would not only yield more insight, but would also keep me actively engaged with the patient in a way that I might not be if I just succumb to the frustration.

Instructor: These wonderings are a good example of thinking about how our images of the work of analysis and our associated feelings can have very real effects on the way we experience and engage in the work. How we envision the work we are doing can change the whole scene, emotionally and interpersonally. We might think of that as our transference to the work of analysis.

Ezra: I think transference is vitally important but I think the way we tend to hold it in mind leads me to sometimes feel like the pendulum has swung to the transference now spoken about as if it's the only thing about analysis that's important. I believe that it's truly important but something happens when we act as if one thing is the only thing that's important. I see that happening with transference. Some analysts say they only work in the transference. We could overdo our focus on that in ways that lead to a forced approach.

Instructor: That's a good point. Addressing the transference, while crucially important, as if it's the only important thing about analysis may lead to the problems for us, like what you described. The transference requires time and space to develop and excessive zeal can interfere with that. When we see that in ourselves and others, we have to wonder if there are unknown anxieties about the transference in the analyst.

Psychoanalysis is composed of an immense breadth of variables and we have to be mindful of the risks of being reductionistic and indoctrinating when we idealize certain parts of psychoanalysis over others. We will delve into this more deeply when we discuss the Dora case in the weeks ahead. And yet, we also legitimately hunger for a clear, convincing, integrated, well-defined conceptual image of psychoanalysis, one that does not come at the cost of impoverishing the complexity, unpredictability, and the art of what we do.

Trying to do all the things that have been recommended for analysts to focus on and integrate them into a coherent definition of what psychoanalytic treatment is presents us with a formidable challenge. In the face of potential overwhelm, we are tempted to reduce psychoanalysis to more simplified, less taxing representations.

I am reminded of a story Stephen Mitchell (1988), citing Powers, told when trying to represent the difficult task of the analyst. He said that a beginning musician was trying to learn to play a piece that Stravinsky wrote. He tried and tried to play the piece and finally went to Stravinsky and said he gave it everything he had and he just couldn't do it. He said that it was impossible. Stravinsky understood that of course it was impossible, but that he wanted to hear "the sound of someone trying to play it" (Mitchell, p. 293).

I think this story captures something about the paradoxical aims of analysis for both analyst and patient. Both are meant to try to do something often seemingly contradictory and impossible to achieve, and the analysis ultimately isn't about achieving it, but, rather, observing and noticing what happens when we try to. Of course, this process necessitates that we find a way to become more tolerant of the experience of paradox, to be able to see it as having an important gradient for growth, which is no easy task. Trying to achieve these things can lead to the development of a particular kind of process, what we might call a type of mental freedom or analytic process.

Midge: I feel some relief at that thought. Reading Freud and trying to think the way he does can feel intimidating, at times impossible. It can even lead me to devalue my own thoughts. But it feels like failure is an inevitable part of the work. We will fail to achieve our aims, but that's the starting point for becoming curious about what's going on unconsciously.

Instructor: This is insightful. I think it's something we have all experienced. It is fascinating to think about the process of wrestling with Freud's process of thinking especially how it engages us in a struggle that does at times feel impossible, like we will never get this fully mastered. There are many parallels to the experience of being in analysis, learning about psychoanalysis, and perhaps the struggle of being taught by a Zen master with all of the paradoxical experiences involved there. What you said about the failure as a starting point for the analysis is so important to keep in mind. The experience of failure, of obstacles, clues us in to the operation of unconscious dynamics to be identified and explored. Failure is always an opportunity for discovery.

I want to draw your attention to Freud's (Freud, 1912) comment about how, within the transference-resistance, the patient is "flung out of his real relation to the doctor" (p. 107). What do you think Freud means by this?

Natalie: It's like a deviation from the real relation and that implies a difference.

Eli: Yes, but what is it meant to be a difference from? It makes me think of some kind of baseline against which the transference-resistance stands out.

Instructor: Maybe we could think of the real relation as part of the analytic frame, like an imaginary line, something relatively stable, from which to see deviations.

Ernest: We could think of the frame as like the working relationship, like an acknowledgement that one person is the patient working with the analyst to understand the patient.

Reyna: The real relation maybe involves the reality that someone is in treatment and is operating from an acceptance of the set roles, the manifest roles of patient and analyst collaborating to understand the patient's mind, what's going on unconsciously.

Instructor: There is a realness to that, an accepted, shared reality between analyst and patient that might allow us to experience and notice a shift, a movement like what Freud described that can feel jarring, like a change of scene.

Midge: It can feel like the patient suddenly seems alien, like they're no longer in the same reality as the analyst.

Ezra:	I think that's what an encounter with the unconscious feels like. I was working with a patient to try to understand and reflect on her erotic feelings for me. At first, we were both trying to think about it as part of a larger pattern in her life, when suddenly she noticed a very small framed picture of my wife on my desk and exploded in rage.
Eli:	That example conveyed that both therapist and patient appeared initially to be in the realm of their real relation, namely their working relationship, and then suddenly no longer so.
Ezra:	It was as if I had betrayed her and it did feel shocking.
Instructor:	Here we have a vivid image of what Freud was saying about the patient being flung out of her real relation to the analyst. As Freud described near the end of this paper, the therapist and patient were reflecting together, but then what was a past pattern to reflect upon intruded into the present and the present/past distinction vanished, at least for the patient, and to a lesser extent maybe for the analyst as well. The patient, in a way, hallucinated a lover who betrayed her. The unconscious fantasy became the most real thing for her and it was shocking for the analyst as well.
Bethany:	What I wonder is what this patient's reaction did to the analyst. How real it did it become for you, Ezra?
Ezra:	I felt scared, and guilty, like I really did betray her. I felt all that at the same time that I knew it was irrational. I also felt rattled and confused.
Instructor:	This reminds me of Freud's comment about how the unconscious is not remembered in the way in which analysts prefer it to be remembered (Freud, 1912, p. 108).
Ernest:	I am suddenly aware of feeling a desire for the work to be calmer and more reflective.
Instructor:	This is another important tension, a duality that Freud is speaking of here. The work is fascinating, but when we get pulled into the intensity of things that disturb our sense of what's real, that's a whole other kettle of fish.
Natalie:	It is a relief to not feel alone in that feeling, an experience that can sometimes feel shameful.
Instructor:	What feels so shameful about it?
Natalie:	It feels like a contradiction to my desire to be an analyst, almost like it means that I'm not good enough, not analyst material.
Instructor:	It is striking how something so natural to feel, so human, can come to feel like such a damning realization. It does underscore how important it is for us to have a space where we can shed our pretenses and get real with each other about what it actually feels like to do this incredibly difficult work.

How do you feel about the idea of the analyst and patient playing prescribed roles with one another, the way we talked about their associated work functions?

Eli: It led me to think of the analyst as helping the patient to see what's going on unconsciously and the patient speaking as freely and openly as possible as serving a function of providing a line to notice deviations. It's interesting to think of the way those roles might help us do something that serves the analytic work.

Instructor: I wonder if you're implicitly contrasting that way of thinking about the roles to some other way of seeing it.

Eli: When I think of prescribed roles, something about that feels inauthentic.

Midge: Maybe it depends on our reasons for playing the role. If I am playing the role of being an objective, neutral analyst and really believe that it's possible to be that, then this for me would be a false place to be.

Instructor: What version of playing those roles wouldn't be false for you?

Midge: It wouldn't be false if I know I'm playing the role for a reason, because it helps with the actual analytic work and that the patient may actually need me to play that role in order to do the work that they need to do.

Bethany: That's interesting. It reminds me of being a parent. There is an aspect of that which also involves playing a certain role because children actually need that, like the asymmetry of the parent/child relationship.

Instructor: That's a nice connection to what Midge was describing clinically. We can miss, and so many analysts do miss, the clinical value of these analytic postures that Freud recommends, like neutrality and evenly suspended attention when we take them too literally and lose the play of it, as well as the pragmatism of it, e.g., how it can actually serve the patient's analytic needs.

Ernest: If we think of the frame suggestions that Freud is recommending as certain positions or postures that he has found conducive to the analytic process, we don't have to get caught up in the idea of whether these positions are achievable or not. That's not really the point.

Instructor: Could you spell out what the point would be?

Ernest: It would be whether or not these positions serve the aims of analysis.

Instructor: Some of the aims that come to mind for me are whether or not they help us identify unconscious dynamics, facilitate the development of transference, free the patient up to associate more unabashedly.

Midge: The idea of having a notion of the role we're trying to play reminds me of what you said earlier about how, both in analysis and in teaching, we enter the situation with particular aims in mind, but there's a kind of looseness with which we hold those aims, knowing from experience that things will play out differently than we imagine and we can't know ahead of time exactly what form these interactions will take. But the roles are still helpful in that they give us a clarifying reference point from which to notice and appreciate the movements that stray from them.

Instructor: That is a very clarifying and valuable summary. The roles may also give us a sense of having something to ground ourselves in, something to hold onto, although in a loose way, as Midge said. We can aim for that role and give it up when it feels necessary to do so in order to further the work.

When Freud speaks of transference as resistance in this paper, he is referring to the way that transference can seem to be an obstacle to the patient being able to consciously remember the repressed material. As the patient's associations converge more and more closely around the repressed complex, that is, the repressed group of intense, affectively embodied ideas and memories from childhood, the transference is used as a kind of last ditch defense against conscious recognition of what is becoming nearly impossible to ignore. The clinical example I will provide will involve an illustration of this.

Presentation of clinical hour: (6-Year-old girl in psychoanalysis)

Patient: Oh, I know, let's play that we are part of a college and my friend Sally and I are students going on a trip far away and you're the professor who is coming to chaperone us. What's the name of a place in France?
Analyst: Paris.
Patient: Okay, let's go to Paris, France.
Analyst: Why France?
Patient: I'm not sure. I heard it's beautiful there.
Analyst: So, we're going to be world travelers.
Patient: Yes. Let's pack our bags and get ready to leave. Okay, I'm ready. I'm going to watch a movie. This is going to be a long flight. Now we land and I am sharing a room with Sally. You're in a room in another part of the hotel. The first thing we'll do is explore and gather information about Paris and then find a place to have lunch. So anyway, Sally and I are going out to lunch. Why don't you go find a different place to have lunch?
Analyst: I see. So I'm on my own. Okay, I can take a hint.

Patient:	No offense. It's just that Sally and I would like to have some private time and besides, you're the professor and you might want to go away and do your own studies.
Analyst:	Now you imagine I might want to leave you behind.
Patient:	Yeah. Go on.
Analyst:	You're being active about it, leaving me, telling me to shove off before I say anything about wanting to go off and leave you.
Patient:	I guess so. I don't know. I think we're just being thoughtful.
Analyst:	Trying to imagine what I want and maybe leaving me before I can leave you.
Patient:	Are you trying to tell me something?
Analyst:	Do you think so?
Patient:	Yes. I really do think that.
Analyst:	The way you're picturing it, one of us is bound to feel left out. Either I leave you or you leave me.
Patient:	(starts to do handstands) Hey, check this out. (shifts to yoga poses).
Analyst:	I wonder if you felt uncomfortable when I was talking about feeling left out.
Patient:	No. Look at this. (does a cartwheel).
Analyst:	I was thinking that our playing lately has a lot to do with leaving. Today, we're talking about going on a trip, you and Sally leaving me to go to lunch and imagining me wanting to leave you.
Patient:	Yeah, but that's just today though. What do you mean lately?
Analyst:	Well, yesterday, the way that woman in your play, Molly, after telling lies, got kicked out of town and our meeting the day before that when you were talking about a woman trying to leave you and you were punching and kicking her.
Patient:	Oh yeah. I kind of remember that. But that was a long time ago.
Analyst:	A long time ago?
Patient:	Yeah. I can't believe you're bringing all those things up. That was like on Monday. (said in a Valley Girl tone) Like whatever. (makes the W sign with her hands)
Analyst:	I think you're feeling afraid of what I'm going to say about all this stuff about a woman leaving.
Patient:	No. Hey look at this. (she grabs a blanket and jumps on top of the desk and starts dancing, pretending that the blanket is a skirt)
Analyst:	Wow. You're really working very hard to distract us from the idea of a woman who leaves. I think you feel nervous about what I might say.
Patient:	(laughing excitedly) No I'm not. (she starts to do cartwheels)
Analyst:	All this stuff about a woman leaving and being angry at the woman leaving makes me think of your mother.
Patient:	No! I have an idea. (she turns two chairs over and joins them together to form a kind of shelter that resembles an igloo. She gets inside the structure.) Okay, no talking.

Analyst:	No talking?
Patient:	No talking.
Analyst:	You must not have liked what I said about your mother. It's hard to talk about her.
Patient:	I said no talking and I mean it.
Analyst:	(quiet) (there are a few open spaces in the shelter and she extends her hand out of one of the crevices)
Patient:	Can you put a pillow in the crack?
Analyst:	Sure. You really want to seal yourself up. You want to be completely away from me right now. No talking allowed.
Patient:	No. You can sing to me.
Analyst:	What would you like me to sing?
Patient:	I know. I wrote something on my iPad, a few songs. I'll get it. (She retrieves her iPad and shows me two songs she would like me to sing and then goes back into the enclosure that she created with the chairs).
Analyst:	Okay, I'll try, but I'm not a great singer.
Patient:	That's ok. Sing both songs.
Analyst:	Okay, here it goes: "Girl, I can't believe nothin you tell me. Look me in the eye so I can see if you're lyin. I don't need you anyway. I'm better than you. Fine, just go and don't come back."
Patient:	(laughing) The singing is terrible. It doesn't go that way at all. Sing the next one.
Analyst:	Okay. "They tell me I'm stupid, that I can't keep a bitch with me. I don't care because I am looking for something really good, someone great, someone who'll never ever lie to me."
Patient:	That was better. You actually have a pretty good operatic voice.
Analyst:	You know, these songs are also both about lying women who leave. That keeps coming up.
Patient:	Oh yeah. That's weird. But in the first song, I tell them to go away.
Analyst:	I see. They didn't leave you. You left them.
Patient:	Yeah. (she comes out of the self-created enclosure and then ties my shoelaces together and laughs) Okay, get up and try to run.
Analyst:	I guess you're showing me that it's impossible for me to leave you.
Patient:	No. Just try to do it. (laughing)
Analyst:	I'll fall and maybe get hurt if I do that. Maybe then I'd get what I deserve for trying to leave you.
Patient:	(laughs) You'll be punished severely for trying to get away from me!
Analyst:	I'm getting a sense of that. You mean business.
Patient:	I'm just kidding though.
Analyst:	Yes and no. I do think that you are very angry and hurt inside about a mother who did leave you. Those feelings come up very strong when I leave you, like my not being here last week.

Patient:	How much time is left?
Analyst:	We're going to have to stop for now.
Patient:	Okay, Bye.

Class Discussion

Instructor: In this case, a 6-year-old girl had a very powerful early bond with her mother. Her mother abandoned her and her family when she was three and she never heard from her again. In the session that I just presented, she is at a point in her treatment when the complex of feelings, memories, and ideas revolving around her early relationship with her mother are permeating her play and her associations.

On the conscious level, she is rejecting of my attempts to draw her attention to this. However, her efforts to reject me begin to transform into an actualization of her maternal transference. It's as if the resistance itself is permeated with the very thing that she is struggling to flee from. Freud viewed this as a compromise between the forces in the psyche pushing toward consciousness and those that are compelled to maintain repression.

As the defenses become weakened through interpretation and greater self-revelation, the transference will be utilized to maintain the resistance. While this transference appears on the surface to be resisting my interpretive efforts, on a deeper level it allows for the old ghosts of her past to come back to life in the present moment of the analytic relationship where they can become available for reflection and psychic work.

Reyna: It seemed to me that you were determined from the outset to speak to the theme of leaving and being left. It made me wonder if that had been something you spoke of earlier in the analysis.

Ezra: That's interesting. I thought about therapeutic zeal, like was there a feeling of pressure in you to address that dynamic with her.

Instructor: These are insightful observations. What comes to mind for me is that prior to this session, I had experienced a great deal of counter-resistance or shutupness about speaking directly to the matter of her mother having left her. The theme itself had become ubiquitous in her play and at the same time, something in me was unable to speak to it. I suspect the zeal you both notice in me had something to do with that internal struggle.

Bethany: The way the patient jumped on the desk and danced seemed seductive to me. It made me wonder if she was reliving something from the past in her transference in that moment.

Natalie: Yeah, like was she exposed to something seductive as a younger child. Was her mother seductive in some way?

Instructor: These are useful questions. What that brings to my mind is her way of trying to hold onto an abandoning object. It also leads me to think about the way seductiveness can be utilized as a way of defending against a threatening repressed idea that is coming into consciousness, like trying to deflect attention elsewhere.

As we noted with regard to the transference as resistance, this seeming flight from an idea may also be revealing something about her internal relationship to her maternal imago. Everything that happens in analysis can be seen as a compromise formation, that is, the unconscious wish and the defenses may be combined in the same action.

Ezra: What I found fascinating was how there was no way for her to escape the dynamic that she was trying to get away from, namely the painful memories associated with her mother. It seemed like everything she did, in her efforts to run away from that led her back to it.

Midge: That reminds me of the transference as resistance. In the transference, when something is pushing toward becoming conscious, part of the transference can be enacted in the present in a way that keeps the past at bay, at least initially. But it does still give form and shape to what is being repressed.

Instructor: I agree. Relatedly, it struck me that when I commented on how the theme of lying women who leave re-emerged in the songs she chose, her reply was that it was "weird." It reminds me of Freud describing a similar experience of his own in his paper "The Uncanny" (1919) when he described a walk he took in an unfamiliar place wherein he kept unwittingly ending up on the same spot on the same street, no matter how hard he tried to figure out his position (p. 237). We might think here about how such a situation can leave one feeling as if their fate is inescapable.

I think the young girl's recognition of the repetition and her comment on it being "weird" was a flicker of a moment of her becoming acquainted with her own experience of her unconscious repetition, a moment that perhaps felt uncanny.

Like Freud, no matter how hard she tried to get away from it, she kept finding herself, in spite of herself, returning to the same place.

Natalie: This is a good example of the value of the patient experiencing that for herself.

Instructor: Yes. Experiencing herself trying to get away from something and finding herself back in the same situation repeatedly allows her to have an experience of this unconscious force in a way that may provide a sense of conviction to the interpretations I was trying to make.

Reyna: It might also increase her sense of conviction of the unconscious force itself operating in her mind.

Instructor: Quite true, like becoming aware of both the force compelling her to repeat the experience and the force trying to escape it, analogous to Freud's own experience.

Natalie: I imagine the repressed as being similar to an invisible force field. You don't know it's there because it's invisible, but if you try to push through it, you suddenly have an experiential realization of its presence.

Instructor: That's a really apt metaphor. It's in the very act of trying push it away that we feel the unconscious force. That's what Freud means by becoming acquainted with the resistance.

Midge: That's interesting. What you said about becoming aware of the force and trying to escape it led me to wonder about becoming aware of the futility of trying to escape the repetition. There is something about that, I think, that could ultimately lead to a kind of surrender.

Instructor: That's something we can wonder about. How do you imagine that serving the aims of the analytic work?

Bethany: I think it could lead to a number of things that would serve analytic aims. If you have an experience, with conviction, that everything you have been doing to avoid emotional pain is in vain, then you might be able to begin to give that up, as Midge was saying, and then start to reflect on the situation you find yourself in. You might stop fighting it and it could ultimately lead to more insight about your suffering and the role you play in it.

Eli: That quality of giving up seems interesting to me.

Instructor: What is to be given up?

Midge: I think it's the fight against oneself. The more you fight against these unconscious impulses and their emotional pain, the tighter the bind locks you into the repetition. It's like trying to leave an internal object and clinging to them at the same time.

Eli: Simultaneously trying to leave an object and unconsciously clinging to it reminds me of a woman I was seeing in therapy who, after much struggle, decided to leave her husband. A few days later, she wasn't able to walk and her doctors were unable to find anything medical to account for it. She was stopped in her tracks by the realization that, in spite of her conscious intentions, there was a force inside her that could not let go.

Natalie: Eli, when you said that she was stopped in her tracks, it got me thinking about the value of that itself. It led me to think about patients who are so active in their efforts to escape something painful. There's a kind of frantic, desperate quality to it and being stopped like that can be the best thing, when you really have to reckon with the internal conflict. In a way, you're forced to.

Instructor: Your comments here are compelling. We can think about the unconscious repetition of the same experience, the compulsive force driving one to repeat. The interpretations that I had been making with this patient played a role, I think, in activating and intensifying her defensive attempts at flight. First, they provided points of contact for her unconscious longings for this abandoning object and then a flight from being aware of that. In this hour, she could even begin to recognize something weird going on. These are the kinds of experiences that, over time, contribute to a sense of conviction about the internal nature of the conflicts that we unconsciously put ourselves in. What you were describing about being stopped, even forced to stop, is interesting. In some ways, in the case I described to you, I was chasing the patient, who was running from painful memories. That chase involved showing her that what she was running from was what she was simultaneously running to. These were moments of her being temporarily stopped in her tracks. Consistent with what you've been describing, those moments, bit by bit, enabled her to begin to become acquainted with her inner conflict.

Shifting gears, I would also like us to think about the idea of the unobjectionable transference. Freud believed that the patient's affectionate, positive transference was a kind of fuel for the analytic work. He did not think it was to be interpreted or analyzed, but rather utilized as a silent suggestive influence upon the patient in the direction of encouraging them to collaborate in the work of analysis, for example, to continue to associate, to speak in the face of emotional pain, in part because they have this affectionate bond with the analyst, trust them, feel safe with them, and want to please them. In a way it is kind of like the patient doing analysis, enduring the pain of it in part because they seek the love of the analyst. This is a form of suggestive influence, but in the service of the patient engaging in work that is intended to lead to their own increasing mental freedom and autonomy.

Do you have any reactions to Freud's description of the unobjectionable positive transference? Do you see any problems with it?

Midge: A positive transference might be defensive, and hide more hostile feelings and fantasies.

Instructor: Do you have any ideas of how we might be clued in to an apparent positive transference that is being used in a primarily defensive way, as Midge was warning us about?

Ezra: For me, it has to do with whether it feels genuine or not.

Natalie: I would question it if it starts to sound too one-sided, if I felt like something was missing from the picture, that it didn't seem balanced.

Reyna:	I try to listen to how I'm feeling and what I'm noticing about the patient's positive feelings, like is it exaggerated, does it feel real to me, or does it irritate me?
Eli:	I feel troubled by our tendency to view the positive transference in an either/or binary kind of way.
Instructor:	Can you say more about that?
Eli:	The positive transference, like anything else we encounter in analysis is going to be a mix of many streams of motives, including hostility as well as love.
Bethany:	I'm thinking about how the positive transference can help the patient to reconnect with the analyst after some experience of hostility or resistance. It could help the patient reconnect with an experience of the analyst as a caring person, after having felt mistrustful of them.
Midge:	I can relate to that. There are times when I really hate my analyst but then a small thing, like seeing a look of genuine concern from him on the way out the door can remind me of other, warmer feelings about him, like oh he is a good guy, not the devil incarnate that I was feeling he was.
Reyna:	What you said about the look of genuine concern led me to think of how powerful in can be when the analyst doesn't respond to the patient's aggressive feelings with an aggressive reaction of their own.
Natalie:	I thought something like that happened in the case that you presented. The girl wanted to get away from you and stop you from talking. But when you said she wanted to get completely away from you, she suggested that you could sing to her. That felt like she was reconnecting with some part of you that she could trust and feel safe with.
Bethany:	In that case she was prescribing a role for you that would help her feel safe.
Eli:	I thought that you're willingness to do that, to sing for her, could be seen as a gesture, a willingness to make contact with her on her terms. I see that as facilitating the unobjectionable component of the transference.
Ezra:	I'm struck by the comment "on her terms" because the way you were initially trying to connect with her was threatening to her and she proposed another way. Being open to that does feel important to me because it suggests that you are willing to do something for her, to stretch.
Midge:	It is interesting that you said that you're not a great singer. I'm wondering why you said that?
Instructor:	I'm happy to tell you about that, but did you have your own ideas about it?
Midge:	Yeah. I thought you were letting her know that you were willing to do something for her that was uncomfortable for you. You were showing her your vulnerability.

Natalie: Then she wouldn't be the only one doing something uncomfortable. Maybe she would feel less alone in the experience of struggling with uncomfortable feelings.

Ernest: Singing to her also reminds me of something a mother might do when putting her child to bed. I wonder if she was getting in touch with softer feelings toward her mother in that moment even though the lyrics were expressing her anger.

Midge: That's like what Eli was saying about how the positive transference can be a combination or compromise involving different affective experiences. It's interesting, you can see both hostility and affection toward you in a number of ways. One moment she tells you that your singing is terrible. The next she says you have a pretty good operatic voice.

Ezra: This is leading me to think about the many ways that we make use of positive, supportive aspects of our relationship with our patients in part to make the analytic work more tolerable and possible for them.

Instructor: How do you see that?

Ezra: After you sing for her, she is much more receptive to noticing that it is true that she is continuing the theme that she had rejected earlier, of lying women who leave.

Natalie: Yes, and her defenses seemed to lower after that, like when she tied your shoe strings together and told you to run.

Midge: That felt playful to me which I associated with her feeling safer. I do think she was able to do that because she felt safer after you were willing to do something for her that was uncomfortable for you. It may have made you less threatening, and then she could even play with you more freely, so freely that she continues the theme that was so painful for her to face earlier.

Ezra: She was, at that point, able to directly express her anger and wish to punish you for leaving her, even with a playful threat. It was in the form of humor which I imagine made it easier for her to express it, but it still felt like an important movement for her to be able to do that.

Instructor: These are all great points. The idea that we make use of supportive aspects of our relationship with patients in ways that compensate the patient for painful aspects of the work is very interesting. How much of that we do intentionally and how much of that happens more unintentionally is an open question. This touches on Midge's question for me about why I told the patient that I'm not a great singer. That was a spontaneous remark. I was feeling some discomfort about singing. But, I think you're right that it did convey something to the patient about my willingness to do something for her that was uncomfortable for me.

Bethany: I'm thinking about the things we do in our work that we don't necessarily intend to do, like your spontaneous remarks about not being a good singer. It's especially interesting when those unintended actions appear to move the treatment forward.

Instructor: Is there anything in particular that interests you about that?

Bethany: It makes me really curious about what is it about those things that move the treatment. Like is it just random luck or well is there more going on, like what is going on for the analyst unconsciously in such moments?

Eli: That does make me ask if there was something going on in that interaction between the patient and the analyst that maybe did provoke a reaction.

Reyna: It's possible that Louis had feelings about the patient reacting so strongly to his interpretations and maybe that played a role in his comment about being a bad singer, like maybe you were feeling bad that you caused her upset.

Ezra: And that reaction might have shifted her feelings, made you more of a sympathetic object in her transference.

Midge: I wonder about the role the patient plays unconsciously in provoking responses in the analyst that lead to movement in the treatment. Ezra talked about the patient grooming the analyst to take on the role of an internal object. What I wonder about is whether the patient may be able to groom the analyst to take on a role that is somehow in line with their own unconscious ideas about what's curative.

Bethany: I see it as an interaction between the patient and analyst, some way in which they were each playing a role unconsciously in creating a scene that would help the patient feel less persecuted.

Instructor: This is a fascinating line of thought that you are pursuing. There are many moments when we engage in a particular way that we experience as unintended, like the comment I made about not being a good singer. We can wonder, as you have been, what is happening on more subtle channels of communication between patient and analyst. Is there some kind of unconscious communication occurring in such moments, aiming to negotiate an interaction that can move things forward?

In this paper, Freud emphasized that the most common types of transference utilized for resistance were the negative transference, where hostile feelings toward the analyst predominate, and the erotic transference, wherein sexual feelings prominent. Here, he is concerned that the negative, hostile transference can be a danger when extreme, as with paranoid patients, leading to the destruction of the analyst's capacity to have any influence over the patient.

Freud (1912) talked about how the transference resistance can lead to a dramatic shift in the patient's attitude toward the analysis. The patient "is flung out of his real relation to the doctor," and this can lead to a dramatic shift in the patient's attitude toward the analytic work, making the patient much more difficult to reach than had been the case before. The analyst's words lose their capacity to impact the patient when this shift occurs (p. 107).

Freud is describing a very real phenomenon. Once the transference resistance emerges, there is a very dramatic change in the patient's frame of mind. Conscious intentions to participate in the process of discovery fall away like dry leaves in a windstorm. There's an analogous version of this for the analyst that Freud will describe in his Transference Love paper.

On page 108, we have a very different view of the transference, and it feels like a very important shift. Freud is now seeing something about the transference that has potential clinical value in and of itself, framing it as something more than a mere obstacle to be removed as quickly as possible in order to get to the forgotten memories.

Here, he is saying that the repressed, unconscious complex seems not to want to be remembered in the verbal, reflectively conscious way that we may prefer it to be remembered. He is speaking to a compelling force to actualize our repressed complexes, to bring them to life and reincarnate them in the form of the present moment relationship with the analyst. He goes on to imply that this is where the life and heart of the work of analysis resides.

Do you have any reactions to the kinds of frustrations and disturbances we have been discussing? Can you relate to these experiences?

Reyna: I imagine Freud was feeling frustrated when he talked about resistance at first. I wonder about the experience of frustration in the analyst as maybe inevitable, in spite of our conscious rational understanding about what we are trying to do.

Instructor: I think you're onto something important. Can you say more about your understanding of the kind of frustration you're getting at?

Reyna: It could be part of a learning process, as we were describing earlier in our experience of learning about Freud. In clinical work too, we will experience moments when something feels confusing and we feel stuck. In those moments, before we are able to get what that obstacle is about, there will likely be frustration.

Ezra: I think that's right but I also think that our frustration may at times reflect a need to shift from pursuing one aim to another. Like, I might be in a position of trying to get my patient to become aware of something that I think I see and he may react in a defensive way. I have to give up the first aim to be able to move to being curious about the defensiveness.

Midge: That's interesting. I thought about a patient who has been telling me for quite some time that he can't ask anyone out on a date, but we had not been able to identify his fears. Then one session, he alludes to it and I quickly seized the moment to explore it, and then he gets really angry with me. I was so frustrated at first. I did have to give up my longing to get to the bottom of his fear before I could get curious about his anger at me.

A Note on What Happened

At the end of this meeting, I was struck by a number of unexpected directions which the dialogue took. The students' candidness in sharing their struggles in reading Freud, e.g., sharing their feelings of shame associated with encountering difficulties in understanding felt very important to me, leaving me reflecting on ways in which we might work with those feelings together. I was quite heartened by their sharing of their own clinical struggles in relation to what we were reading. In that sense, they were struggling right alongside Freud, as I had hoped. The discussion about how the analyst is shaped by the patient's transference did lead to increasingly complex and fascinating considerations of the ways that patient and analyst transference intersect and even appear to form a kind of interactive compromise, one that may be unconsciously communicated between patient and analyst. The critique of Freud's use of concepts that seemed alienated from social relationships did feel to me like an invaluable link to invite students to fill in those gaps with their own experiences. My aim in presenting the clinical case was primarily to illustrate the concept of transference and resistance. The dialogue went far beyond that, e.g., in their consideration of the ways in which analysts' unintended actions can move the treatment forward, leading to interesting speculations on underlying, interactive unconscious processes which may be involved in these phenomena.

References

Freud, S. (1912). The Dynamics of Transference. SE 12: 97–108.

Freud, S. (1919). The 'Uncanny'. SE: 217–256.

Mitchell, S. (1988). *Relational Concepts in Psychoanalysis*. Harvard University Press.

Roazen, P. (1971). *Freud and His Followers*. Da Capo Press, p. 31.

Terentius, P. (1880). *The Hauton Timorumenos or Self-Tormentor, of Terrence*. Thomas Shrimpton and Son; Whittaker and Co.; Simpkin, Marshall and Co.; Kessinger Publishing.

2   Working Through, Resistance, and Therapeutic Action

A Note on My Intentions

In my approach to the teaching of this paper, "Remembering, Repeating and Working-Through" (1914), I wanted to have the students reflect upon Freud's idea of working through, specifically with regard to the work that the patient is meant to do within the analysis. I aimed to continue to encourage the trend from the last class of linking Freud's concepts to one's own clinical and personal experiences. I intended to draw attention to Freud's conception of the role of interpretation and its relationship to overcoming repression. I wanted us to continue to think about Freud's concept of resistance. In addition, I sought to consider the role that transference neurosis plays in keeping untamed drives and memories within the borders of the analytic relationship. Finally, I also wanted us to consider important changes in technique heralded in this paper, e.g., the caution not to deliberately focus on anything in particular, but rather to follow the patient's associations wherever they lead.

Instructor: Freud's paper, "Remembering, Repeating and Working-Through" (1914) begins with a reminder of where psychoanalysis started, his work with Breuer to use hypnosis in their efforts to help patients recount the circumstances that preceded their symptoms and to do so in such a way that would be emotionally charged. He speaks of how the catharsis would bring about a release of tremendous tension.

   By catharsis, Freud meant that the treatment would lead to a discharge of pent-up, pathogenic affects. The hypnosis facilitated the patient to bring traumatic memories to mind, to relive the situations to which these affects were connected. He speaks of the abandonment of the cathartic method and how it was replaced by the work the patient had to do to overcome their resistances to remembering.

   Lawrence Friedman (2019) posits that Freud was looking for something in this new free association and interpretation model

DOI : 10.4324/9781003610977-3

that would compare to the powerful effect of catharsis. We will discuss this further into the paper and we might think together about what that could be for Freud, as well as what that might be for each of us in thinking about our own psychoanalytic work as analysts and patients.

One question that comes up here is whether the power of catharsis is replaced by the patient's pushing through and speaking, in spite of the resistance, as Freud (1914) suggests when he says, "...the element of abreaction (emotional discharge) receded into the background and seemed to be replaced by the expenditure of work which the patient had to do in being obliged to overcome their own criticism of their free associations" (p. 147).

Note the emphasis here on the work the patient must do. This is a very interesting development. Freud appears to be talking about working through as involving the courage to struggle with one's resistances and eventually push through and speak and remember what we feel must not be spoken and remembered.

Does this notion of working through, one involving the struggle with one's own resistance have any resonance for you, given your own experiences?

Ernest: I've felt this in supervision. It would become clear what I needed to say to the patient, but I would feel too scared to say it, and much of the work then would involve trying to face that fear, to talk about it, to explore it, and to keep trying to struggle through whatever was keeping me from saying it until I could finally say it.

Midge: I wonder if that struggle in the analyst to say what he's afraid to say could have something mutative about it for the patient?

Instructor: It sounds like you have something in mind about that.

Midge: I think the patient would, on some level, maybe not consciously, pick up on the work the analyst was doing to get there and maybe something about noticing the analyst's struggle would be emotionally impactful.

Eli: I'm not sure if this relates to what Midge is getting at, but it brought a patient to mind who seemed to get worse when I interpreted things that I heard from my supervisor, especially if I hadn't done some internal work on these ideas first. That might be an example of a patient picking up on whether or not I struggled to say what I had to say.

Instructor: Very interesting. And what do you mean by internal work?

Eli: It's hard to define that, but mostly stewing with it, engaging in some conversation with myself about it until I could say it in a way that felt like my own thoughts and voice. What she said made sense to me, but I had to sort of find it for myself, find my own path to it in a way, say it but go through my own emotional process to say it, not just repeat what I was told.

Instructor: So, I want to mark a theme here that feels important. It has to do with the private emotional work that the analyst does in order to make an interpretation that is impactful to the patient and how this work the analyst does is analogous to the work the patient does, what Freud talks about as working through. Eli's vignette illustrates the way an undigested interpretation, e.g., something that one hears from a supervisor, that hasn't yet been worked over in one's mind, can actually lead to disturbances in the patient.

Bethany: Sometimes when we are experiencing the patient as being resistant, it really is our own resistance that we are seeing in a projected form.

Instructor: An excellent point. When we have the idea that the patient is being resistant, we can begin to wonder if we are reacting and shying away from something that feels threatening for us.

Early on, Freud reasserts that the goal of psychoanalysis, despite the change in methods, is still about remembering what has been forgotten. However, he is also saying that the transference has pride of place as the most important type of resistance. He is defining the relationship between the analyst and patient as one where the patient repeats their forgotten past in the form of action and the analyst interprets this to help the patient become conscious of what has been forgotten. Here, it is clear that Freud's thought about interpretation is that it is meant to assist the patient to become conscious of what is repressed.

Does this make sense to you? I am wondering how you think about interpretation in your own work. Maybe some examples come to your mind.

Natalie: I usually think of interpretation as something that helps the patient to make sense of their suffering, something that gives form to what might be a state of confusion or disorganization. It is meant to help the patient to be able to think the unthinkable by putting words to it that approximate the underlying emotional experience.

Ezra: I see the interpretation's role as providing a stimulus for further thought, for more associations, to get something moving. Interpretations can trigger memories that have been repressed. An incorrect interpretation can move things forward too, pushing the patient to come back and counter what he heard in ways that can shake things up.

Instructor: Is it the case that the analyst's interpretations are always ultimately in the service of making sense of something, of increased understanding? Do you think there is anything problematic about this view?

Reyna: That way of putting it seems reductionistic to me. An interpretation isn't always about understanding, but sometimes it can even undo an understanding that has become fixed. It can cause confusion by challenging or contradicting an assumption that the patient is stuck in.

Instructor: That's a great point, Reyna. Sometimes my analyst could provoke that feeling in me by simply asking me "why." I also like Ezra's comment. These remarks give more breadth and complexity to our conception of interpretation.

I would like to highlight an important tension in these ways of thinking about interpretation. On the one hand, we can think of interpretation as serving an organizing, ordering function, of pulling things together to provide an understanding of something confusing, as Natalie described. On the other hand, an interpretation can undo understandings and serve the function of creating disorder or disorganization, of breaking up understandings. We might think of these opposing functions as working together interactively, each serving important roles.

Midge: I want to bring us back to a conversation we had a moment ago about the work the analyst does to be able to speak to what he feels must be said. I think that what I was trying to get at was something about that process in the analyst that demonstrates something to the patient about how to do the work of working through.

Instructor: How do you imagine it playing out? Can you picture a scene that illustrates that?

Midge: I was thinking of it as sort of showing the patient how to do it, not in a conscious or even deliberate way, but sort of unintentionally, a felt and perceived experience that the patient could unconsciously draw upon.

Ernest: That reminds me of ways that we might be subliminally influenced by observations that we don't even consciously know we are making.

Ezra: I'm thinking about our previous conversation, what I called grooming that can occur when patient and analyst are sort of provoked subtly to take on certain roles, all of which occurs unconsciously.

Instructor: These are fascinating ideas. Consistent with what Ernest and Ezra have described, I want to emphasize the part where Midge said that "showing the patient how to do it" is not conscious or deliberate. I do wonder about that piece. There is an element of not trying here that feels important. The analyst is processing their experience, working through something, out of necessity, due to discomfort, but at that early stage of the process it is not in the conscious, intentional service of teaching or showing the patient something. It's located in the analyst's personal struggle, we might say driven by the pleasure principle, with trying to cohere something in the form of trying to put it into words that do not yet feel speakable. In fact, I wonder if that may be part of what makes it more possible for the patient to make use of it. There is an implicit, unintended interpretation in it for the patient to receive, but it is not directed to the patient in the way one might when later making a deliberate, conscious interpretation that is meant to enlighten the patient.

Bethany: That reminds me of play therapy when children are able to consider something that is said through a character telling it to another character in the play. They might not be able to hear it if the therapist said it directly to them. There is an indirectness about it that could make it easier to take in, in a way maybe bypassing defenses that would otherwise be deployed if it was obvious that the analyst was intending to interpret to them.

Natalie: That's a really interesting way of looking at this. Also, if I am in a struggle with the patient and I am focused less on coming up with something to say that will impact the patient, but more on my own efforts to give expression to an experience that I'm having, that might free me up in a way that's less pressured.

Eli: That reminds me of Midge's example. Sometimes I feel relief after making an interpretation to a patient. I wonder if that might have a beneficial effect on the patient's state of mind, maybe making it easier for the patient to expand and associate more freely.

Instructor: What do you think would lead the patient to be able to do that?

Eli: The patient's felt sense of my mental state seeming calmer might be an indication to the patient that there is more receptivity in me, more room in my mind, an increased tolerance to hear more of something that I previously felt defensive about.

Instructor: Another very interesting point. I was thinking also, that if the patient is anticipating a hostile reaction from the analyst, such an interpretation that is cathartic for the analyst would likely lead to an experience of the analyst that stands in contrast to what the patient is anticipating. That may exert a therapeutic action.

Ezra: This conversation has me thinking a lot about what we often perceive as resistance in the patient. We've been talking about the ways that the analyst deals with their own struggles within the analysis and the potential impact that has on the patient. The work the analyst has to do is very similar to the work we are trying to get the patient to do. It does seem to me that our own difficulties in doing that work could very well result in what we see as the patient's resistance to doing the work.

Natalie: Right, like are we displacing our own resistance onto the patient, in an effort to maintain some esteemed position of being the analyst who is trying to get at something, like a denial of the trouble we're having.

Reyna: That idea of the resistance viewed as an interpersonal manifestation of an intra-psychic conflict does lead me to think about how often there is a kind of antagonistic tension between patient and analyst.

Eli: Antagonism makes me think of fighting. So, is the patient's inclination to fight the analyst in certain moments an externalization of an internal antagonism having to do with an intra-psychic conflict?

Natalie: That makes sense to me. Like when the girl you presented last week was pushing you away and telling you not to say anything, there was aggression in that, and it seemed to have to do with a conflict in herself, connected to her refusing to having anything to do with thinking about her mother.

Ezra: That makes sense, but I'm also thinking about what Reyna said about there being an antagonistic tension between patient and analyst. So, if that's true, what is the analyst's antagonism about?

Midge: There are a lot of possibilities. When the patient directs at the analyst an internal hostile attitude say against certain repressed unconscious ideas perceived as threatening, that is going to have some impact on the analyst.

Ernest: It's interesting though, because when I heard the idea of the patient's resistance as an interpersonal manifestation of an inner conflict, it felt relieving to me, sort of like a different way of thinking about something that can feel like an attack.

Instructor: A different way?

Ernest: A way that is less personal, like I can think the patient's attack on me isn't really about me so much, but more of an attack on their own unconscious, something threatening within them that I am getting close to.

Eli: I can see how that vantage point would give the analyst more perspective and make it less likely that he'd be reactive. On the other hand we may not see that in the moment. There may be moments when it all happens so fast and we feel attacked and find ourselves reacting more personally.

Midge: These kinds of tensions between patient and analyst involve the analyst making room within themselves to use their relationship with the patient as a container for the conflicts that the patient needs to work on.

Instructor: That idea of the analyst finding a way to make room within the relationship for the patient's conflicts reminds me of what Freud (1914) said about how the patient may express very strong impulses before the transference is able to provide a containing function (pp. 153 and 154). One implication in what Freud is saying here is that the transference can keep these untamed drives and untamed memories within the borders of the analytic relationship where it can be subjected to reflective scrutiny and gradually become more conscious, emotionally processed, and integrated. The work within the transference can also protect the patient from the dangers of acting out, of the repetition compulsion outside one's analysis where the risk of destructive harm is greater.

Ezra: The way Midge described the analyst making room within themselves to use the relationship as a container so that patients can work through these conflicts is fascinating to me. The making room must have so much to do with what gets triggered in our own transference reactions to the patient's antagonism.

Natalie: I think the making room is going to involve the analyst working through vulnerable areas in themselves in order to be able to allow the patient to make use of them within the transference relationship.

Instructor: I think that's true and I would add that the emotional experiences that we struggle with in the process can be put in the service of interpreting the nature of the patient's struggles.

Ezra: That reminds me of acting, how actors, when they are playing a role encounter personal vulnerabilities, the reemergence of pain they've felt in their lives and they try to use that in their work, rather than fight against it.

Reyna: I really like that and I can see how analysts likewise might be initially inclined to fight against their own painful feelings. Those moments really put to the test our own relationship to analytic work.

Instructor: How do you see that playing out, Reyna?

Reyna: Children are much more influenced by what their parents do. I wonder if something similar happens in analysis. How the analyst responds to their own emotional pain will communicate a lot to the patient about the analyst's belief in the treatment they're offering. I would think that the analyst's responding defensively could diminish the patient's trust in the process.

Midge: The analyst might deny that and treat the resistance as occurring solely within the patient. That could have unfortunate consequences in terms of the analytic process.

Instructor: Unfortunate consequences?

Midge: The analyst might have an overvalued notion of where the patient needs to go and interprets the patient's speaking of something else as a resistance.

This could lead to a power struggle and maybe even oppress the patient into having to submit to some idea of himself that isn't congruent with his own experience.

Instructor: That's a very important point for us to keep in mind. I think you are approaching the dangers of therapeutic zeal again which can create many of the types of deleterious effects you described.

As we discussed, the patient's transference will inevitably link up with some aspect of the analyst's transference and this makes the work much more personal and important, raising the stakes for the analyst. It is true that the patient's reliving through the transference will also stir up our own transference, and so the work of speaking the unspeakable will involve something very personal within our own struggles. This lends itself to the analyst having more skin in the game, so to speak. And as you have been describing so well, how the analyst deals with these struggles will say a great deal, in action, about their attitude toward analysis and their unconscious.

Freud (1914) says,

> ...there has evolved the consistent technique used today, in which the analyst gives up the attempt to bring a particular moment or problem into focus. He contents himself with studying whatever is present for the time being on the surface of the patient's mind...
>
> (p. 147)

This is an important development in technique, where Freud is suggesting that we follow what is most active in the present moment of the patient's mind.

The analyst is now cautioned not to deliberately try to focus on anything in particular. There is a quality of trying to let go of our own desires in order to be free to follow the current of associations wherever they lead and to stay with whatever is most immediately alive and present. The analyst is positioned here as non-directive which is an analogue to the patient's position to say everything that comes to mind without goal directed attention.

Eli: Sometimes I feel compelled to try to bring the patient back to something that felt important in the previous session, but it always feels forced and not convincing for the patient. I feel like I could be encountering a frustration that Freud encountered himself.

Instructor: This kind of comparison to your own clinical experience is a great way to try to feel our way imaginatively into what Freud may have been grappling with clinically in the process of developing his technique.

Freud (1914) says,

> ...we may say that the patient does not remember anything of what he has forgotten and repressed, but acts it out. He reproduces it not as a memory but as an action; he repeats it, without, of course, knowing that he is repeating it.
>
> (p. 150)

The repetition, which previously had been described as an obstacle, a resistance to remembering is now viewed as a form of remembering.

How does it feel to think of things in this way versus how Freud spoke of the transference resistance at the beginning of "The Dynamics of the Transference" (1912) paper?

Ernest: My own experience with this paper involves a shift in attitude in thinking about the transference as less of something to be overcome and more of something to be curious about, something of clinical value in and of itself.

Instructor: Ernest's comment reminded me of something we talked about earlier, that is, the repeated experience in analysis of encountering what seems to be obstacles and overcoming this initial view in order to re-find one's curiosity about what we had felt as nothing more than an impediment. In a way, this process involves a limited view transforming into a more expansive, complex perspective. A sense of frustration and feeling stuck may be the prelude to the shift to a higher plane, a broader vantage point. It seems to me that the precursor to this shift is a kind of giving up and accepting that the force we are trying to overcome is stronger than our conscious aims. This is one area within which we will be tested in terms of our attitude toward our own unconscious processes.

Can you think of experiences you've had of encountering obstacles and subsequently being able to move from a limited vantage point to a wider lens perspective on what was going on?

Bethany: I take on blame for the patient's resistance, feeling like if I were doing better analytic work, the patient would not be manifesting the resistance. My supervisor helped me to see that what was happening was not an indication that I had failed, but was actually a sign that something was starting to move.

Midge: The idea of resistance seems to have fallen into disuse and I wonder if that could contribute to a misunderstanding of processes in the patient that look like bad news, namely a tendency to interpret resistance as a sign of a failing analysis, even a tendency to evoke more personal, moral ideas of failure.

Instructor: Freud (1914) said that the modifications of analytic technique leads to the replaying of past experiences in ways that can feel quite dangerous, even leading to the patient's symptoms worsening. This is a very important warning about the new treatment model. To Midge's point, when we don't keep these concepts in mind, e.g., the resistance, we may be more inclined to feel that we are failing in such moments.

        This can be quite scary for the analyst, especially given that this will likely also stir up repressed areas of conflict within the analyst. The "blood of recognition" (Loewald, 1980, pp. 248–249) will occur in both patient and analyst leading to the mutual, interlocking transferences of each of the involved parties. Freud (1915) will speak to this again in the "Observations on Transference Love" paper when he speaks of the analyst's inclination, when this emotional heat reaches a certain threshold of intensity, to try make the patient suppress the transference.

Bethany: This may be about the analyst feeling compelled to do that to keep his own sleeping dogs asleep or put them back to sleep.

Midge: That might play out in very subtle ways that we aren't even aware of.

Natalie: I'm thinking about the intensity of the repetition. I wonder if that's part of what can lead us to do things that attenuate feelings that reach a high pitch of intensity.

Ezra: I am sure we each have our own Achilles in terms of what feels threatening, especially when things get emotionally intense. For me, I've noticed that when patients are enraged, I do tend to respond in ways that tone things down.

Bethany: Yeah, I can relate to that, but for me it's when hopelessness and despair become overwhelming, I move away from it or try to interrupt it. My own feelings keep me from being curious about it.

Reyna: It's really hard to be curious when you feel you're in danger. Reflexively, you want to get away from that feeling.

Instructor: Consistent with your comments here, Freud said that our tendency to do that can at times be like bringing old spirits back to life without learning anything from them. These fears in the analyst can clue us in to the inception of the transference neurosis, that moment when the patient's and analyst's transferences intersect and both parties can feel a strong desire to escape this fate. As a graduate student once said, upon hearing his colleague present a very difficult clinical moment, wherein she said that she wanted to quit the treatment and perhaps her training altogether, "Houston, we have transference."

On the same page, Freud speaks to a shift in attitude that can occur in the patient, and the analyst, I would add, when in the grip of the work in the transference, one where the patient experiences his suffering as something meaningful and worthy of his respect. He's also talking about a shift in attitude toward one's unconscious, one that is less dismissive, one wherein the patient may begin to experience a sense of conviction regarding what is being said and shown by himself and the analyst. That is similar to the shift in ourselves from viewing a seemingly stuck point in an analysis as a mere obstacle to an object of curiosity and potential insight.

When the affective experience in the here and now of the transference is joined with the words spoken, there is a greater likelihood of a moving and potentially transforming experience. This joining of affect and words is a new edition of Freud and Breuer's original cathartic treatment in the early days of hypnosis.

This is when speech which may have felt hollow and unconvincing becomes filled, imbued with very real emotional experience. There is the hollow speech that seems to work against abreaction, the speech that dulls one's mind into a kind of comfortable numbness. That stands in marked contrast with speech that has emerged from a struggle with one's resistances, speech that moves.

What do you imagine the therapeutic effect of this joining of the emotional experience of transference with spoken words?

Midge: It reminds me of our earlier discussion of the impact on the patient of the analyst's version of working through. What if an interpretation that emerges from the analyst's emotional work to say it, especially if we've had to overcome our own sense of danger, is a way of joining the emotional experience with spoken words, something felt as having more conviction in it. The analyst might be perceived as having conviction, or as you said, skin in the game, about what they are saying to the patient and this could be heard differently by the patient.

As Eli described earlier, the patient might also see for themselves, within the analyst's affective response, that speaking from this place of emotional struggle leads to relief.

Instructor: What Midge is saying can be seen as an example of filled-in or imbued speech in contrast to a more hollow speech that is not grounded in the experience of the analyst's emotional work to say it. We have to wonder how the analyst's speaking from a place of joining words with emotional experiences impacts the way in which the patient receives the communication. We can also think about the resistances in the analyst that inhibit speaking from this position. This also once again touches on the issue that the patient and analyst are struggling with similar forms of resistance.

This analogue that we read in Freud's writing between the early technique and the new one reminds me of an important insight that Ernest shared about the way Freud writes and how we read him as very important. He noted how Freud often changes his thinking, even within a single paper. It is very interesting to see how Freud's ideas are continuously moving into new forms, new ways of thinking, while also not discarding many of the older ideas.

Note Freud's emphasis on the work the patient must do to express what they feel must not be spoken. The work necessitates an expenditure and discharge of energy. We see Freud's model of abreaction taking on a novel clinical form. And these new concepts begin to hint at ideas yet to come. So, with Freud you often get the past, present, and nascent future conceptualizations all coexisting side by side.

Reyna: This reminds me of what we talked about earlier about trying to imaginatively engage Freud in dialogue. Freud himself seems to be in dialogue between different phases of his own thinking.

Instructor: That's a great way of putting it and an important observation.

Eli: Freud's process of thinking involves both conservative and progressive tendencies.

Instructor: Can you flesh that out more? Where do you see that playing out?

Eli: Even when Freud is in the midst of developing new ideas, these are in tension with his older views, and that seems to be a very useful tension. It might be like a strategy Freud uses to keep his thinking sharp and in a kind of continuously creative tension.

Instructor: That's an excellent point. He also creates a similar tension in imagining critics in argument with him as he writes. We might think here about Freud's capacity for staying with conflicts within his mind, staying with these tensions, and using them as having important clinical implications. In some ways, it represents the intellectual counterpart to the kind of capacities that are crucial for the emotional work of analysis.

Your experience of reading Freud in and of itself can be thought of as an exercise that is related to your struggles to become an analyst. Do you see any connection between your struggles to read Freud, grappling with his concepts, and your efforts to practice psychoanalysis clinically?

Ernest: In my own struggles in reading Freud, it's hard to stay with him as he goes into one idea and then changes course so often, at times seeming so ambiguous and even contradictory.

Instructor: How do you think about those experiences in the context of what we have been discussing?

Ernest: The idea that Freud's way of thinking represents important analytic capacities led me to wonder if the process of reading Freud and working to increase my tolerance for these tensions in the writing, the ambiguities, the contradictions, might in some way help me to bear those experiences clinically.

Instructor: The way you just described that Ernest reminds me of the idea of negative capability, fundamentally involving our capacity to tolerate uncertainty. I am also thinking about Hans Loewald's work. Loewald spoke of how he read Freud in a way that allowed him to experience Freud as a living presence. Loewald would juxtapose Freud's early thoughts with his later conceptualizations, bringing them into tension with one another, allowing them to come into living contact with one another, sometimes to transiently reconcile these tensions or to maintain them creatively in the service of generating new ideas, or to create new vistas that are more comprehensive, coherent, and developmentally complex. But these tensions appeared to keep Freud's ideas in continuous motion. This is a dialectical approach. We're looking at these ideas in their process. A new idea comes into being out of the tension with other ideas that may appear to be in contradiction. The novel idea does not completely eliminate the previous idea, only parts of it, while integrating other pieces that are still useful.

We can see something similar happening within our dialogue here in that we tend to return to previous ideas in the novel context of the present moment and these ideas can take on new shades of meaning over time.

Reyna: That itself sounds a lot like something that I think happens in analysis. We repeatedly revisit ideas that have come up previously and these older ideas exist in tension with the new context that we are in. That process must change our perspective, making it more rounded out and complex over time.

Midge: I just thought of another link between this kind of tension of ideas and the tensions involved in the analytic process. It reminds me of the tension between the repetition compulsion and the struggle to keep it in the psychical realm and also the tension between interpretations that bring material together in ways that convey understanding versus those that tend to undo understandings.

Instructor: Those are important links. It also seems to me that we are facilitating a dialogue in the patient between seemingly opposed parts of themselves and between different time periods in their lives and that maybe that itself is also in part generative of an unfolding analytic process. It is analogous to the kind of internal dialogue that Freud lets us in on in his own writing. These tensions bring the experience of contradictions to the fore which may press one toward a shift, a movement away from a static position.

Bethany: I'm thinking of something being cut off from circulation. Repression pushes ideas out of circulation, it cuts something off that can't join with other ideas in consciousness and deprives us of an important tension that is generative and growth promoting. In some ways we bring these repressed ideas back into circulation with other ideas within consciousness. It's disturbing at first. It perturbs a comfortable but inert one-sidedness in our thinking, but it also can spark movement and generate new ideas with more layers to them.

Instructor: I love what you said, Bethany. I also see a connection between what you're describing clinically and what we've been experiencing reading Freud. Freud and his way of thinking unsettle a more comfortable, but perhaps inert one-sidedness in our thinking. And as you said, it is also clearly sparking a movement in our own reflections and generating new ideas in our dialogue. Those new ideas come out of your own unique struggles to make use of language and metaphors for grafting onto Freud's ideas through your own experiences and prior knowledge. In these ways, you are bit by bit making these ideas your own, that is, thinking for yourselves.

In terms of clinical psychoanalysis, what I hear a number of you saying is very important and reminds me of how we are facilitating a dialogue between ideas that were repressed in early childhood and our adult conscious reasoning. What was intolerable and impossibly dangerous to think about in our early years is more likely going to be more thinkable for our adult conscious mind to synthesize.

Ezra: I just imagined a conversation between our adult self and our child self and this reminds me of the idea of being the kind of parent to that past child self that I needed. I was thinking about what kind of parent little me would be able to find relief from. Maybe I can learn to be that for my little me.

Instructor: That metaphor seems useful and emotionally resonant.

The piece on page 152 of this paper about the shift in the patient's attitude through the experience of the transference reminds me of some things Freud (1920) said in the paper, "Beyond the Pleasure Principle." He warns us that merely making an interpretation will not necessarily lead to the patient being convinced of what we are saying. The patient is required to relive it in the present in order to acquire their own sense of conviction, adding that we may wish that the patient do something tamer, e.g., recall the past in a way that is more clearly distinct from the present.

Can you think of any examples when you have wanted the patient to behave differently only to subsequently discover that what they were doing was actually important to move the treatment forward? Or has something like this happened in your own analysis?

Reyna: I felt frustrated with a patient who seemed to refuse to see the way they were repeating an abusive relationship. But then later I could see that it was playing out between us. I was blaming and, at times, even browbeating him for not seeing something when it was also me that was not seeing something going on right there between us.

Instructor: These humbling moments are so crucial in our learning about psychoanalysis.

Freud (1914) said that, in this novel technique, the analyst has to be able to expect to deal with tensions continuously in our efforts to direct the patient's tendency to enact his impulses toward reflection on what is pushing toward consciousness.

Here Freud is depicting the relationship between the analyst and patient as one between reflection and action. The patient is seen as driven to enact an unconscious fantasy while the analyst is portrayed as always trying to get the patient to notice what they are putting into action and to reflect on it, eventually to see, with conviction and feeling, the forgotten past that they are reliving.

The patient must be given license to express whatever is pushing to be actualized in the transference. Later in the paper, Freud (1914) said, the transference is "allowed to let itself go in almost complete freedom and is required to display before us all the pathogenic impulses hidden in the depths of the patient's mind" (p. 154).

Natalie: I just noticed something I didn't see when I read this paper, Freud's use of the word "almost" in the piece you just quoted.

Instructor: That's a great catch. What do you think is significant about it?

Natalie: Freud was talking about another important tension of allowing the patient freedom but within important limits as well.

Instructor: What do you think the limits might be?

Natalie: I think it has to do with the analyst actively bringing the patient back to reflect on the dynamic meaning of what they are doing and maybe also what the analyst and patient are doing together.

Midge: The analyst actually needs the patient to repeat the past so that her words are in close proximity to the patient's emotional experience. That would carry more emotional conviction for the patient and analyst.

Eli: I agree, but I wonder if our resistance to the patient's repetition might reflect our resistance to our own unconscious.

Bethany: It occurs to me that our resistance to our own unconscious is a resistance to life. The repetition is life; it is coming to life of something that has been repressed, buried.

Midge: That brings to mind our earlier discussion of feelings of danger and our tendency to tone things down when they get intense.

Ernest: I think that's why we are doing this work. Even though we might feel we didn't sign onto this when it gets really rough or when it feels too real, maybe that's what we precisely did sign on for, unconsciously.

Instructor: Like maybe it's not just an accident of fate that we are doing this kind of work. That does help us to experience our work more personally, as congruent with a personal path that we are on, especially during the difficult times when we may not feel that way.

Freud speaks to the transference as something that the analyst must give almost complete license to express as fully as possible and that the analyst is meant to handle the transference through interpretation in such a way that this regressive enactment can be kept under some frame or containment. He says that the patient's symptoms will gradually take on a new transference meaning and what was once an intra-psychic structure within the patient's psyche will become more fully manifest in the transference relationship with the analyst. Freud called it a transference neurosis.

Later, in "Beyond the Pleasure Principle," Freud (1920) added that the analyst has to try to facilitate the patient's repeating of his past experiences but also to be able to pull back from it and look at it from a more distant perspective. He uses the word aloofness to describe that latter step.

I was struck by what Freud described about helping the patient to both re-experience their repressed memories through regression and to maintain some degree of aloofness. Freud is describing the analytic dialectic between being free to regress and relive unconscious fantasies within the transference and then being required to step back and reflect critically on what has been playing itself out.

Freud (1914) then says that the analyst pointing out the transference resistance to the patient is not enough to alter the situation. He said that

> One must allow the patient time to become more conversant with this resistance, with which he has now become acquainted, to work through it, to overcome it, by

continuing in defiance of it, the analytic work according to the fundamental rule of analysis.

(p. 155)

Freud's revision shifts the emphasis of therapeutic action to what the patient is able to achieve through the struggle to put into words what had been repressed and deemphasizes the role of the analyst naming the resistance through interpretation.

Can you think of any implications for our work of this changed emphasis? Can you think of any benefits and/or problems with it?

Reyna: This way of putting it helps me to take in the idea that the interpretation is not something that we do to the patient, but it feels more like something the analyst extends to the patient. The patient still has to do something on their end to meet that, to work toward reaching it and making use of it. I'm realizing now that I was holding a kind of one-direction psychology with regard to interpretation as a kind of medicine offered to the patient without taking into account the work the patient has to do. I'm realizing how a mutative interpretation is really a two-way street. Also, the work that the patient is not doing allows us to identify resistances that would be important to bring to the patient's attention.

Instructor: Great points. The two-way street also reminds me that the analyst must listen very carefully to the patient's allusions to how they are perceiving the analyst. These often contain important interpretations for the analyst.

When we discussed Freud's view of working through, I focused primarily on the patient's private experience of struggle and effort in dealing with divided intentions within themselves. Am I missing something by emphasizing this piece?

Natalie: I think what's missing are the many actions the analyst engages in that set things up for that to happen, like interpreting the transference and other forms of resistance. I think that these things we do facilitate this private struggle, often serving as stimuli that ignite that struggle. Reyna spoke about this when she talked about how the work the patient isn't doing clues us into the resistance, something we can bring to the patient's attention.

Ezra: I agree with this but I am also curious why that felt important to say.

Instructor: It sounds like you have your own idea about that.

Ezra: Yes, it might be hard for us to acknowledge that there is much that moves the work forward that we cannot attribute directly to our own interventions.

Instructor: Why would that be difficult to acknowledge?

Ezra: It could leave us feeling less important, less of a direct causal agent in helping the patient overcome his suffering, and maybe less in control of what happens and that feels terrifying.

Instructor:	Any ideas about what might be terrifying about that?
Ernest:	It feels scary to think of the analytic process as having a life of its own. It makes me feel more like a passive bystander watching something happen without being able to be certain that it's going to be for the good.
Reyna:	The way you described it reminds me of my own experience in my analysis. I observe and speak my own thoughts as they emerge and follow that path without knowing where it will lead and I often don't feel any control over that process. Also, I can feel things moving with a life of their own and I have no idea what that's going to ultimately look like, but I have a sense that much will be different than it is now.
Instructor:	What Ernest said about feeling like a passive bystander watching a process ensue that has a life of its own captures a very real part of what it's like when that process takes flight. Reyna's example, I think, does demonstrate an important experience of being in analysis when we begin to notice and hear our own associations as a kind of flowing process, driven by forces outside our conscious control. The loss of control can be scary, but also exciting and quite novel. In such moments we actually become more interesting and mysterious to ourselves. We can see, though, that change, something we want to happen and don't want to happen, can also frighten us, not only for the patient but for the analyst as well, especially early on in one's training, but certainly not limited to that.

A Note on What Happened

At the end of our discussion of this paper, I was left stirred up with many wonderings about some of the unexpected places we traversed in this discussion. The focus on Freud's idea of working through led to a consideration of how analysts themselves similarly struggle to speak to what feels unspeakable. I was struck that this focus followed on the heels of my speaking last week about my own experience of struggling to speak in the case that I presented. This evolved into thinking about the private emotional work that the analyst engages in in order to make interpretations that are impactful to the patient. The idea of needing to digest something learned from a supervisor before making interpretive use of it reminded me of the question of how it is that we make something we learn our own. This idea came up again a little later when we talked about how new ideas emerged out of the students' own personal struggles to make use of language and metaphors conducive to latch onto Freud's ideas through their own experiences and prior knowledge. In these ways, they were in an early process of making these ideas their own.

My drawing students' attention to Freud's conceptualization of interpretation led them to consider their own views on interpretation, based on their clinical experiences. For example, they talked about how interpretations can help to make sense of the patient's suffering, give form to states of confusion and disorganization, and the idea that interpretations can undo understandings that had become fixed. The notion that the analyst's emotional work to speak from a place of their own felt experience led to speculations about the possibility that patients may be able to make indirect use of their own experiences of the analyst's process of working through resistances. This led me to think about the importance of reciprocal impact in analysis and teaching, that is, that there may be mutative aspects of patient and analyst and students and teacher, experiencing being impacted and having an impact on one another. Students explored the idea that Freud's way of thinking itself, as manifested in the text, appeared to demonstrate important analytic capacities. A fascinating question was posed, reflecting on how the process of reading Freud and working to increase tolerance for the tensions in the writing might in itself be a kind of training for being able to tolerate those experiences clinically.

References

Freud, S. (1912). The Dynamics of Transference. SE 12: 97–108.
Freud, S. (1914). Remembering, Repeating and Working-Through. SE 12: 145–156.
Freud, S. (1915). Observations on Transference-Love. SE 12: 157–171.
Freud, S. (1920). Beyond the Pleasure Principle. SE 18: 3–64.
Friedman, L. (2019). *Freud's Papers on Technique and Contemporary Clinical Practice.* Routledge.
Loewald, H. (1980). *Papers on Psychoanalysis.* Yale University Press, pp. 248–249.

3 Erotic Transference

A Note on My Intentions

I approached the teaching of this paper, "Observations on Transference Love" (1915), wanting to explore the intense feelings that analysts often experience in the face of the erotic transference. One aim I had here was to see if the students could make use of their own experiences to resonate with the difficulty Freud was struggling with. I wanted to actively invite students to engage with Freud in a way wherein they would be grappling in a process of problem-solving alongside of Freud, thinking about similar problems they encounter in their own clinical work. Toward that end, I wanted to present a case involving erotic transference that I struggled with, hoping that the students would feel free to comment on their observations of the clinical interaction. I also aimed to have us think about the role of regressions to early states of mentation within the analyst as an important context for understanding fears that emerge when encountering erotic transference.

Instructor: Freud (1915a) mentions how "obligation of professional discretion" held back the development of psychoanalysis from being able to tackle this issue openly (p. 159). He is, in part, referring to the transference situation in the Anna O case of Breuer, mentioned in the footnote at the bottom. Breuer was an admired mentor of Freud's and played a very important role in collaborating in early discoveries that began the psychoanalytic enterprise. Freud's love of Breuer would eventually turn into intense disappointment. Freud was to come to feel a strong contempt for what he experienced as Breuer's turning away in the face of the erotic transference with Anna O and, relatedly, his subsequent abandonment of psychoanalysis.

Freud felt that Breuer was not able to maintain the necessary mental state of aloofness to recognize the universal nature of the erotic transference that his patient experienced toward him. It's interesting here, to think about how Breuer, in the grip of a very concrete experience of the patient's erotic transference, was not

DOI : 10.4324/9781003610977-4

able to make a jump to a wider perspective about the universality of the erotic transference.

Breuer also worried about what he might have done to seduce the patient into having this reaction. This whole experience had a profound effect on Freud and certainly influenced his thinking about the erotic transference and his image of the position the analyst is meant to aim to hold when dealing with these phenomena.

I wonder if we can relate to what we've heard from Breuer's experience.

Midge: This reminds me of what we talked about last week, of how easy it is for analysts to experience a personal reactive response to the patient's transference. It's interesting that Freud was so critical of Breuer taking Anna O's transference so personally and then he seemed to take Breuer's countertransference quite personally.

Ezra: That's an interesting parallel. I'm curious about the work that we have to do to deal with that this tendency to take things concretely and personally. Something gets triggered in us that is similar to the patient's struggles.

Eli: I would like us to try to think about strategies that could be helpful for us in dealing with erotic transference. There's something about this phenomenon that feels especially difficult.

Instructor: Freud (1915a) is very aware of this difficulty when he warns us about the counter-transference. He says that the analyst has to see that the patient's passionate erotic feelings are a result of the analytic setting and not about the analyst in a more personal sense.

Here Freud is trying to provide a viewpoint that is meant to help analysts to ward off a self-centered focus on such feelings, the egocentrism that can lead to the type of over-personalization of the erotic transference that Breuer found himself mired in. We might think of this, keeping in mind Eli's question, as a potential strategy for dealing with the emotional difficulties encountered here.

Ronald Britton (2003) discussed a related phenomenon he called the erotic counter-transference neurosis, when the analyst tends to see every interaction with the patient as imbued with sexual feelings. Britton emphasized the effects on the analyst's sense of reality and perception, especially in the lapses in the analyst's thinking that coincide with this type of counter-transference.

Does any of what you're hearing so far resonate at all with your own clinical experience?

Eli: I feel quite anxious dealing with patients' erotic feelings. I'm not totally sure why.

Ezra: I find it really interesting to think about, but it does feel very challenging to speak to directly within the clinical situation.

Ernest:	I can relate to Breuer's fear of being seductive. If I notice that a patient may be having erotic feelings toward me, the idea of trying to speak to it feels itself seductive, like I'll be seen as engaging in a flirtation.
Natalie:	I worry that the patient will react angrily or feel humiliated if I try to speak to erotic feelings in a way that feels rejecting to them.
Instructor:	I appreciate you sharing these feelings. I think it will be useful to keep this in mind as we continue to go through the paper. Let's try to think about what it is that is so anxiety provoking and challenging for us about this issue.
Bethany:	I wonder about trying to make a distinction between times when we are able to see the bigger picture, to have a perspective on the dynamics playing out and other times when we aren't able to.
Midge:	I think it's connected to having some kind of footing or hold on something in one's mind, but when the patient repeats the past in the present, it can really impact the analyst in emotionally powerful ways.
Natalie:	I think the analyst gets pulled into a state of mind much like the patient's where everything can feel quite present and real.
Instructor:	What do we mean by real here?
Ernest:	I think it has to do with the impression that the patient's feelings and maybe the analyst's feelings could become real in that they could act upon those feelings.
Reyna:	It helps to have something like these ideas about erotic transference or a supervisor's voice in mind, or Freud's comments in this paper, like an analytic third. We could think about these as strategies as well.
Instructor:	Can you say more about what you mean by an analytic third? What would that look like in this case?
Reyna:	In this context I'm thinking of it as something or someone in the analyst's mind that is outside of the relationship with the patient and that allows a reference point beyond the twoness from which to look at things.
Natalie:	That reminds me of how being in a romantic relationship, especially at first, like falling in love, when you spend almost of all of your time with that person, and you don't have a lot of contact with other people, it can start to feel like being merged with the other person in a way that no longer feels good.
Ezra:	That's a helpful image. In that scenario, you can start to lose contact with reality and find yourself in a kind of fantasy world. As Freud once said, falling in love does have a kind of madness associated with it. We can lose our bearings on what's real.
Eli:	Turning to friends, family, and other people in our lives can help us reconnect with a greater sense of reality and perspective on things, similar to what Reyna was getting at.

Bethany: I would add that the analytic community as whole may serve a similar function, like when we get together in groups and talk about our cases. It can help to have the trusted group or community in mind as a kind of caring watcher.

Instructor: The method or strategy that Reyna described is one that makes use of imagination, imagining an internal presence that you can engage with in some kind of inner conversation about what's happening in your interaction with the patient. Reyna is describing a very useful function for the creation of a wider lens for looking at what's going on. It's a way of expanding one's field of vision and providing space to think about what's happening more soberly and critically. It involves imagining an internal interlocutor to engage with, one that can generate a creative and mind-broadening interaction. Also, Bethany's point about discussing our cases with others that we trust, e.g., in groups, can assist us in that process.

Freud (1915b) speaks to where the patient would likely be left were the relationship with the analyst to lead to an actualization of sexual feelings. He says that the patient would remain imprisoned by her neurotic affliction and retain a correlated difficulty in her "capacity for love which it involves" (p. 161).

Freud is emphasizing the damage to the patient that would result from a boundary violation. This is something we are all familiar with. Do you agree with it? Do you hear anything missing in this account that we might need to think more about?

Ezra: We often talk about how the actualization of sexual fantasies in analysis is damaging to the patient, and I completely agree with that, but we don't often talk about how it impacts the analyst. We were just talking about what happens when we fall in love, how it impacts our sense of reality, and how we can lose our bearings and find ourselves in a merged state of mind, one of being immersed in fantasy. It does feel important to focus on understanding these dynamics.

Eli: It seems like we tend to shun analysts who commit boundary violations and it even extends to discussions of the issue that appear more about moral condemnation than a more scientific approach to studying the issue in order to understand it more dispassionately. I don't think it serves us very well in terms of understanding the dynamics involved. It seems similar to Freud's condemning reaction to Breuer.

Midge: I agree. That kind of condemnation seems fear driven to me and it doesn't help us learn more about the process of how such violations can happen. It has a kind of "not me" quality to it, like the rejection of the boundary violating analyst reinforcing the illusion that the rest of us our immune from it which I think only heightens the actual danger of losing one's perspective.

Reyna: Again, we return to fear. When I think about the idea of shun-
         ning analysts who commit boundary violations, I think of a fear
         of contagion, like their transgressions become a danger to the
         whole community.

Instructor: Consistent with what you are saying here, Freud (1915) said,
         "I am in the happy position of being able to replace the moral
         embargo by considerations of analytic technique, without any
         alteration of the outcome" (p. 164). I think that our attitude as
         analysts, and one that Freud embodied, was to approach every
         subject from the perspective that all human phenomena are
         potentially understandable, and to beware of moral condemna-
         tions that obscure exploration of deeper human truths hidden
         within the subject of our inquiry. The attitude of excessive moral
         scrupulosity implies defense and it is not an analytic approach
         in that it tends to shut down thought.
             Freud (1915a) speaks critically of analysts who try to warn
         patients ahead of time about the erotic transference. Do you
         have any thoughts about why the analyst is inclined to prepare
         patients for the erotic transference?

Midge: Freud said it robbed the transference of spontaneity. I wonder if
         maybe that's the point.

Bethany: I agree. I think the analyst is trying to ward off feeling caught off
         guard and surprised by the patient's transference.

Instructor: There is something upsetting to the analyst's equilibrium about
         that experience of finding oneself suddenly, unexpectedly in the
         grip on an erotic transference. It's something we feel we must
         prepare for.

Ernest: It's easier to keep a coolness about these things when it's from a
         distance. If you expect it and the patient expects it, then maybe
         you can talk about it in more of an "as if" kind of way.

Instructor: What would the "as if" give the analyst?

Midge: It might give the analyst a more clear distinction between what's
         happening in the present and what's coming from the past.

Instructor: Can you think of other ways in which the analyst might be able
         to find the clarity of the distinction between past and present?

Midge: I think that it can help when we are able to think about how the
         transference is, as Freud tells us, a repetition of the past, and that
         part of that process of encountering the transference will involve
         transient moments of confusion about past/present distinction.

Eli: This seems like another technique like the one about conjur-
         ing up an internal third, be it a theory, an idea, or an imag-
         ined internal interlocutor. What I wonder about is the analyst's

disinclination to turn to such techniques even if he knows they are there in his repertoire.

Instructor: That's a new take. Why might the analyst be so disinclined?

Eli: The analyst might be enthralled, really in the grip of a very intense, passionately gratifying experience that he does not want to step away from.

There might be something that feels dangerous in a thrilling kind of way that the analyst doesn't want to relinquish.

Instructor: I want to highlight Eli's comment because it is introducing something we have not looked at. So far, we've talked about the sense of danger and threat that the analyst experiences when dealing with erotic transference.

Here, we have something else to think about, namely, the allure that the analyst may be swept up in and not want to give up. It may be a kind of painful pleasure that even has an addictive quality. He may disavow his learned techniques and their associated clarity for the sake of keeping this passionate excitement. Let's keep this in mind as we continue to go through the text.

Bethany: That idea links up with something I was thinking about when you were talking about our attachment to our internal objects. I was thinking about how entrenched these transferences can be and how difficult it can be to help patients let it go.

Midge: That's interesting. You were talking about patients and Eli was giving an example of that with the analyst. In his view, the analyst may not want to let go of whatever object is ignited in him by the patient's transference.

Natalie: This is reminding me of my work with a patient who was quite stymied in his life and really bound up internally with a very cruel and demanding internal object. He had long separated from his mother and had very little contact with her, but he still couldn't let her go. He talked to himself and treated himself overall in the same ways she treated him. Her presence was always with him judging and criticizing everything he did. I felt so frustrated by it. I think, for me, what was so vexing was that it touched something similar although not quite as paralyzing in myself.

Ernest: What you were just describing Natalie is the kind of thing I often have a hard time knowing about when it's happening. It can take me a long time to even admit it to myself. I think that does contribute to the kinds of distress and confusion that come up in these situations.

Instructor: It can take time and reflecting a great deal in and out of our sessions to begin to get a glimpse of these very well defended vulnerabilities in us. Natalie's example reminds us that it's not only the patient's past/present distinction that collapses, but also the analyst's. Freud (1915a) describes this kind of experience of first encountering the erotic transference. He speaks to how both patient and analyst lose their grasp on the analytic situation. He says, "There is a complete change of scene; it is as though some piece of make-believe had been stopped by a sudden irruption of reality—as when, for instance a cry of fire is raised during a theatrical performance" (p. 162).

Here, I think, consistent with your comments, he is alluding to the experience of a loss of the distinction between inner and outer reality. I think an implication here is that there is something peculiar about the emergence of erotic transference that can alter the clarity we have of our sense of reality, for both patient and analyst, making it all the more difficult to have a clear sense of what is going on. We enter another dimension, a different temporal reality.

We can wonder again here what is meant by reality?

Reyna: I think it has to do with differentiating between past and present and between inner fantasies and outer reality. But I like the idea of different temporal realities.

Natalie: I think it has to do with the distinction between the real treatment roles of the analytic relationship and the fantasied one. Although the fantasied one has reality associated with it as well, like the way it alludes to real truths from our past experiences.

Bethany: The disturbance reminds me of watching children playing, especially when the play suddenly shifts into something that isn't play anymore, like when a pleasant play experience where the kids are having fun turns into a bitter fight.

Instructor: That's a great example of the suddenness of how the play space and analytic space for play can suddenly turn into something that is perceived concretely or with literality. Here there is a loss of the capacity to play or associate imaginatively with what the interaction may mean in a broader sense. We are seeing Freud here trying to warn us of the dangers involved in working with erotic transference and of how easy it is to become confused and myopic, losing the broader perspective.

Given all the warnings that Freud is making, we are justified in hypothesizing that the analyst must subjectively experience some sense of threat associated with erotic transference. This is also consistent with experiences that you have mentioned in your own clinical encounters. What leads to this feeling in the analyst? When we are in a situation that feels dangerous and it's not clear what that is, we may feel confused, most likely more frightened by the unknown, it's likely that we will project some unrecognized part of that danger onto the external situation.

Freud here seems to be locating the danger as coming from the patient, at least in these moments of his writing.

Freud (1915a) is returning to reflect on the counter-transference, a movement from the projection of threat onto the patient, to an observation and criticism of how the analyst is responding to his fears. He says,

> To urge the patient to suppress, renounce, or sublimate her instincts the moment she has admitted her erotic transference would be, not an analytic way of dealing with them, but a senseless one. It would be just as though, after summoning up a spirit from the underworld, one were to send him away without asking him a single question.
>
> (p. 164)

At the bottom of the page, he warns that it may be a very slippery slope in allowing our feelings of love free rein. So now, it's the analyst's feelings that are to be kept in check. In the Joan Riviere translation of Freud (1915b), she translates this as Freud recommending that the analyst keep himself "indifferent" to the patient. With this advice, it's as if the analyst's feelings in and of themselves are a source of danger.

These recommendations of keeping feelings in check and making oneself indifferent may sound like defensive reactions to one's feelings.

Bethany: I wonder though if it's not only defensive but maybe Freud is talking about a technique for managing these feelings. Freud might be saying that it's important to let yourself feel this love, but maybe only up to a certain level, maybe only so far, like far enough to use it interpretively. This could relate to what Eli was speaking to, like not looking at the sun for too long or you may be blinded to the true underlying forces behind the transference.

Natalie: This reminds me of Freud's comment about how the transference is given almost complete freedom to express itself. That tension we talked about between an emotional re-experiencing of the past and then stepping back to think about it seems consistent with what Freud is recommending for the analyst as well.

Instructor: That is a really great way of putting it. Does anyone have any ideas about why that may be important?

Ezra: It would allow the analyst to be aware of the feelings without being overwhelmed or taken over by them. He's not repressing them, so he knows about them, but he's also not consumed by them. I was thinking about the comparison that Natalie just made. The idea that the analyst makes use of the tension between being free to regress within one's own transference but within limits is interesting. I often hear how important it is not to gratify the patient. Here we have the counterpart in the analyst putting limits on their own gratification.

Reyna: I think it's also related to the analyst keeping in touch with the reality of his role, as we were talking about. It's for the patient to give free expression of their feelings, to allow the transference full license to express itself, but not for the analyst. It's not the analyst's analysis.

Instructor: So, I want to draw your attention to what you are describing as specific strategies for the analyst to be aware of his feelings, be in touch with them, actually feel them, but also to regulate them in ways that allow him to keep his footing in reality. It's not about denying feelings, but feeling them within limits, like enough of a taste of the feelings to know what you're dealing with. Also, what Natalie and Ezra spoke to is the idea that the patient and analyst may make use of a kind of oscillation between the freedom to relive their transferences but within certain limits.

Midge: I think it's also important to keep in mind what we were discussing a few moments ago about how the patient's transference to an object they are unable or unwilling to let go of may activate something similar in the analyst.

Reyna: Yes, and in that case, the analyst would have to become aware of that, and work through it to some extent to be able to even make use of the regulatory strategies we've been thinking about.

Ezra: That's really important because we could easily lose our bearings and focus on the patient's difficulties and be blinded to the role we're playing in clinging to a particular kind of interaction.

Eli: The analyst keeping these feelings in check is not only for the analyst's protection, but it also can be more directly related to what the analyst is trying to achieve clinically.

Instructor: Can you spell that out more? What do you think the analyst is trying to achieve in doing that?

Eli: Freud said (1915a),

> The more plainly the analyst lets it be seen that he is proof against every temptation, the more readily will he be able to extract from the situation its analytic content…the patient will then feel safe enough to allow all of her pre-conditions for loving, all the phantasies springing from her sexual desires, all the detailed characteristics of her state of being in love, to come to light; and from these she will herself open the way to her infantile roots of her love.
>
> (p. 166)

Midge: There are similarities between parents and children I think. It reminds me of how important it is for parents to be able to be relatively proof from the temptations to respond to their children in excessive, judgmental, and reactive ways, in that such reactions can lead the child to feel a dangerous omnipotence that can lead them into inhibiting themselves excessively.

Instructor: That is a very interesting analogy. One question here is how the analyst can demonstrate this proof against temptation and still retain a private awareness of all the feelings that are active in her/him?

Natalie: Sometimes it is hard to feel these things without becoming afraid of acting them out, and that could lead to actions on the analyst's part that lead the patient to feel unsafe.

Instructor: What are you picturing?

Natalie: I was thinking about defensiveness when it's obvious to the patient that the analyst is uncomfortable and trying to appear as if they're not. I also think that a lot of patients notice feelings their analyst is having but don't say anything about it.

Instructor: That's a good point and the kind of mixed message that could lend itself to a disturbance for the patient, even a kind of gaslighting. What you said about patients noticing the analyst's feelings and not speaking to it is so important. We do need to listen and look for signs of that and try to bring it into our dialogue when we see it. Another thought that occurred to me relates back to Eli's earlier comment about the analyst's enthrallment with their own erotic feelings. The recommendation of indifference may be a strategy aimed at helping the analyst to find a middle position, one that does not deny nor indulge in the erotic feelings.

On page 166, Freud (1915a) goes into more detail about what the patient would be denied, from a treatment perspective, if the analytic relationship were to become an actualized sexual one. I spoke about this earlier, so I will only briefly say that Freud is talking about the way the patient's repression would remain in place and this would keep her limited to the narrow confines of living that her neurosis affords.

There would be a missed, precious opportunity to bring these repressed influences into consciousness in a way that could open up a freer mind and freer existence. Freud refers to this as mental freedom. The analysis would ostensibly offer the chance of freeing the patient to love in less unconsciously dictated ways beyond her control and open up other possibilities in her life. I will give a clinical example to illustrate this.

On the same page, Freud (1915a) defines more clearly the optimal position for the analyst to strive to hold. He said that the analyst must not gratify the erotic transference, but he also must not suppress it. Freud is articulating a middle position where the analyst does not indulge and does not suppress. It's also a clear image of a position meant to keep the analyst's eye on the psychic reality of repressed unconscious fantasies.

Here I think Freud is advocating a position for the analyst and patient to occupy, analogous to play in children where one can emotionally experience the illusion, while at the same time recognizing that it is not fully real. The feelings, the experience, the external replication of our inner world is very much emotionally real, and yet there is also a way in which we are in a kind of simulated reality within which there is an inner necessity to play something out in order to know something that can help the patient move forward developmentally.

Metaphorically, we can think of it as a kind of rift in time, a break in the sense of time as we normally conceive of it, allowing for psychic travel to earlier dimensions of experience.

Bethany: If the play space collapses, the patient's opportunity for working through their resistance and overcoming repression is wasted. That's the fire in the theatre, when the necessary as-if-ness or simulated roles are interrupted and those fantasied roles we have implicitly agreed upon are broken through, analogous to a play disruption in child treatment.

Reyna: That reminds me again about the quote we looked at earlier, when Freud (1915a) said, "...it is as though some piece of make-believe has been stopped by the sudden irruption of reality...." (Freud, p. 162). It's very interesting here, because the reality of the analytic situation is what is disrupted by the erotic transference which is depicted as the irruption of reality.

Midge: I'm glad you repeated that because I was confused by that quote initially. Right now, the phrase "as though" feels very clarifying for me. The "as though" for me captures how something has reversed in the scene where the treatment itself and its roles suddenly come to feel less real than the erotic fantasy.

Instructor: That's an important piece to highlight. In that case, we can see that there's a regression to a level of literality wherein one can no longer see through the transference. The complexity of thinking is collapsed and regressed to concrete mentation, to developmentally earlier forms of thought. There is also a failure to perceive the rift in time that I was speaking to a moment ago.

Bethany: I am thinking about different levels of reality involved in the analytic work. There is the work itself, what it is we are consciously aiming for, like making space for the transference to unfold and come to life, so that we can work to make it conscious for the patient, but then much of what emerges is a fantasy, not real in the literal present day sense, but very real in terms of the patient's emotional experience and in the context of their developmental history. And also likely to feel very real emotionally for the analyst.

Ernest: Listening to what you just described, Bethany, has me thinking about how much there is to attend to and how confusing it can feel when we're in the midst of all those levels.

Instructor: That is very true. We are continuously in a position of oscillating between being immersed in the psychic reality/fantasy playing out in the transference and stepping back to reflect critically on what is happening. Relatedly on page 168, Freud is able to step back again from what he has been saying thus far and turn his critical eye on himself. He takes a second look at the arguments he's been making, that the transference love is not genuine or real love and he sees the flaws in this argument. Freud is able to see that, with the exception of the focus on resistance and the associated clinical aims of analysis, the other arguments against the genuineness or realness of the patient's love are rather weak.

Midge: I'm still grappling with trying to think about what is it exactly that is so frightening for the analyst when confronted with the erotic transference, wondering about the incest taboo and how this is replicated in the frame of analysis.

Instructor: Midge is touching on something that is difficult to wrap our minds around in terms of what the nature of the fear is for the analyst. The analyst's subjective sense of danger in the face of the erotic transference is one that figures prominently in the paper. Freud is issuing many warnings to us of dangers lying in wait for us in dealing with this type of transference.

I was also thinking about your comments sparked by Eli's remarks about the analyst's possible feelings of enthrallment, our own erotic transference to the patient and how that can lead us to actively turn away from known techniques for regaining a wider lens on what's happening, such as a third position or vantage point and the titration of one's feelings by keeping them within manageable limits. Let's keep these issues in mind as we listen to the following clinical hour.

Presentation of clinical hour:(Adult woman in analysis)

Patient: Wow! You're all dressed up! (I was dressed more formally than usual). (Long Silence)

I'm thinking that I don't want to get into what we talked about yesterday. I think I don't want to get back into that again. It felt hard to be in that place yesterday.

Analyst: You've alluded to what happened for you yesterday but haven't mentioned specifically what you have in mind.

Patient: (Angrily) You should remember! You don't even remember what happened yesterday! You have to ask me!

Analyst: (I'm taken aback and notice I have an irritated tone in my response) What makes you think I don't remember what happened yesterday?

Patient: You wouldn't have to ask me if you remembered. You're asking me in that way that you do, making it seem like an interpretation to cover up that you really don't remember.

Analyst: Well, a lot happened in yesterday's session and I asked you to know specifically what was on your mind. (feeling defensive)

Patient: (angrily) You are so irritated with me! You shouldn't get so irritated with me! I don't feel good when you get so mad. It doesn't help me when you get into these moods. Now I don't even want to talk to you about anything anymore! (long silence)

Analyst: (pause) You're right. I did get irritated with you when you accused me of trying to cover up what you perceived as my forgetting what happened yesterday. I wonder if you may have wanted to provoke me so that you could avoid having to get into the details of what was so hard for you about yesterday.

Patient: If I did that, it wasn't conscious. I didn't intend consciously to provoke you. I was just telling you how I felt. I don't think it's fair to me that you got so mad and mean to me. Now I don't even want to talk about yesterday or anything else with you. I don't trust you and how you'll react. (we are both quiet with arms folded)

Analyst: (I notice the patient lying down with her arms folded tightly and notice that my arms are similarly folded and this is followed by a shift in feelings in myself. I hear in my tone of voice that I am no longer sounding irritated)

It strikes me that this kind of thing we're both experiencing right now has happened a number of times. I'll respond to you in a way that you feel is wrong, like just now when I was irritated with you, and then you respond as if I have committed a terrible, unforgivable sin against you, like I've betrayed you and you can't talk to me ever again.

Patient: (shift in affect, no longer sounding angry) Yes. I know it. It feels exactly like that to me too. It's like you acted badly against me, betrayed me, and I don't want to talk to you ever again. I feel mad, hurt, and right. Very right. It's like you are the bad one and I am in the superior position, judging you. And I just get quiet. I sit there silently, sometimes not so silently (laughs), judging you and it feels like I'm winning, like morally I'm better than you, that you're the one who's out of control. I feel morally superior to you like when I think you're the freak, not me. I'm the good one and I can dismiss what you say about me. But it also feels so good to make up with you after I feel like you've wronged me. At first I feel like I can't ever forgive you, but when I do forgive you and talk to you again, it feels so great. I feel so warm and close to you again.

Analyst: When you feel wronged by me, things get cold and distant between us and when we reconcile you can then let yourself enjoy feeling close to me again.

Patient: They somehow go together. The cold feeling of hurt and anger and the really good, warm feeling of being close to you again. It reminds me of what I told you about with my father. He treated me the way I treat you, like I betrayed him and he shut me out. I desperately tried to get close to him again. I couldn't stand to be shut out like that and feeling so bad, like I must have done something so awful and unforgivable. I treat you like you've done something so awful to me and like I can never talk to you again.

Analyst: I think you felt shut out by me today when you first walked in the door and commented that I'm all dressed up today.

Patient: When I saw you dressed so nice, I imagined you were going out on a date. It made me feel mad at you and left out. Thinking about you going out and spending time with another woman makes me feel like I'm not special to you, like I'm nothing to you. I wanted to fight with you. I am always trying to push these feelings away. I feel like if I admit them to you then you win, you have the control over me.

Like yesterday, when you said that I was having feelings about you being away, I didn't want to admit that. I acted like you were being really weird, turning it into something it wasn't, that you were being creepy. I wouldn't accept anything you had to say and I kept making fun of you. I feel foolish about that now.

Analyst: I think that you acted that way to dismiss any consideration of how you felt about being away from me because it made you anxious to talk about wanting to feel close to me, as if there's something wrong or dangerous about that.

Patient: Saying goodbye to you, even for a short time, feels like losing you in the way it felt breaking up with a lover. I feel like it's going to be really hard for me to not be able to meet with you for so long. I don't know why I couldn't let myself tell you that when you tried to bring it up yesterday. But, it really bothers me that you won't miss me, that the nature of our relationship makes it impossible for you to have any feelings for me. It feels so one-sided. Me missing you and caring about you, but I don't mean anything to you emotionally. I don't affect you.

Analyst: Your earlier complaint about my irritation with you suggests that you are aware of being able to affect me.

Patient: I can tell that you're emotionally involved with me. I know you care about me and I think you'll miss me when I'm away. I keep doing that though, telling myself that you don't care, that you're not involved with me or affected by me at all.

Analyst: I think you have mixed feelings about how involved you want me to be with you emotionally. On the one hand, you want me to care about you and be affected by you, but I think the thought of us being involved in an emotionally close way scares you which is why you need to portray me as unfeeling and uncaring. It reassures you that we're not going to get involved together in a way that feels dangerous to you.

Patient: That makes me think about what I said about missing you like a lover. There are times when I feel closer to you in a way that makes me feel guilty, like I'm doing something wrong and it feels bad. I feel better, less scared if I think of you as a robot with no feelings. It's safer to imagine you as not caring or feeling anything for me.

Analyst: Yes, and I think you've noticed that when you accuse me of that, I seem to respond with irritation, at least sometimes like today.

Patient: Yes, and that's when I feel like I am special to you, like I can get under your skin in a way that none of your other patients can.

Class Discussion

Midge: I wonder about your own erotic transference to the patient and the role that played in this repetitive enactment. Was your irritation with her both a defense against and expression of a regressive form of your erotic longings for the patient, suggesting that the underlying erotic feelings might feel dangerous to you on some level?

Instructor: That's a very astute observation. A question that comes to my mind, one we've been grappling with, is how do we account for this kind of felt danger? What is behind the danger that Freud is working so hard to warn us about and prepare us to face in this paper? What are we analysts so afraid of? And more directly related to Midge's observation, what do you think I was afraid of?

Natalie: I think there's a parallel between what the patient was afraid of and what you might have been afraid of. She was afraid that if she allowed herself to express her longings for you, some line could get crossed and those feelings could be actualized. Fighting with you became a safe way to give form to those passions, in a way that assuaged her fears as well. And I imagine maybe something very similar was going on for you. You seemed as inclined to fight her as she was to fight you. I'm also thinking of the incest taboo. In the transference we do come to represent parental figures and early erotic longings for such figures. The threat of actualizing those longings is a repetition of those early incestuous fears.

Instructor: First, Natalie, I think you're exactly right in your assessment of the kinds of fears involved for me and the nature of the compromise formation between the patient and I. You're touching on a crucial issue in our work, namely that the patient and analyst both experience the recrudescence of our unconscious dynamics in the work and that will inevitably lead to enactments.

Midge: Consistent with what Natalie brought up about the analyst's unresolved attachment to their own incestuous objects, I wonder if your interaction with the patient might have been a repetition of an early incestuous tie, one that may have felt both exciting and dangerous for you.

Instructor: That's a very important question and you're onto something. We have to ask ourselves these kinds of questions throughout our work. Otherwise it is very tempting to attribute to the patient elements of our own struggles in ways that defensively obscure the role we're playing in the enactment. I do think we see some of that playing out with me in the beginning of the hour especially.

The incest taboo also brings us into thinking about the Oedipus complex. We can also wonder about something else, also related to the developmental stage of the Oedipus complex, something your comments approach, that is, the alterations in the analyst's state of mind when confronted with erotic transference.

Recently, I mentioned a paper by Lee Grossman (2015) called "The Syntax of Oedipal Thought in the Case of Little Hans." This paper was useful for me in thinking about Freud's transference love paper, especially with regard to the dangers experienced by the analyst in the face of erotic feelings.

Grossman speaks to the particular forms of thinking that are prominent during the oedipal stage, for example, the egocentricity illustrated in Britton's example mentioned earlier, the confusion of thought and action or what is often referred to as the belief in the omnipotence of thought, the capacity to anticipate terrifying consequences associated with one's thoughts and feelings, and the projected attribution of motives. In Freud's paper, I think that his warnings to analysts allude to the activation of these forms of thought in the analyst along with the accompanying subjective sense of danger.

I think that when we are dealing with erotic transference, it's not uncommon to experience dangers having to do with a transient manifestation of feeling and thinking that we've crossed a line in our excitement. We may experience moments of confusing the boundaries between thought and action that can be quickly disavowed and covered up with a facade of analytic technique.

Midge: I'm trying to get a sense of how we would notice that, moments when we've regressed to oedipal level thinking, e.g., equating thought and action. What I wonder is how we might notice it in a way that would not lead us deny it?

Instructor: Does anyone have any ideas about Midge's interesting question?

Natalie: Well, if there's excitement involved, to me that sounds related to something erotic, an erotic feeling. That seems like it could be a clue that something's going on if you could catch it soon enough.

Instructor:	I'm interested in "soon enough." What does that imply, I wonder?
Ezra:	For me, that implies defense. Like if we can catch it before our defenses kick in and obscure the whole thing.
Eli:	When you said that, I was asking myself, are we just doomed to see these things in retrospect or will we ever be able to catch them in a way that enables us to make use of it in the moment?
Bethany:	I don't think we should be too quick to disparage seeing things in retrospect. I do see that process as a kind of training or practice for acquainting ourselves with the kinds of defensive reactions that we have in situations like this.
Instructor:	Training and practice for noticing our defenses and anything else?
Ernest:	For being able to notice something in the actual moment as it's happening like Eli was getting at.
Instructor:	And this retrospective practice would help us do that?
Natalie:	I think it could. I know you're going to ask how it could do that. I think that each time we engage in these retrospective reconsiderations of the clinical hour, each time we see a little more about how we reacted, what we were defending against, and we might acquire more acceptance of the feelings we were experiencing.
Instructor:	And how would that be helpful do you think?
Midge:	I think if you are more accepting of these feelings, you're going to be more likely to notice them and less likely to defend against them when your with the patient. I do think that would expand our capacity to make use of the experience toward understanding and interpreting what is going on in the transference and give us more of a sense of calm in the room.
Eli:	I also think that all those things you just described, Midge, would likely contribute to a feeling in the patient that these emotions are not unthinkable, not so terrifying that we can't talk about them.
Ezra:	I'm thinking about the clinical hour again in the context of what you were saying about childhood mentation. There were moments when you and the patient were locked into an irritated exchange. The way each of you spoke to each other seemed very concrete.
Instructor:	I think you're right but I want to make sure I understand what you mean by concrete here?
Ezra:	The focus was kind of literal and about what the other person did or didn't do, like did you remember or not or did she provoke you or not. It was kind of funny, like each of you was saying you did it and no, you did it, but you were both doing it.
Instructor:	That's a good point. I see what you mean. Yes, I think that illustrates the kind of regressions that can occur in the work, to a more primitive form of mentation. In this case the projective attribution of motives. We were both projecting onto one another in that moment.

Ernest:	Relatedly, it was interesting to see the moments of you being entangled in that surface level with the patient that Ezra mentioned and then beginning to speak to something that felt deeper than that.
Instructor:	Do you have any thoughts about what might have led to that shift?
Ernest:	The comment on the repeated pattern shifted from comments about whether the individual, you or her, did something or not, to the interaction between the two of you, what you were doing together and as part of a more enduring, larger, reciprocal pattern.
Reyna:	It did seem like a shift in the kind of thinking the two of you were engaged in, like a transition to a view with more perspective and active movement.
Natalie:	The interaction had more "as if" to it. The "as if" of playing something out that was no longer feeling literally true in a concrete way, but maybe metaphorically true, like it represented something deeper, an unconscious pattern maybe or a repetition of a broader dynamic, and one that was actively unfolding.
Midge:	What enables us, I wonder, analyst and patient, to make this kind of shift in our thinking?
Bethany:	The shift in your thinking seemed to follow noticing something similar between yourself and the patient, that you were both silent and had your arms folded.
Instructor:	That moment did feel like stepping back and seeing that something similar was going on for both of us. How do you think that could lead to such a shift in thinking?
Eli:	It might lead to a sense of empathy with the patient and for yourself, that you were both feeling defensive and maybe hurt and angry, and that it could be talked about openly.
Midge:	It is an image that includes the two parties and becomes a widened perspective in that sense. It's like a scene of the two of you being part of something together.
Natalie:	That reminds me of a third position outside the two of you in opposition. Once you could identify it out loud, the interaction itself becomes a third point outside of one to one relationship. You looking at both her and yourself together in the same frame sort of simulates an outside party observer and that creates more space to think.

A Note on What Happened

At the end of our discussion of this paper, I was left thinking about the tension between my own interests coming into this class and moments of novelty in what I was hearing in the students' reflections, the unanticipated ideas that came up in our discussion. Students related the topic of erotic transference to their own struggles. I went into this class very much interested in thinking about the nature of the kinds of fears that tend to come up in the face of erotic transference. Strategies for dealing with these fears were proposed, e.g., having the supervisor's voice in mind, being able to engage in an internal dialogue with an imagined other, both conjuring up an analytic third, an imaginary presence in an effort to expand one's field of vision and sense of reality, being in contact with one's analytic role, retrospective analysis and post-session critique of clinical hours. There was a comment made about how analysts may turn away from known techniques in order to maintain an erotically gratifying experience, one linked to an incestuous object. In our discussion of the clinical case, students were able to identify evidence of my own erotic transference to the patient, a parallel between the patient's transference and my own, as well as ideas for noticing when one is experiencing regressed mental states. What impressed me greatly, something that was developing in the group, was a growing appreciation and acceptance of the complexities, tensions, and struggles involved in the practice of clinical psychoanalysis. I can see in retrospect that I entered this paper with my own interests and agenda, e.g., to think more about the analyst's subjective sense of danger when encountering erotic transference. The feeling I was left with was that it was an agenda I did not succeed in holding as loosely as I aim to do. This may have also influenced the relative absence in our discussion of pleasures and feelings of delight that analysts can feel when encountering erotic transference and how those feelings are intimately related to the sense of danger which often accompanies them. I was left thinking about how important it is for me to work to toward being as aware as possible of my own interests and the potential of those interests to impact and limit the free flow of the class dialogue.

References

Britton, R. (2003). *Sex, Death, and the Superego: Experiences in Psychoanalysis*. Karnac Books.

Freud, S. (1912). The Dynamics of Transference. SE 12: 97–108.

Freud, S. (1914). Remembering, Repeating and Working-through. SE 12: 145–156.

Freud, S. (1915a). Observations on Transference-Love. SE 12: 157–171.

Freud, S. (1915b). Observations on Transference-Love. *The International Psycho-Analytic Library No. 8*, Sigmund Freud Collected Papers Volume 2, 377–391.

Grossman, L. (2015). The Syntax of Oedipal Thought in the Case of Little Hans. *Psychoanalytic Quarterly*, 84 (2), 469–478.

4 What to Do When Repression Is Unavailable?

A Note on My Intentions

I wished to have students reflect on the clinical hour in the context of Freud's papers on Negation (1925), Fetishism (1927), and Splitting of the Ego and the Process of Defense (1940). I aimed to try to have us think about disavowal, castration anxiety, traumatic overstimulation, and negation and to begin to play with making some experiential distinctions between neurotic, psychotic, and perverse operations. I wanted to have us to think about what kinds of defenses are utilized when repression is not available. My aim in underscoring a moment of seeming contradiction in the dialogue was to enable us to grapple with this tension together, a version of struggle that is analogous to the kinds of struggles which led Freud to write the papers we had just read. It was also analogous to the kinds of struggles and tensions I experienced in my work with the case that I presented.

Instructor: This time, I propose that we begin with a clinical hour, loosely holding these papers in the backs of our minds, without being too intentional about applying them. Let's just see what comes up as we listen.

Presentation of clinical hour:(young adult man in analysis)

Patient: I had a dream last night that I was in here on your couch and I was talking to you, saying something and then you said something to me. What was said was not clear. It feels blurry. But I remember having the thought that you thought that what you said to me was a normal interpretation but I thought that you were giving away some factual detail about yourself. I pointed that out to you, asked you if you were aware that you just gave away something about your personal life. Did you intend to give it away or was it a slip on your part?

  Whatever it was you said, I can't remember what it was, it would have been contradictory to anything I've learned about proper analytic technique. I thought it was an indication that you

DOI : 10.4324/9781003610977-5

regard our work as finished, that it was time to end. As I talked about that with you, you got up from your chair and started to walk to the door. I saw that you were wearing shorts, a Hawaiian shirt, and a baseball cap. You said that we could have a relationship now. Then I noticed the side of your face. Your cheek was opened up and flesh was exposed up to your eye socket. That was the dream. (pause)

This is going to sound ridiculous, but I was just thinking about how you corrected me yesterday when I was talking about the tv show, "The Big Bang Theory," the two characters, Sheldon and Penny, how I thought they represented logic and emotions, respectively, and the tension between rational and emotional life. I referred to Penny as Amy and you corrected me saying that it was Penny that I meant to say. When you said that, I felt excited, like I found out something about you, that you're a nerd because you watch that show and that felt so funny to me, I couldn't stop laughing. I did feel that you exposed something personal without meaning to, but then I wondered if you did want to tell me that you're into Big Bang Theory. I thought that maybe you wanted to share that with me. It felt like you were doing something you shouldn't be doing.

Analyst: Something not proper.

Patient: I'm feeling that way now, like you did something wrong, but yesterday, it felt so funny, I couldn't stop laughing. My stomach hurt so much from laughing. It felt like it was too much for me but I kept wondering if it's something you did on purpose.

Analyst: Did I intentionally let you see something about me that I shouldn't let you see?

Patient: In the dream, I felt like a line got crossed and it meant that the analysis was over and then I saw you in that crazy outfit, in shorts and a Hawaiian shirt. It was like, Oh boy, anything goes now. We could even end up having sex. This is too much. It was hard to breath. Yesterday, I was laughing so hard. I don't know why I'm so hung up on this, but there is something about this question of did you do it on purpose, show that to me, what you said.

Letting me see something you shouldn't let me see reminds me of my stepmother, how she would walk around naked. I felt excited when I caught a glimpse of her. Sometimes I couldn't help myself and had to masturbate. Sometimes I would imagine that she knew that I was doing that and that she wanted me to and even liked that I was masturbating after seeing her. Most of the time when she walked around naked, I wouldn't let myself look at her. I couldn't see what was right in front of me. I knew she was naked and visible to me but I could blur my eyes and look to the side and not notice anything but the blurry image.

Analyst: When you were telling me the dream, you mentioned that what I said to you in the dream seemed blurry.

Patient: (pause) I feel like what you just said is taking me away from where I was going. (pause) It felt like an intrusion. Maybe I'll just say what I was thinking before you said that. I was thinking that I don't want to know too much about you. I don't even look at you when I come in or leave the session.

Analyst: At the end of the session in the dream you saw something quite disturbing when you looked at me.

Patient: Yeah. The gash on your cheek was all opened up like someone took a knife and sliced the side of your face and it was totally exposed up to the eye socket. It was like it had been there the whole time but I had never noticed it before. It was really gross and disgusting.

Analyst: A gross and disgusting gash of exposed flesh.

Patient: (laughs nervously) That sounded sexual. Oh god! I know what you're thinking. You're always thinking everything is about sex. You think it's a vagina. (laughs more nervously)

I have never felt easy and comfortable around them. Maybe that's why I'd rather get off in a way where I don't have to see it. I feel that the safest sex for me is when it's phone sex, when I don't have to see the woman at all. The times when I am able to have sex in person, I have done it in ways that allow me to not see the vagina. I just focus on watching my penis going in and coming out.

Analyst: Especially coming back out again.

Patient: (taken aback) What? What do you mean?

Analyst: If you keep an eye on your penis, you can make sure it comes back to you safe and sound.

Patient: Oh, yeah. I wish I could feel safe when I have sex. I was just thinking about how I feel after I climax and get soft. It's the worst feeling. I know this is completely irrational, but I always feel afraid that I won't ever get another erection again. (pause) This feels really important to me. I hope that I will be able to remember what we're talking about today.

Analyst: Like with your penis, you're afraid you won't be able to hold onto these ideas.

Patient: I was thinking that if I write this stuff down after we meet, then I can have something permanent to hold onto and take with me.

Analyst: Something permanent that you can hold onto, that can be yours to take out whenever you want to.

Patient: I want to be in control of it, to feel like it's a part of me that totally belongs to me, my own possession.

Analyst: Part of you, part of your body.

Patient: Hmm. When you said that it jarred me. I keep feeling like you're pushing your ideas onto me. When you say something to me here, it's real time. I have a hard time hearing it or even responding to it. So often I have the feeling of not being able to see what it is you're talking about. But when I leave I can often remember what was said and I can write it down. Then I can think about it later when I'm alone and it doesn't jar me anymore. It's easier to think about it when we're not physically in the same room.

Analyst: I think you do feel a danger when I say something to you. It doesn't feel safe to be in live contact with me, in the same room together, like anything could happen if things get too lively between us. In moments like that, later you can write it down and take a de-animated version of me with you so you can go off and enjoy it safely by yourself.

Patient: When I write down what you say and read it later, it's like a thing that I have totally under my control, something I can't have taken away from me. It's sort of part of you too, a thing I can do whatever I want with whenever I want. It's very strange. It makes me feel like I don't need you or anyone, like I'm totally self-sufficient.

Class Discussion

Reyna: The patient's thought that he could really have sex with you shows how his thinking can quickly feel so real, like the difference between thought and something really happening, like his feelings and thoughts are undifferentiated from action in his mind.

Midge: It was undifferentiated in the manifest content of the dream, but he seems clear about the differentiation consciously within the clinical hour.

Instructor: That's an important distinction. A neurotic patient, for example, would be consciously able to make that differentiation, but we would see signs that on deeper unconscious level he acts as if that is not the case.

Natalie: It sounds to me like he's had early experiences when his feelings of sexual excitement became overwhelming.

Ernest: That reminds me of a question I had about whether the patient was right about his stepmother being intentionally seductive. The patient appeared to be picturing you as seductive when he wondered if you showed him something about yourself on purpose.

Bethany: The patient's feeling taken by surprise, jolted after your comments, might be a reenactment of something from his past. He could feel like you're disclosing something about yourself, something private, similar to his stepmother showing herself, seducing him and he could feel like he has to look away from what you're saying the way he felt he had to look away from her naked body.

Natalie: He's curious about it and excited to get this little piece of information about you, but he has a different reaction later, a feeling that you were doing something wrong in sharing it with him.

Ezra: I'm thinking of the patient's disgust at the image of the gash on your face. The cut on your face leads me to think of castration, how Freud talked about the boy turning his gaze from the female genital because he sees it as a castration and fears it will happen to him. I wonder if the patient was defending against a desire or excitement that he experienced as dangerous, too dangerous to experience in your presence, but one he could possibly experience more safely alone. It's like he was in a terrible dilemma of feeling sexually excited but terrified of being castrated for it and he had to find a way around that. Also, his feeling cut off by your comments could be related to the danger of being cut off on a deeper level, like the fantasy of being castrated.

Eli: He may need to think about things alone because he is so afraid his thoughts and feelings will make actual things happen, even if he isn't conscious of that. This isolation of himself could be a way of controlling himself when his thoughts lead to the danger of being actualized.

Reyna: Ezra's comments on castration leave me feeling like something is missing here. I wonder if the danger of actualizing his wish is really a fear of castration. His reaction of feeling interrupted when you speak is of being cut off. But also, there's something that feels dangerous to him about seeing something he feels he should not see. In his past, he did see something that as a child was too much for him to process. So I'm not sure if it's castration, but I think if it is, it's not only castration.

Natalie: That's interesting because it does seem that, for him, at that young age, experiencing his stepmother's nudity and seductiveness, was a traumatic experience. He saw something he felt he should not see. And when Louis revealed something personal, it was triggering to him, overexciting at first, but more horrifying in the dream. I'm thinking of the gash on your face as symbolic of something traumatic, more than just the site of the genital. He did say at one point that he felt that you were trying to push something onto him. That leads me to think of the stepmother's exhibitionism around him.

Bethany: That's interesting. I wonder if the excitement itself maybe was not a purely sexual one. What if the excitement was more a defense against something that felt overwhelming to him, like a sense of transgression coming from someone who is meant to protect him.

Midge: That makes sense to me. The patient is relating to you as a thing in his relating to you through his writing, but you're also sort of a transitional object, like he's trying to relate to you in a way that feels safe. It reminds me of what Freud said about the patient needing to be sure that the analyst is proof against any seduction in order to feel safe. I wonder if the patient maybe isn't yet convinced that you are proof against any seduction, particularly given the traumatic experiences he has had with his stepmother. He takes small things that hint at something about you as an impingement. I imagine that's similar to what he felt when his stepmother exposed herself.

Ezra: I'm thinking about times when, after the fact, I realized that I said something to a patient that was revealing about myself, but the point I was making could have been made without doing that. I do wonder if moments like that can make patients feel anxious about our boundaries. It strikes me that there are many ways that such disclosures on the surface may seem banal, but they actually could lead patients to feel misused. Very small things may feel that way, like when your analyst mentions something important to them, but not really relevant to what's going on for you.

Reyna: Maybe the patient is in an intermediate stage toward being able to see you as a more of a safe, whole person. He might need to relate to you as a de-animated object on the way to being able to relate to you as a whole, three-dimensional, alive person. Treating you as a thing is a way of trying to protect himself from the experience of feeling his boundaries violated.

Natalie: Related to that, I also think you're revealing something about yourself, if not excessive, might be a way of gradually moving the patient in the direction of being able to make some kind of closer contact with you. It's tricky because the patient's treating you as a thing is likely to feel frustrating in the sense of leaving you deprived of a feeling of having contact and engagement.

Instructor: Your comments here are very insightful and pick up on important dynamics in this case. You immediately noticed how dangerous his thoughts feel to him, as if thinking something could make it happen. This seems implicit in what he's saying, alluding to his unconscious mentation, while you also noted that consciously he is able to differentiate between thought and deed.

You've zeroed in on the possible etiology to this conflation of thought and reality, that is, the overstimulation he experienced from his stepmother when he was a child. A child who has experienced frequent overstimulation will encounter difficulty making use of repression to deal with thoughts that are felt to be dangerous. They'll have to use other defenses to deal with their perceived dangerous thoughts.

Midge:	When I think of neurosis, I think of repression, of painful thoughts being pushed and kept out of consciousness. So, if there is a lot that seems excessively available to consciousness, it leads me to wonder if maybe we are dealing with something other than neurosis.
Instructor:	Interesting idea. You might be right. Can anyone think of any alternative explanations for the patient having so much accessible to consciousness?
Eli:	We could be looking at a patient who has done a lot of work in psychoanalysis and has much more access to previously repressed material.
Ezra:	That makes sense to me, although I'm wondering if this patient might have initially appeared to be neurotic but maybe over time seemed to be operating from a more perverse place, as Freud wrote about in his Fetishism paper.
Instructor:	Could you spell that out a little more or would anyone else like to describe what Ezra might mean by perverse place, given what we read for today?
Ezra:	What Freud said about the splitting of the ego, especially how someone might use such defenses to turn away from a threatening perception that they remain conscious of, so it's not repressed because they are still conscious of it. They can know it but sort of not know it. This reminded me of your patient's ability to not see what was right in front of him.
Instructor:	Your struggle to make these diagnostic distinctions really illustrates how challenging this can be. I have had other experiences which led me to question my early impressions of the patient as primarily neurotic. There are clues for us to attend to in this hour that may help us to flesh out the picture that you've begun to articulate.
	As several of you noticed, the ideas we discuss are very much available to his consciousness. He can deny them but he's still aware of them. He relies primarily on disavowal, something we expect to see with patients functioning at a perverse level. But, we also see disavowal among patients at other structural levels, neurotic or psychotic, for example.
	Disavowal involves stripping a perception of its significance, acting as if you didn't see it, hear it, feel it, like it never happened. You perceive something and you're fully conscious of it, but act as if it has no meaning or consequence for you. It's a conscious refusal to acknowledge it as important.
	Freud said that you cannot repress perceptions. For example, with this case, as Natalie said, there was near constant sexual overstimulation when he was a boy. It is impossible to forget that.

Bethany: It's interesting, given the overstimulation that he experienced. I felt a sense of detachment, a disconnected feeling in my experience of listening to this hour. I wonder if that's how he defends against the threat of feeling overstimulated. I also wonder if you felt connected to him. I'm thinking about what Natalie was saying that it's likely that you felt frustrated in the way he was treating you as a thing.

Instructor: Great questions. Your observation, Bethany, about the detachment as defense against overstimulation is very perceptive. This patient has described how he needs his sexual objects to be absolutely still and to make no sound in order to have sex in a way that feels safe for him. We can think here about how he did not feel protected from an object that in many ways he felt violated by. There were times when, during the early phase of the treatment, I felt that I had to be something like an inanimate object for this patient to tolerate the analysis. I had long moments with him, of feeling that I had to restrain my own reactions, natural responses, comments, even movements that would make sounds which would disturb him greatly.

    The challenge was to stay alive and seek opportunities to, bit by bit, make observations and interpretations, in a gradual, non-traumatic way. It was also important to openly explore his startled reactions to what he experienced at times as my invasiveness, an analogue to having felt violated as a child. This allowed him a gradual building up of a sense of safety and trust in the relationship.

Midge: That leads me to wonder if you have any ideas about what might have been going on in you when you corrected the patient's mistakenly referring to Amy when he meant to say Penny?

Instructor: It's an important question to ask ourselves, when something like that happens. What I suspect is that it was due to the tension and frustration that I was experiencing in holding so much about myself in abeyance with this patient, some yearning in me to connect in a way that felt real and alive, some desire in me to be more animated. It felt to me that it sort of just busted out unpredictably, but in a way that was relatively manageable and seemed to create some movement. I speculated that at least some of those moments signaled that the patient was ready for more contact. That may have been a rationalization on my part. That feeling of yearning for a more animated connection was a point of intersection between my transference and his.

    Some of you brought up the issue of castration anxiety when thinking about this patient. In Freud's paper, "Fetishism" (1927), he states that "the boy refused to take cognizance of the fact of his having perceived that a woman (his mother) does not possess a penis" (p. 153). The idea is that the boy experiences the sight of the female genital as evidence of castration and this intensifies his own terror that this will be done to him. Freud explains that the boy has both retained the belief that his mother has a penis and simultaneously given up that belief.

Do you think castration anxiety is an important part of this case or any cases?

Bethany: I can believe that what Freud said there does happen. I'm also wondering about what exactly makes that realization traumatic? I don't think it's traumatic for every boy.

Instructor: Let's see if we can play with that question.

Reyna: In the case we're talking about, there was a traumatic experience, one that was both exciting and overwhelming. So there was a sense of danger, but I do wonder if the sense of danger was really primarily that of castration.

Natalie: Right. There may have been fears that preceded that and maybe they even primed the boy to have such a reaction.

Instructor: What do you think those fears may have been?

Eli: I think that the whole scene is filled with seduction. I imagine the boy felt tremendously excited and at the same time terrified that something could actually happen sexually. I think that could be one kind of situation where something like castration anxiety could emerge.

Instructor: Where do you imagine the castration anxiety coming into the picture?

Ezra: I wonder if it might be related to the fear of an actualization of his erotic feelings and then a fantasied punishment for his imagined crime.

Reyna: Kids do tend to blame themselves when parents are putting them into difficult situations. His thoughts may have been loaded with self-incrimination for his sexual lusts, without realizing that he was being provoked to have those feelings.

Midge: The way Reyna just put that is very interesting and has me thinking about what might prime a boy to link his sight of the female genital to the threat of castration. If he is already thinking about being punished for his feelings because they feel like actions, he might be more primed to see that threat embodied in that way.

Bethany: If you are carrying so much guilt and badness, you're likely to be on the lookout for any sign of impending punishment and in this case the imagined punishment of castration does have a link to where the erotic excitement is most felt, in his penis. It would then feel so terrifying that you would want to hide from the perceived threat and try to not see it.

Instructor: That touches on an important etiological consideration here, and one Freud speaks to in his considerations of splitting of the ego and fetishism, is that you cannot repress a perceptual experience that keeps getting repeated, as was the case with this patient's experience of his stepmother. You have to protect yourself in a different fashion. That involves looking away in some manner. There is a wide variety of defenses that can be used to play this function. They fall under the category of what today we would call perverse defenses (Grossman, 1993, 1996, 2023).

Freud is saying that, in a general, broad sense, in neurosis, when dealing with the threat of conflict, the ego will tend to side with reality against the instinctual impulses. For example, an oedipal wish is perceived as dangerous. The associated wishful thoughts are experienced as a danger in reality in that one's wishes could result in being killed/castrated or in the death of a loved parental object; so, the wish will be repressed, pushed, and kept out of consciousness. In a psychotic situation, there is a refusal to relinquish the wish as well as to accept the reality.

The patient that I presented can have the idea that he and I ending the analysis and having a sexual relationship. He also has a sense of as-if-ness to that fantasy. It's not concretely real to him the way it would be with a psychotic patient. I worked with a psychotic patient, for example, who saw another patient leave my office smiling. The patient abruptly, angrily, stormed out of the waiting room. For her, it was a massive betrayal. Her fantasy that we were having an exclusive, romantic relationship was experienced as an actual fact. There was no as-if about it.

One thing to note is that Freud is talking about particular types of defensive processes that are available to the ego when repression is not possible. Moments when repression is not available are something that every human will experience, while some will experience that scenario more than others depending upon the circumstances of one's development.

Your dialogue has added an important social, environmental context to consider when thinking about the danger of castration, the considerations you make about how certain early experiences might prime a child to be at a greater risk of experiencing castration anxiety.

Natalie: How does negation fit into all this? It seems similar to disavowal in that it fits in with the issue of what is the ego to do when repression is not available.

Instructor: In Freud's paper on Negation (1925) he defines it is a rejection of an assertion that has been made. For example, when one speaks of wishes, thoughts, and feelings that had previously been repressed and then disowns what one has said. It represents a moment when an unconscious idea or wish begins to assert itself into consciousness. It can allow the patient to play with ideas that might otherwise be impossible to consider.

Reyna: There is something about this concept of negation that seems kind of creative and playful to me. Negation can potentially create more space for possibilities, for thinking the unthinkable without having to be so afraid of the consequences.

Bethany: Like you were saying, it does remind me of play, and the way something can be held in mind, but without necessarily officially endorsing it. That seems like it would have clinical value.

Instructor: How so?

Ezra: It reminds me of when we were talking about practice, how retrospection can be a form of practice that enables you to move toward greater self-acceptance. Here, negation could allow you to practice familiarizing yourself with an idea that you hold which you aren't yet ready to own up to.

Ernest: That leads me to think about how negation might be seen as a kind of transitional object. It's existing between an idea and taking responsibility for the idea being your own.

Instructor: Interesting. Can anyone think of an example of that?

Midge: I was thinking about a situation with a patient who used both negation and projection. She often said that she wasn't angry. She would say that I was angry. It did seem to me that she was moving toward the idea of being angry, but in a gradual way. It wasn't yet tolerable for her to admit it. She sort of had to slowly saddle up to it.

Reyna: I really like that way of putting it. It reminds me that there are a lot of things like that in analytic work. Like things that play out in the transference and there may be a lengthy stretch before we can acknowledge where those feelings come from, like the 6-year-old girl who would be angry with you for leaving her and how she needed to not know it was about her mother for a period of time. It was too painful to plunge into that. She had to build up to it and the transference work did provide a kind of intermediate space, similar to what negation can provide.

Eli: Midge's example made me think about a patient that often told me that I was angry with her. It did make me angry. Now I'm wondering if my getting angry might have made it difficult for her to do what Midge was saying, to slowly saddle up to owning her own anger.

Instructor: That's interesting. Does anyone have any idea about how that would work in light of our discussion?

Bethany: The patient might need the analyst to show that they are comfortable with the very thing the patient is so frightened to acknowledge within themselves. If the analyst shows that he isn't tolerant of those feelings attributed to him, the patient may take that as confirming his own fears about harboring such feelings.

A Note on What Happened

After this class, I found myself working to digest some of the class' reactions to the clinical case that I presented. There was a moment of tension between two opposing ideas, a tension between the idea of the patient manifesting a neurotic structure versus the sense of surprise at how much the patient appeared to be conscious of. This was an important tension for us to grapple with together, an in vivo version of the kinds of struggles I imagine Freud contending with himself. Their ideas about how castration anxiety, in this case, may have been primed by a prior traumatic overstimulating experience, were interesting to ponder. The concept of castration anxiety was explored against the backdrop of the patient's sexual overstimulation, leading to ideas about how the social/environmental context can be useful when considering the subjective experience of a danger of castration. A student commented on how the patient appeared to relate to me as a thing, perhaps as a way of feeling safe. A question was posed about whether, in that way, the patient may have been trying to make use of me as a transitional object, first in a de-animated way, on the way to seeing me as a more whole, three-dimensional person. Another student posed the question of what led me to correct the patient and this moved us to consider the role played by my own transference to the patient. Our discussion of negation led the students to look at the concept as a way of playing with ideas that might otherwise be unthinkable. The thoughts that students raised about negation were fascinating to me in that they opened up new ways of thinking about the concept. The idea of negation as a transitional object was brought up, looking at negation as existing in a liminal space between thinking about an idea and taking responsibility for the idea as one's own. Another student similarly said that we may play something out in the transference for some time and need this lengthy stretch before being able to acknowledge where the ideas and their associated feelings are coming from. An analogy was made to an idea that came up recently of the use of retrospection as a form of practice enabling the analyst to re-look at his own clinical work as a way of moving toward gradual self-acceptance of certain self-observations that may be difficult to own up to.

References

Freud, S. (1925). Negation. SE 19: 234–239.

Freud, S. (1927). Fetishism. SE 21: 152–157.

Freud, S. (1940). Splitting of the Ego and the Process of Defense. SE, Vol. XXIII: 273–278.

Grossman, L. (1993). The Perverse Attitude toward Reality. *Psychoanalytic Quarterly*, LXII, 422–436.

Grossman, L. (1996). 'Psychic Reality' and Reality Testing in the Analysis of Perverse Defences. *International Journal of Psycho-Analysis*, 77, 509–517.

Grossman, L. (2023). *The Psychoanalytic Encounter and the Misuse of Theory*. Routledge.

5   Early and Late Freud
A Dialogue

A Note on My Intentions

In this class, I aimed for the students to keep in mind our prior readings of the technique papers in the context of reading "Fragment of an Analysis of a Case of Hysteria" (1905). My hope was that we would have an experience of feeling the tensions between what Freud had subsequently learned through experience and prior struggles that helped him get there. I also wished for this kind of exploration to lead to students being able to speculate about similar struggles and learning in their own clinical work.

Instructor:	Let's now begin to think about Freud's Dora case in the context of the recommendations we read about in the technique papers.
	We've been working with the idea that it is only by an appreciation of the struggles that Freud was contending with that we can grasp the principles behind his concepts, the specific tensions that gave rise to these ideas.
Natalie:	Thinking about our own clinical struggles in the context of what we imagine Freud struggling with does make Freud feel more human, less idealized, and more reachable.
Eli:	It's been interesting to notice some of the ideas that bring up feelings of discomfort or even threat, as well as noticing the aspects of clinical work that feel intimidating, like erotic transference.
Reyna:	Listening for the struggles that we have has increased my sense of empathy for listening to others presenting their work as well as for myself in my own work.
Ezra:	I agree with what Natalie was saying about how thinking about Freud's struggles makes him more accessible to us as a human being, someone who struggled in ways that are not so far removed from our own efforts and difficulties.
Ernest:	At times Freud has come across, in his writings, as so certain. It does help to think about his difficulties, especially when they relate to our own. It somehow brings him closer to our lived experience.

DOI : 10.4324/9781003610977-6

Midge:	I think that makes us more human too, in that it becomes easier to admit to having these struggles.
Eli:	There is something about this felt connection with Freud's struggles that actually seems to make talking openly about our difficulties easier.
Instructor:	I'm very glad to hear that. Now that we have read Freud's technique papers, I think it could be useful to go back in time to consider Freud's paper, "Fragment of an Analysis of a Case of Hysteria" (1905) juxtaposed to Freud's technique papers to speculate about what Freud's treatment of Dora was like and what he learned in the time between that case and his later technique papers.
	My hope is that we can try to imaginatively bring the Freud of the technique papers into dialogue with the Freud who treated Dora. I would like us to try to see if we can notice those tensions in Freud and to look at similar tensions in our own work, our own attempts to engage in psychoanalytic clinical work past and present, our mistakes and regrets and what we have tried to learn from them.

Reflecting on Freud's Dora Case

Instructor:	Just before Freud started treating Dora in psychoanalysis, he had abandoned his seduction theory, that is, the idea that all neurosis was caused by actual sexual trauma. He shifted his focus to unconscious sexual fantasies from early childhood. He had also just published his most important work up to that date, "The Interpretation of Dreams" (1900a and 1900b). Dora began the analysis at age 18. She was in treatment with Freud from October until the end of December of 1900.
	Dora's father was having an extramarital sexual relationship with Frau K. Herr K was actively trying to seduce Dora from the time when she was 14 years old.
	Dora suffered from a wide range of physical symptoms, including headaches, loss of ability to speak, difficulty breathing, coughing attacks, depression, and suicidal thoughts. Dora attempted to obtain the help of her father in dealing with the unwanted advances Herr K was making upon her. Her father did not believe her reports of what Herr K was doing. Freud did not trust Dora's father and believed that he wanted Dora under control.
	Is there anything about the beginning of the text that struck you?
Midge:	I was thinking about Freud's (1905) comment on page 12 that manifest symptoms do not tell you what the underlying structure

is. This really does distinguish psychoanalysis from the mainstream approach today of organizing diagnoses along the lines of manifest symptoms rather than underlying structures.

Bethany: I also appreciated Freud's (1905) comment about dreams being "… one of the roads along which consciousness can be reached by the psychical material which, on account of the opposition aroused by its content, has been cut off and repressed…" (p. 15) what Freud referred to as the "indirect method of representation in the mind" (p. 15). This made me think about how much psychoanalysis makes use of indirect methods for gaining access to the unconscious, like dreams, slips of the tongue, allusions, symptoms, mistakes, transference. It's a subtle, artful approach that works with ambiguity and hints. It's not limited to what the patient says directly.

Eli: Freud describes different forms of hiding that we can expect to encounter from our patients, like intentionally withholding information, forgetting as one is speaking, filling in gaps, altering the chronological order of events, and the use of doubts.

Instructor: Does this bring to mind any clinical experiences of your own?

Ernest: I worked with a patient who would become confused and doubtful of everything precisely in moments when certain themes began to become more clear, like when his sadistic pleasure was more salient. At first, I would become confused too, confused about his confusion. I kept trying to be more clear which only made things worse until I finally realized the function that his confusion served.

Ezra: I was thinking about Freud's (1905) comments on page 26, where he said that

> The experience with Herr K—his making love to her and the insult to her honor which was involved—seems to provide in Dora's case the psychic trauma which Breuer and I declared long ago to be an indispensable prerequisite for the production of a hysterical disorder. But this new case presents all the difficulties which have since led me to go beyond that theory.
>
> (p. 27)

Freud here, as we discussed earlier, is recognizing the importance of psychic reality.

Instructor: This is an important piece to mention. Do you have more to say about it?

Ezra: It led me to think differently about how Freud moved away from trauma. I thought Freud abandoned the reality of sexual abuse, but I now see that it is more complex than I thought.

Instructor: This is an important realization. Freud's abandonment of the seduction hypothesis resulted in his increasing focus on how psychical fantasies and psychic defenses play a key role in the formation of neurotic symptoms, eventually concluding that it was inner, psychic reality that was of primary importance in understanding the construction of neurosis.

Midge: I am thinking about Freud's (1905) comments about the reasonableness of Dora's complaints, and how Freud said, on page 35, "When the patient brings forward a sound and incontestable train of thought...the patient uses thoughts of this kind, which the analysis cannot attack, for the purpose of cloaking others which are anxious to escape from criticism and from consciousness" (p. 35).

This led me to think about Freud's comments on the importance of psychic reality and how easy it is to be seduced into thinking that a traumatic experience is the sole cause of the patient's difficulty when this seemingly incontestable idea itself can be used as a way of hiding more subtle inner workings that are playing out.

Ezra: That's interesting. I noticed when a patient was telling me about an interaction he had with his boss, I found myself agreeing with him that he was treated unfairly. I still think that's true and it was important to validate that, but it was one of those sessions when I didn't feel like I could offer much in the way of noticing what might be going on for him unconsciously. I do wonder if the focus on something sound and incontestable deflected attention away from more subtle allusions. Like, it never occurred to me until now that he may have been implying some feelings he has toward me.

Natalie: Herr K appears to be a villain in this account and I think in many ways he was. As Ezra said of his patient's issue, it seems incontestable, but Dora's symptoms, as with all neurotic symptoms are complex and formed from multiple determinants, so we don't want to jump on the most obvious thing in our efforts to understand the meaning of the symptom.

Instructor: Does everyone agree with what Natalie is saying here? Can you think of any problems with it? Are we leaving anything out?

Eli: I agree but it's also important not to be dismissive of the patient's subjective experience of her difficulty. If she feels Herr K and her father have wronged her, and I also think there's a lot of truth in that, it would be harmful to her to invalidate that. We would be at risk of gaslighting the patient. Also, Freud is saying that inner psychic reality is paramount in thinking about symptom formation, but I don't think that rules out the external reality, in this case, again the issue of trauma, playing at least a contextualizing role in that process.

Instructor: Well said Eli. And I like the way you're continuing the thread of our previous dialogue about how the social/environmental context can prime and contextualize symptomatic processes.

Ezra: Freud takes into account multiple sources of influence, like how a symptom can be caused by various determining factors. This idea of overdetermination of symptoms is very helpful. Sometimes I find myself looking for the one cause of the symptom and becoming over-wed to it. I guess we can err on either side of the environment/psychic reality continuum. Sometimes I find myself thinking that one particular traumatic event caused the pathology. Other times, I'm more exclusively focused on the patient's underlying fantasies.

Bethany: I really resonate with that. Either side on its own can be an impoverished picture, an incomplete story, not that it will ever be complete, but it's easy to single in on a favored way of seeing things if we're not careful.

Natalie: On p. 64, Freud (1905) asked Dora to "take the dream bit by bit and tell me what occurred to her in connection with it. She had already had some training in dream interpretation" (p. 65). I wonder how it is we can train patients to interpret dreams.

Instructor: This is a very good question and it has broader implications for how we train patients to work analytically. Freud (1905) offers a clue about asking Dora to "take the dream bit by bit," that is, to break it down into smaller pieces and allow herself to associate to those parts of the dream. Another example of training the patient was on the same page, "Now, I would like you to pay close attention to the exact words you used" (p. 65). Consistent with previous conversations we've had, I think about how the analyst implicitly shows the patient a way of processing their own struggles is another way of training patients to work analytically.

Reyna: In that case, part of the training is about helping the patient to become a better listener of themselves, to become more attuned to hearing hints of what's going on unconsciously. I guess we show them that by being open about how we are listening to them.

Midge: We engage in a kind of teaching, not to be overdone or be too didactic, but we do show patients how to listen to themselves, how to become better observers of so many things going on with them. I agree with how you put it, Reyna. I think we also show patients how we listen to ourselves too.

Instructor: Can you think of some examples of that?

Midge: We show patients how we listen to their dreams, their associations, the timing of when things co-occur and maybe noticing what's going on within ourselves at times, as well as in how we make sense of the interactions we have with our patients. I show patients how I listen to myself when I catch myself saying something to a patient that says something about how I am engaging with them. Like, I noticed myself talking to a patient in a way that sounded to me to be a kind of pontificating. I hated the way I sounded to myself, but I thought it was worth telling the patient what I heard because I thought it said something about what was going on between us.

Ezra: I love that example and it reminds me that Freud also teaches or trains the patient to work analytically by showing his thinking to the patient, showing how he links things up and putting the story together, and what he hears as he's listening.

Instructor: These are all excellent examples.

Let's keep in mind Midge's example of noticing how she was speaking to her patient and how that could be communicated to the patient to open up an exploration of their interaction, and the timing of when things co-occur and Ezra mentioned linking things up. This also reminds me of the importance of the analyst noting and listening to the sequence of what we hear from the patient's associations. The sequence will tell you so much in terms of pivotal moments in a session when one thing follows another. They clue us in to the way things can be meaningfully connected. The contiguity and contrast allude to a connection that we and the patient may not otherwise notice. It provides a context or backdrop that allows us to notice the potential meaning of so many otherwise incomprehensible phenomena.

Bethany: Freud would point Dora toward noticing the exact words that she was using and they often were words or phrases she used in another context. They provided important clues to understanding the latent meaning of otherwise quite ambiguous remarks, or comments that would have remained ambiguous due to their being isolated.

Ernest: I notice how much Freud shows us in this writing about the very careful, detailed way that he observes and thinks about the material, what he sees, hears, and how Freud has learned from experience that there are many ways that patients tell us and show us what's hidden in them, if we can listen carefully enough and with an open mind, without preconceptions.

Eli: Often it seems that Freud is listening for analogies, like when he notices a resemblance between two questions that Dora poses, he's clued into a deeper connection and can use that to interpret it. He looks for connections between the patient's thoughts continuously.

Instructor: I hear your comments here as remarking on how much Freud shows us in this paper, about his way of listening, observing, his strategies for organizing his observations in such a way that enables him to hear the intimations and allusions to the repressed material. There is so much for us to learn here. Some of you mentioned Dora's grievances and ways she was mistreated. Is there anything about this paper that raises concerns or problems for you?

Bethany: I was thinking about how when Freud is approaching Dora's dreams, there are times when Freud appeared to be moving rather quickly in his interpretations.

Instructor: What led you to think that?

Bethany: It was clear that Freud was very much aware of Dora's resistance, but not helping her to become more acquainted with it, at least not in the way he taught us to do in his technique papers.

Reyna: He seemed to be under the pressure of the therapeutic zeal that he criticized in his later writings.

Ezra: I felt that Freud was imposing meanings that he had arrived at that Dora was not very near to being able to connect with her prior understanding of herself. She wasn't able to struggle with it in the way that we need patients to do, so that she could arrive at a conviction about it that was her own.

Instructor: Ezra, That is very well said. Can you say more about what you mean by imposing? Do you mean imposing meanings that didn't seem to fit the material for you?

Ezra: It was more of an imposing related to Dora not being ready for them, maybe a timing issue, but much of the content, as well as the way he arrived at his inferences seemed convincing to me.

Instructor: One thing I'm hearing is that Freud is doing most of work of discovery here, deriving insights, whereas Dora is not afforded much space to do so herself. I also hear your experience of the treatment of Dora leaving you with the impression of Freud interpreting her dreams continuously and over zealously.

Your comments reminded me of a quote of Steven Ellman (1991) having said in regard to this paper, "His manner seems more that of a prosecuting attorney than an analyst" (p. 14).

Ernest: I had the feeling of Freud pressuring Dora to submit to his way of seeing things, listening to her only long enough, to impose his ideas onto the material.

Eli: There's a parallel between Freud's imposing his ideas on Dora and her experience of Herr K forcing himself on her.

Bethany: I wonder if we may be having an experience of Freud that identifies with Dora's experience of Herr K within her transference to Freud.

Ezra: I'm reminded of the postscript where Freud spoke of having missed the transference. Why might that be? It makes me wonder about my own experiences of missing the transference and my resistances to recognizing the transference that we encounter.

Natalie: I think he also missed a possible enactment of a power struggle between Freud and Dora.

Eli: I was thinking this is a good example of the analyst excessively interpreting and how that can defend against noticing the transference.

Instructor: Any ideas on how excessive interpretation could do that?

NATALIE: When I have been preoccupied with coming up with the right interpretation, I wasn't thinking about the quality of the interaction that was going on between the patient and me. I get too focused on getting it right because I'm thinking that's what's going to help the patient.

Ezra: Yeah, that helps me to see how there's an inward focus to that. If I'm intensely trying to come up with the right interpretation then I'm in my own head, kind of alone, no longer in it with the patient, and my attention is narrowed to my own efforts to say the right thing.

Reyna: There was a one-way quality of the relationship, where Freud was to exert an influence on Dora without being open to being influenced by her.

Midge: Related to what Reyna said, I thought that Dora seemed to disappear as an agent, a true desiring subject with her own mind, her own subjective experiences. In some ways, reading about this treatment, it seemed like it was Freud's theory on center stage, not Dora. It's striking because it is very different from what Freud recommended in his technique papers.

Bethany: I'm thinking about our previous discussion about how our desires, the desires of the analyst, can derail the development of an analytic process, one that the patient is actively involved in.

Eli: It can be so difficult to contend with our own ambitions in the work. I'm thinking about my own need to feel successful and helpful, and how frustrating and demoralizing it can be when it feels like the treatment isn't going the way I want it to go. I am aware of often wanting the patient to be impressed with my interpretations. I know that's not what the work is about, but I still feel that a fair amount. I think I have had the idea that unless I say something really profoundly enlightening, the patient won't be affected sufficiently to change.

Instructor: These are very important struggles to think more about and keep in mind as we continue to talk. It does relate to how Freud repeatedly encountered disappointment in his work, as we all do, often discovering crucial insights about psychoanalysis in the process. We have our desires and associated fantasies about what the work should look like and then we experience something very different in actuality. And as Eli was describing, it's human to want to be impressive and we have to be accepting of ourselves here, while also reminding ourselves of the kind of process we are aiming for, which includes the nature of the work that we are trying to cultivate in the patient.

Ernest: It feels so important to strive to maintain curiosity in the face of these disappointments and even a sense of failure, to remember that there is always something to learn in those moments.

Instructor: I think this is a crucial point that we find ourselves returning to.

Midge: I was thinking about how Freud was a product of his times, and I wonder if there are parallels between Dora's experience of how she was treated by men in her life, her father and Herr K, that Freud may have repeated.

Instructor: What do you notice?

Midge: It has to do with what Freud missed seeing in her transference and I wonder if he was so focused on his own ambitions for the case that he lost sight of the patient's passions in the room with him and maybe in her life as well.

Instructor: Could you say something about what you think were some of Freud's own ambitions for this case?

Midge: If we look back where Freud talked about his objectives for this paper, to make use of the case as a supplement to his book on interpretation of dreams, to show how dream interpretation can be used in analysis, to stimulate interest in the complexity of psychological events in the formation of hysteria, and to show the role of sexuality in the formation of symptoms. These preoccupations of Freud may have played a role in deflecting his attention away from the transference.

Ezra: I can relate to that if it did go that way. I'm thinking about the excitement I feel when I see something playing out with my patient that I'm particularly interested in, especially if I'm reading about it and/or writing about it.

Instructor: Could you say something about how that excitement and interest affect your work?

Ezra: I will get so into the content I'm hearing from the patient that I forget to even think about what's going on in my relating with the patient. It always hits me right after the session or in supervision when my supervisor says, "that is all very interesting, but what about the transference?"

Eli: What Ezra is saying reminds me of some experiences I've had with patients who are able to get a sense of what I am interested in. They'll tell me things that I immediately get excited to hear and my fascination with it does deflect my attention. It's only after the session is over that I am like, wait a minute, I totally neglected to say anything about something I should have drawn attention to.

Midge: That's interesting. I wonder if that can be a kind of defense or resistance on the patient's part. It does exert a certain level of control over the analyst.

Instructor: We can be so busy trying to understand what's going on with the patient, that we don't notice that they are reading us as carefully as we are trying to read them.

Bethany: I also wonder about the misogyny of Freud's time and how that might have affected the work. Dora was treated very poorly in my opinion by Herr K and by her father. I get an overall sense of her being used by the men in her life. Even though I think Freud was trying to help her with her symptoms, he also had his own ambitions for how he wanted to use the material from this case and in that sense may have replicated some misogynistic dynamics already at play in Dora's life.

Instructor: That's a very good point, Bethany, and you have an argument to make there. Relatedly, it's interesting to reflect back to a reference Freud made in his Dynamics of Transference paper, the first paper we read. He referred to a book written by Gabriele Reuter called "From a Good Family" (1896). I wonder if any of you have read it. Freud thought that this book was an accurate illustration of some of the conditions that give rise to neurosis.

I read the book and found that it also illustrated a convincing account of what life was like for women in Freud's time. The main character, Agathe, was an intelligent, passionate person with a strong spirit. The attitudes of her social class and the larger cultural attitude toward women impacted her in ways that led to the impoverishing of her internal world, and the sense of possibility. Her knowledge and desire to learn were actively suppressed. For her, every love interest served as a beacon of hope that she might be able to make use of them to expand her constricted world and have a meaningful life.

The authoritarian indoctrination that Agathe received about what it meant to be a woman, i.e., to be subordinate, submissive, self-sacrificing, and intellectually inferior won out in the end. She was never able to overcome the subsequently internalized dictate to live her life for others. In line with the point Bethany raised, we might wonder about some of these cultural dynamics which were operative during Freud's time and the impact of such social forces on one's clinical work.

Natalie: I was thinking about how Freud (1905) said transference was the hardest thing in analysis, that interpreting is actually much easier for us, making inferences from what the patient tells us. The transference seems to be a very slowly evolving process, so slow and subtle, that it takes a lot of work to tune into it and even notice it happening.

Reyna: We are also very much a part of the transference and we need to have a capacity to step out of something that we are mired in to be able to see it more distinctly. That is really hard when you're in it. It's easy for someone else listening to the hour to hear it.

Ezra: I think part of what's easier about the "explanatory arts" of interpreting dreams is that there is a more clear differentiation between the analyst and the patient, but with transference, there is a shared merging and that gets more entangled and harder to sort out. But what Reyna said about someone outside the hour being able to hear it does bring to my mind the value of the analyst writing and listening to their sessions after the fact.

Instructor: You both raise important points here. I also want to emphasize the observational strategies that Freud shows us in this paper. Freud was able to construct remarkable insights about what was motivating Dora, how her symptoms formed psychically, and her underlying conflicts. He gave us a very deep and convincing narrative that he was able to put together. Remarkably, Dora even seemed, at the end, to be able to accept some of what Freud was saying.

              This discussion we had about this case also serves to remind us that in spite of the brilliance and correctness of much of what Freud was able to uncover and put together interpretively, there appeared to be clinical difficulties in linking Freud's interpretations and Dora's ability to receive them and, as Ezra said, do the work that she needed to do to be able to arrive at her own sense of conviction about these ideas.

              It is an important lesson in terms of thinking about how there is so much more involved in analysis than the analyst's knowing what's going on inside the patient and communicating that. This touches on the art of the work, the work of forging a scaffolding between what we are able to learn from listening, observing, and interacting with the patient and the patient being able to come to see it for themselves in an emotionally convincing way. This has a lot to do with the analyst being able to make use of their emotional flexibility in order to provide a connectable bridge between themselves and the patient, wherein they are speaking and listening at a level where both parties are relatively on the same affective wavelength.

Natalie: When we're focused on finding the right interpretation within ourselves, it becomes so difficult to remember that whatever we have to say to the patient has to take into account so much of where they are at emotionally.

Ezra: That's true. Like if I'm criticizing myself, feeling like I'm failing to help my patient, I'm not thinking about his experience in a way that's separate from my own anxieties.

Midge: I think that that kind of self-criticism is often related to having come into the session with our own agenda, like when things aren't going the way we wanted them to go and it feels hard to let that go.

Bethany: Yeah, letting go of what we wanted to happen opens up more attention to what is actually happening with the patient.

Eli: And not being able to do that can lead to a great deal of oppression of the patient.

Freud's Technique Papers

Instructor: Your comments here are very much related to what Freud said in the technique papers, so that we can think about the Freud who worked with Dora juxtaposed to the Freud of the technique papers. Please feel free to jump in as the spirit moves you as I am talking about these references.

In "Remembering, Repeating and Working Through" (1914), Freud says…

> there has evolved the consistent technique used today, in which the analyst gives up the attempt to bring a particular moment or problem into focus.
> He contents himself with studying whatever is present for the time being on the surface of the patient's mind…
>
> (p. 147)

This was a very important development in Freud's technique. The analyst is told to follow what is most active and present in the patient's mind, to pursue their lead, to let the patient's desire guide the way.

The analyst is meant to not have goal-directed attention. These recommendations are a striking antithesis to how many of you experienced the way Freud engaged with Dora, for example, as often directing her to focus on what he wanted her to attend to, often interrupting her attempts to associate. Freud's desires, specifically his handling of those desires, in the treatment, as in all treatments, was an important part of treatment to think about.

Midge: This is reminding me how much I loved the Freud who wrote "The Handling of Dream-Interpretation in Psycho-Analysis" (1911). In that paper, Freud could see that his interest in dreams and his therapeutic ambitions in trying to interpret them fully was a big problem. He had to give up his own ambitions, his own agenda or it would kill the whole process.

Instructor: Here again, this advice stands in contrast to the way Freud insisted on interpreting Dora's dreams fully. Midge, I am curious if you might be able to say more about what you loved so much about the Freud who wrote the paper on handling dreams interpretation?

Midge: It feels like such a relief from some of the things that I feel so much pressure to try to do in my work.

Ezra: I can totally relate to that. It reminds me of what we talked about when our interpretations feel forced and mostly driven by trying to make something happen.

Reyna: The comments Freud makes in that paper feel like permission to not have to try so hard and that feels like a great relief, to simply get out of the way and let things happen, to follow the current of what emerges of its own accord.

Instructor: When we can let something happen, we open more space for attending to the unfolding transference. In "Remembering, Repeating and Working Through" (1914), Freud speaks to a shift in attitude that can occur in the patient when in the grip of the work in the transference, one wherein the patient experiences their suffering as something meaningful and worthy of their respect.

I think he's also talking about the way one's engagement with the transference can lead to a greater sense of conviction. He said, that the transference is "allowed to expand in almost complete freedom..." (p. 154).

Freud does not attend to the transference in his treatment of Dora, and it seems that he does not give her sufficient space to arrive at any sense of conviction with regard to the material of the analysis. He also spoke about the patient becoming acquainted with their resistance and says that the therapeutic action of working-through is really located in the patient being able to continue to struggle to speak in the midst of their resistance and ultimately remember what had been repressed.

This involves the analyst's recognition that putting words to something, telling the patient something by interpretation for example, does not lead to the patient knowing it, that is, knowing it by acquaintance. This seems to differ from his treatment of Dora. At times, he appears in this treatment as the sole mover, the one who single-handedly attempts to force the therapeutic action upon the patient. He made very lengthy interpretations to Dora, as if this could help her to know in a mutative way.

Ezra: I'm thinking about Freud's footnote when he was able to retrospectively think about what he missed in his treatment of Dora, namely attending to the transference. This reminds me of what we were talking about last time about the practice of engaging in retrospective review of our work, trying to think about what we missed.

Bethany:	I like the word practice in this context. It reminds me of athletes, looking at videos of their previous performance, trying to learn something about areas of their work that could be improved. There's something about it that also feels constructive, sort of positive, not self-attacking, but more looking forward, viewing it more as an opportunity for growth, in contrast to self-condemnation.
Eli:	I'm thinking a lot about my own clinical work and how there are so many things that I want to happen in that work. I'm thinking right now about a particular patient who is living what to my mind is a very impoverished existence and I feel so strongly that I want his life to be better. Sometimes it does lead me to work too hard to convince him that his way of thinking is wrong.
Reyna:	I can identify with that, but I also see it as a form of countertransference, one that disguises itself as an attempt to help the patient, when it actually may be repeating a dynamic that feels quite oppressive to the patient.
Bethany:	I wonder about the pressures involved in this for the clinician. We want to help our patients. Sometimes, especially when there are risk factors involved, like with suicidal and self-destructive patients, that pressure can be severe and lead to a greater tendency to try to force something.
Midge:	There are so many pressures that can affect us. What you just described, Bethany, in and of itself, is quite scary, but I'm also thinking about it in the context of training. I wonder about the added pressure of feeling our work to be under surveillance in a sense. In training, we are being observed, by our supervisors, the progressions committee, even our colleagues. It can lend itself to approaching the patient in ways that impose our own agenda on the patient.
Instructor:	Maybe an agenda that you imagine is expected of you. The pressures that you described, e.g., to demonstrate that one is practicing psychoanalysis successfully and how this can lead to an excessive focus on our own actions. This can unwittingly lead to a deflection of attention from the patient's associations, struggles, and divert our focus from facilitating the work the patient must do.

These are both important points demonstrating how our own aims and efforts can become oppressive. For example, in the "Observations on Transference Love" (1915), Freud cautions analysts not to lead and direct patients, not to anticipate what will happen in the analysis or it "robs the phenomenon of the element of spontaneity which is so convincing..." (p. 162). The spontaneous, unbidden experience of the transference is a very powerful one, especially with regard to conviction.

In Freud's technical paper called "Recommendations for Physicians on the Psycho-Analytic Treatment" (1912), he expresses similar ideas:

> The technique, however, is a very simple one. As we shall see, it rejects the use of any special expedient (even that of taking notes). It consists simply of not directing one's notice to anything in particular and in maintaining the same 'evenly suspended attention' (as I have called it) in the face of all that one hears.
>
> (p. 112)

Ernest: I started working on a paper inspired by themes in one of my clinical cases that I found fascinating, but then started to feel the impingement of that work into the treatment.

Instructor: What did you notice?

Ernest: I started to make interpretations that came more from what I was writing and inferring in my paper than from what I was hearing from the patient and sometimes imposing ideas on the patient's comments that she experienced as forced. A number of ideas that I was forcing upon my patient were ideas that, prior to writing this paper, emerged spontaneously.

Instructor: We can see in our dialogue that as we think about the pitfalls that Freud is contending with and writing about, that we have gone through our own versions of these struggles. This helps us to relate more personally to what he's grappling with in these writings. Freud was continually reflecting on his work and making use of these practices to learn and grow from his experiences. We can learn a great deal from this practice and it is central to our development as analysts.

In his technique papers, Freud recognized the importance of being able to let go of efforts to control the analytic process and the inclination to prescribe a direction to the flow of that process, both of which he seemed to have difficulty with in Dora's treatment. The attitude toward analysis that Freud is advocating in his later technique papers is the original version of no memory and desire.

Midge: I love this way of thinking about analysis, but we are always going to find ourselves wanting things to happen in our work. What Freud is recommending here is an ideal. We're never going to reach that, certainly not in any kind of final way. Like we're never going to arrive there once and for all. Nothing is ever fixed in analysis.

Instructor: Assuming that what Midge is saying is true, how do we feel about it?

Ernest: I was feeling really good about the idea that we could engage in the retrospective practice and continue to grow in ways that would ultimately lead to being able to overcome our own impediments. I realize that what Midge is saying doesn't rule out our ongoing growth, but I think I did have the idea of reaching a point where I would not impose my own wants on the patient. Now I am feeling like it's going to be a continuous struggle and that does feel disappointing.

Ezra: There is something that feels seductive about the idea of finally getting to a place where you are a competent analyst, like becoming the thing you have been working so hard to become, sort of like finishing a race. I picture that at graduation, a sense of finally arriving at what I was striving for.

Reyna: Going back to Freud, as an example, he was continually finding problems and re-thinking his conceptualizations. I imagine that Midge is right, that it's going to be like that for us, no matter how much experience we get. I don't feel disappointed by it, although I can also relate to the idea of wanting to reach some marker that feels good in some way, like a sense of having climbed a mountain, a feeling of completion and accomplishment.

Ezra: This reminds me of the problems we've been talking about of imposing an agenda on the patient. I was thinking about it in terms of interpretation. We might have a session when something comes together in the form of an insight and you speak to it and it moves the patient. It really resonates and seems to have an impact. Then later, you find yourself trying to use the same interpretation again, but it has no effect and it just feels forced.

Midge: Yeah. That captures what I was trying to get at earlier. It's not as though we're ever going to arrive at some point, some happily ever after. And I don't actually feel disappointed by that. For me, this way of thinking about our work feels more interesting, unpredictable, and alive.

Ernest: I've been telling myself, when I make mistakes, when I don't know things I feel I should know about psychoanalysis, that I am a work in progress.

That leads me to feel less self-critical. What I am hearing today leads me to the idea that I will always be a work in progress.

A Note on What Happened

Students talked about how comparing their own struggles to Freud's struggles made Freud more reachable, more human, less idealized, increasing their empathy in listening to their own and others' clinical challenges. This process appeared to make it easier to openly acknowledge their clinical difficulties and even to value such open dialogue. The discussion of training patients to work analytically developed an idea discussed earlier. Examples of such training were offered, including the ways we show patients how to listen to themselves, how to observe themselves, the ways we show patients how to listen to their dreams, associations, the timing of when associations co-occur, showing our own thinking to patients, how we link their associations, and, perhaps most importantly, how we listen to ourselves. There were criticisms of Freud's handling of Dora's treatment, e.g., not sufficiently helping Dora to become acquainted with her resistance, imposing meaning interpretively in ways that felt premature, not close enough to what Dora was able to grasp, how he seemed to be interpreting excessively and overzealously. These critiques were making use of Freud's subsequent writings in his technique papers. They also considered social/cultural dynamics which may have been involved in difficulties in this case, e.g., misogyny and cultural oppression of women. There was a realization that telling the patient something via interpretation does not lead to the patient knowing it by acquaintance, i.e., thinking for themselves and making it their own. I thought this idea applies to teaching and learning psychoanalysis as well. The students continued to relate Freud's struggles to their own. This led to a deeper consideration of the value of retrospective introspection of one's clinical work, reviewing our clinical work in ways that allow us to think about what we missed, to look more carefully at areas of our work that can be improved, a constructive critique of our clinical work, analogous to Freud's, viewed as an opportunity for growth and development, in contrast to self-condemnation. This led me to think about the harsh self-criticism that students disclosed at the beginning of the course. I wondered if the constructive retrospective self-criticism could be viewed as a new formation of what had felt like a harsh superego attack. My overall impression was that the kind of dialogue we were engaged in seemed to be an important step in gradually serving to demystify the process of the evolution of a psychoanalyst.

References

Ellman, S. (1991). *Freud's Technique Papers: A Contemporary Perspective*. Jason Aronson Inc.

Freud, S. (1900a). The Interpretation of Dreams. SE 4: 1–338.

Freud, S. (1900b). The Interpretation of Dreams. SE 5: 339–751.

Freud, S. (1905). Fragment of an Analysis of a Case of Hysteria. SE 7: 3–122.

Freud, S. (1911). The Handling of Dream-Interpretation in Psycho-Analysis. SE 12: 89–96.

Freud, S. (1912). Recommendations to Physicians Practicing Psychoanalysis. SE 12: 109–120.

Freud, S. (1914). Remembering, Repeating and Working-through. SE 12: 145–156.

Freud, S. (1915). Observations on Transference-Love. SE 12: 157–171.

Reuter, G. (1896). *From a Good Family*. Camden House.

Part II
Teaching Freud's Later Theoretical Writings

In Part II, we will take a deeper look at Freud's later writings on psychoanalytic theory, with an emphasis on his third major theoretical viewpoint. This third paradigm begins with Freud's paper, The Ego and the Id (1923). Freud's first topography was beginning to yield to the strain of having to account for more and more complexity. We have seen that strain very clearly in Mourning and Melancholia (1917). That paper forecasted many important later developments to come.

The first involved the importance of interactive relationships that become internalized. Relatedly, Freud also turned his attention to the vicissitudes of narcissism and their role in identifications that constitute the internal structures of the mind. Third would be the development of conscience which will become one of the constituents of the later development of the superego and the structural model of the mind. All of these developments raise Freud's theory of psychoanalysis to a more complex level and require a new model of the mind that can account for all of it.

In the topographical model, Freud conceptualized the unconscious as constituted by the drives always pressing for discharge. In the Mourning and Melancholia paper, we have seen that Freud was locating complex internal object relationships, e.g., one part of the self attacking an internal object representation in the unconscious system. He also spoke of unconscious guilt that he will later link to the superego. In addition, the ego was, in the topographical model, associated with consciousness, but Freud was finding it necessary to consider a substantial portion of ego activity occurring unconsciously, e.g., unconscious defenses and resistance.

The structural model represents the mind as divided into three major agencies. The Id is viewed as equivalent to how the unconscious was represented in the topographical model, representing the drives perpetually pressing for immediate discharge. The Ego is viewed as the executive agency of the mind, having to find ways of adapting to the impinging forces of the Id, Superego, and external reality. The Superego is viewed as the internalization of the parental prohibitions and ideals. It is the medium of conscience and ethical

DOI : 10.4324/9781003610977-7

values. A significant portion of the Superego and Ego is considered to be operating unconsciously.

It is also important to note that Freud does not take up the defensive organization of perversion until after his 1926 paper, Inhibitions, Symptoms, and Anxiety. In his earlier writings, Freud often used repression as a generic way of referring to all defenses. He changes this in the Inhibitions, Symptoms, and Anxiety paper and describes repression as a very specific operation. He refers to it as the rendering of something unconscious and keeping it unconscious. It is a rapid and persistent forgetting.

His new position here is that anxiety causes repression as well as other defenses. Within the structural model, Freud is realizing that there are many different types of defenses, beyond repression. One important example of this expansion is one we looked at in our discussion of his paper on Fetishism and his focus on disavowal, a defensive organization focused on conscious experience. The development of our understanding of the ego within the late structural model greatly expanded our appreciation for the breadth of defensive operations available.

References

Freud, S. (1917). Mourning and Melancholia. SE 14: 236–258.
Freud, S. (1923). The Ego and the Id. SE 19: 2–66.

6   Beyond the Pleasure Principle

A Note on My Intentions

I decided to approach the teaching of this paper, "Beyond the Pleasure Principle" (1920) aiming to begin with a description of what life was like for Freud during the difficult time period within which he wrote this paper. I also wanted to provide the clinical context for the paper by revisiting Freud's notion of the repetition compulsion and its association with the trauma of war. There were a number of core concepts that I aimed to cover, e.g., the pleasure and reality principles, the instinct for mastery, the compulsion to repeat, binding, the theoretical problem Freud encountered with narcissism, aggression, and the life and death drives. I wanted to have us notice tensions that came up for us in reading this text and to try to think together about these reactions in order to better understand them.

Instructor: In Jones' (1957) biography of Freud, he tells us that the time period within which this paper was written was a very onerous one for Freud. The years after the First World War were quite crushing in many ways. All normal everyday life in Vienna had come to a halt. Much was nearly unbearable. There often was no heat in the cold winter months and inflation was soaringly high. Jones (1957) said that Freud tried to focus on his hopes for the future of psychoanalysis. Note the importance of the temporal dimension here in terms of regulating unpleasure.

Here is a quote from a letter that Freud wrote (Jones, 1957) at this time:

> And even if our hopes deceive us and mankind remain a victim of their unconscious to the very end, still we have been vouchsafed a glimpse behind the scenes, and knowledge of the truth can compensate us for much we are deprived of and also for much suffering.
>
> (p. 7)

DOI : 10.4324/9781003610977-8

In March 1919, Freud's wife Martha became seriously ill with the Spanish Flu and took many months to recover. Then, he suffered his most painful loss to date when his daughter Sophie died of the same illness a short time later, only a few days after the death of his very close friend, Anton Von Freund. Sophie was the mother of the boy, Freud's grandson, in his Fort Da vignette.

In the fall of 1920 the Vienna Freud had known much of his life was in a state of transition and hardship after the war. In the residue of destruction of the First World War and the pandemic of the Spanish flu spreading across Europe, people were feeling a great deal of uncertainty.

The paper we read on the repetition compulsion is a context to keep in mind when reading Beyond the Pleasure Principle. We read about this concept initially in Freud's paper, "Remembering, Repeating and Working-Through" (1914).

What has been repressed pushes to emerge into the present in the form of symptoms, dreams, transference, and acting out. Freud said that something that has not yet been made sense of, will, like an unlaid ghost, keep returning in the form of repeating.

In this paper, Freud is focusing on forms of repetition that appear to have very little, if any, noticeable satisfaction or pleasure. He was influenced by the trauma experienced by soldiers after the First World War, the lingering symptomatic effects of their experiences of the violence of war.

Suddenly there were many people suffering from traumatic symptoms, for example, the replaying in dreams of frightful moments experienced during the war. These were clearly not wish fulfillments according to Freud. He believed they were phenomena that required a new analysis of the compulsion to repeat.

Freud is thinking here that the repetitive compulsion is an automatic, instinctual process originating unconsciously which compels a person to relive experiences from their past without recalling the past scene which is being repeated. He believes that this primal instinctual urge cannot be fully explained by the conflicting tensions between the pleasure principle and the reality principle. He is viewing this compulsion to repeat as something we are driven to do in disregard of the pleasure principle.

Recall, that when Freud talked about the reality principle, he was referring to the postponement of pleasure as a result of the need to take reality into account. In that instance, he was talking about the postponement of the operation of the pleasure principle by a set of inhibitory mechanisms.

The ego in that circumstance has to change, has to face reality, and it's a painful process. That is not an exception to the pleasure principle, but a postponement of its execution. Freud also explores the way that children repeat in their play, delimiting their experience of painful events thereby achieving relief and pleasure from those experiences. This still falls under the domain of the pleasure principle. In addition, he talked about the instinct for mastery here, the turning of a pain experienced passively into one within which the subject takes an active part.

Before we proceed, I suggest that we check in here to see what struck you about the paper, particularly areas that have emotional resonance for you.

Reyna: I appreciate the way Freud is bringing in the connection between psyche and environment in this paper. This feels like a return to his earliest writings and their focus on the impact of external trauma.

Midge: That's interesting. In a way Freud's paper is partly a repetition of his earlier writing, as Reyna was pointing out, like a repetition of the trauma of hysteria but in a new form, the trauma of war.

Ezra: This leads me to think about the shift Freud made from the seduction hypothesis to focusing more on psychic reality. While I can see the value of that shift and how it did result in thinking more complexly about psychic fantasy and so many internal processes, I wonder if Freud turned away from something that he's now returning to in this paper.

Eli: That makes me wonder if Freud is returning to something that, at the time, became overwhelming to deal with, something he had to push away and maybe the return to it in this paper speaks to Freud having learned over time to return to something in the past with a new perspective.

Natalie: This discussion has me thinking about reading Freud in a way that listens for not only his consciously intended communication, but also how what he is saying could enact the very thing he is talking about.

Instructor: That's interesting. We discussed another version of that in the "Transference Love" paper.

Ernest: Yes, the felt experience of reading the paper is like a way of reliving something that might be similar to the experience Freud was having when he wrote it.

Instructor: Like an unlaid ghost in the text laying there unrestfully.

Reyna: Like the discussion we had when we talked about perversion. I was feeling frustrated when we talked about the Fetishism paper and the focus on seeing the female genital and construing it as a threat of castration. What was left out of the picture was the role of the external environment as an organizing and priming context. The patient you presented had been traumatized. That was deemphasized when thinking exclusively in terms of psychic reality. The ideas of an external trauma priming someone to experience a fear of castration rounded out the explanation for me. This paper may be trying to do something like that, to move to a more full way of thinking about external trauma in relation to internal psychic reality.

Instructor: That's a great example of how our feelings as we read Freud can help us to tune into important subtexts within the writing, that as Natalie and Ernest remind us, might not be consciously intended. These experiences can open up a path to identify something new, like what Reyna is suggesting and as we've seen in other dialogues.

Bethany: Freud's comments on page 20 are quite moving. Freud (1920) said,

> The early efflorescence of infantile sexual life is doomed to extinction because its wishes are incompatible with reality and with the inadequate stage of development which the child has reached. That efflorescence comes to an end in the most distressing circumstances and to the accompaniment of the most painful feelings. Loss of love and failure leave behind them a permanent injury to self-regard in the form of a narcissistic scar, which in my opinion, as well as Marcinowski's (1918), contributes more than anything to the 'sense of inferiority' which is so common in neurotics.
>
> (p. 20)

Midge: The oedipal child has the experience of noticing that the parent who is the primary object of their desire does not belong to them in the same way that they once believed. This process is incredibly painful and, I think, a prototype for subsequent heartbreak and rejection. This whole discussion of the excruciating pain associated with the Oedipus complex helped me to see more clearly what an important developmental phase this is and also how much pain and rage can emerge from it.

Ernest: It reminds me of a moment in my own family when my 5-year-old daughter, after being told that I was going out with her mother, my wife, and leaving her home with the sitter, suddenly attacked her mother in a state of rage, attempting to bite at her breasts.

Instructor: That vividly illustrates the power of the passions involved during this phase of development. I very much appreciate your emphasis of the importance of the Oedipus complex here. Your comments, especially on the intensity of emotions involved when the child notices that the parent who is the object of their desire doesn't belong to them as exclusively as they once believed they did.

This process can be phenomenally painful and the competitive rivalry with the parent becomes quite apparent as the compelling example Ernest gave illustrates. I think you're touching on the scorn, rejection, humiliation, murderous rage, and overall narcissistic injuries associated with the unresolved struggles associated with this stage of development.

Eli: I'm thinking about the experience of the threat of castration being an important part of this phase as well. In the example Ernest gave, the girl was attacking something her mother had that she herself didn't have yet. I wonder about how we might think of a boy, similarly, envying his rival father's penis and wishing to take it from him, only later to fear that he is under the same threat.

Instructor: That's a really good link. Eli's association of castration anxiety with these types of injuries to the self is important. As he described, we can think of castration fears as connected to the projection onto the rival object of what one has fantasized inflicting on that rival. The example that Ernest gave also shows us an act of bodily damage upon the rival object. As Eli said, we might imagine that the child, post projection, coming to fear bodily damage herself.

Natalie: This discussion of castration anxiety is interesting, given that we were just talking about the way external reality, for example, in the form of trauma, might prime us to experience castration anxiety. That notion seems to have disappeared and the focus on psychic reality seems to have become disconnected from external reality.

Instructor: In the example Ernest gave, there was mention of an external reality, namely the experience of the parents, especially the object of desire, leaving the child behind and going out with the mother. Nevertheless, I think you're onto something important here that feels absent from the discussion.

Eli: We weren't thinking at all about the external environment of the family situation. I am not trying to get into what Ernest's family situation is, but in a more general way, if we see a child react with such a strong reaction, it seems to me that it would be useful to think of the whole family context.

Natalie: That makes a lot of sense to me. We might think about a parent who is seductive with a child, and how that could intensify the child's reaction to feeling left behind. Also, that kind of seduction may be quite subtle and may not even be something that the parent is conscious of.

Instructor: These are important points and you can see how, making use of our sense of something missing from the picture can broaden our assessment of the situation. Is there anything else we haven't considered?

Midge: Another important angle that we have to be careful not to miss is the importance of the drives. The forcefulness of Ernest's daughter's reaction, especially given the heightened intensity of the sexual and aggressive drives during the Oedipus complex has to be taken into account. I guess I'm seeing the flip side here, of what can be missed when we focus excessively on the external environment.

Instructor: That's an important point and we can see how tricky our work can be. Our hypotheses can very seamlessly leave out important dimensions which is why it's such a useful exercise to regularly ask ourselves what we might be missing.

Reyna: I was thinking about the way trauma can be collectively denied, like the national erasure of what really happened, in ways that lead to the compulsion to repeat.

Midge: That reminds me of the many forms of collective denial in our culture, like praising war veterans as heroes or speaking of resilience, a way of deploying attention away from their trauma and the exploitation and violent misuse of human life. I think that increases the risk of intergenerational transmission of collectively denied trauma.

Natalie: I was thinking about the ways one can return to the scene of a trauma and experience the collective validation of what has happened, like holocaust survivors who go back to the site of their trauma and how powerfully healing that can be. There might be some kind of therapeutic action about embodiment in the context of experiencing concrete aspects of one's trauma, remnants of evidence of the truth of one's past trauma.

Ernest: The repetitions in analysis reenact traumatic memories, the coming to life of old painful scenes from early childhood in ways that can validate what happened as real, making it tangible, or embodied as Natalie put it.

Midge: I'm going back to think about Freud's remark that something that has not yet been made sense of, will, like an unlaid ghost, keep returning in the form of repeating. I wonder what Freud meant by "made sense of."

Instructor: That's a good question for all of us to think about.

Ezra: It could have to do with the instinct for mastery, the turning a passive experience into an active one.

Reyna: I felt that the boy in the Fort Da game was able to tolerate giving up his wish for his mother because the game enabled him to make sense of her coming and going, like he was able to create a picture of her departure and return that he could hold in mind in order to draw upon as a placeholder for his mother in his mind when she was absent.

Bethany: I really like that way of putting it. It does create a kind of narrative form that makes sense, like creating a story of going away and

	coming back. It reminds me of when I heard my young daughter crying for me but then suddenly stop and calm down. I went to her room and she was gazing at her little framed picture of me. I think of it as a way to remind herself that I would soon be coming.
Eli:	There is an introduction of time into the narrative, a sense of future that allows the present absence to feel more tolerable. That does sound like the reality principle to me.
Instructor:	I see what you mean. It reminded me of the way Freud did the same thing when he thought about the future of psychoanalysis at a time when everything around him seemed so bleak.

Freud is taking a closer look at the pleasure principle, that is, the tendency to lower, keep constant, or eliminate tension, and finding this principle does not account for everything. For Freud it doesn't account for the compulsion to repeat unpleasurable experiences, when there appears to be very little if any yield of pleasure. He is saying that there are certain forms of repetition that cannot be fully explained by the pleasure principle as it stands.

Freud is defining here the most elementary quality of the instincts, that is, their conservative nature ultimately to return to a former state, the ultimate former state being the state of the organism before its own existence. The death instinct is defined as a tendency to reduce all tensions aiming toward a return to an inorganic state. Note the word "tendency" here. Freud is saying that there is a pull in the direction of reducing all tensions, but this does not imply that the aim is attained.

Midge:	A patient I'm seeing was repeatedly abandoned as a young child and repeats that painful experience in her romantic relationships, where she is compelled to torment her boyfriends until they finally do leave her. That then propels her into an inconsolable state of despair and hopelessness. Each time this happens, I try to help her make links to her past experiences of abandonment and, very gradually, to make new connections, and new reminiscences of those earlier traumas come to light along with more associations and painful feelings.
Instructor:	That is an excellent example of the kinds of repetition Freud is exploring here and also you have in a very concise way articulated some very important aspects of the treatment, the kind of working over of these experiences that can occur in the midst of the repetition, but most often only with the kind of assistance you just described.

Note how you bring in the temporal dimension to an experience that feels like an eternal present for the patient. That does shrink the trend toward dissolution to one that has a more bounded narrative encircling it and limiting it. It is a process that effectively puts a frame around it and punctuates the ceaseless, eternal traumatic experience. The many links that you are able to help her make also provide a kind of psychic web for binding which then allows for a gradual piece by piece mourning and discharging of those earlier experiences.

When Freud says beyond the pleasure principle, often these are moments when he is identifying the pleasure principle with the principle of constancy or homeostasis. There is a reduction of tension back to a state of psychic equilibrium. The "beyond" in those instances can be viewed as the surpassing of this stable state into one that throws the psychic system into chaos. One could say that this "beyond" can occur in both directions. It can be the beyond of plummeting of stimulation associated with the death drive or the excessive overstimulation associated with the life drive. Most often, we will see a combination of the life and death drives operating together in such a way that maintains a psychic form of homeostasis.

When Freud (1917) talked about trauma, he said,

> We apply it to an experience which within a short period of time presents the mind with an increase of stimulus too powerful to be dealt with or worked off in the normal way, and this must result in disturbances of the manner in which the energy operates.
>
> (p. 275)

The level of massive increase of excitation and stimulation is excessive in relation to what the psyche can process.

The psyche in this situation is rendered unable to discharge its excitation in accordance with the pleasure principle. The mind has to attempt to gather all of its energy in a desperate attempt to bind or halt, essentially trying to put a stop on the inflowing of massive overstimulation before the pleasure principle can resume its normal functioning. He speaks early on in this paper of a more urgent task of attempting to bind the excessive influx of traumatic excitation that he thought of as an experience which is beyond the pleasure principle. It is viewed as fundamental and taking precedence before the pleasure principle can operate as it normally does in its regulatory capacity.

Midge gave us an illustration in her clinical vignette showing how she helped her patient delimit her overwhelming anguish by locating her repeated trauma in the past, as well as accumulating links to those past experiences to construct a web of associations, once again bringing in temporality and chains of ideas as a way of binding the free flowing excitation and hence moving toward reconstituting the normal operation of the pleasure principle.

Freud thought that this operation of struggling to bind will ignore the associated unpleasure in the service of this more fundamental, elementary function of trying to stop this flow and then ultimately strive to return to a quiescent state.

Ernest: I wonder what would lead to a repetition succeeding in binding energy, in contrast to experiences when it fails to do so.

Bethany: I'm thinking about Midge's example as a reinterpretation of the original traumatic experience in a new context of the present and past combined. Each time it happened, something new was added to it, like seeing a scene in a movie repeated, but from a very different vantage point or perspective with each repetition.

Natalie: I was thinking about a patient I worked with who was very volatile and reactive from the beginning of the therapy. I had to slow her down, often asking her to stop for a moment, so that I could put into words experiences that she was having that felt like a runaway train. I think she gradually started identifying with that stopping function that I provided her. Then we could start to think together about what she was doing in a more meaningful way.

Instructor: Here I think you are all touching upon something Freud talked about regarding the way the ego can at times make use of the compulsion to repeat by working it over associatively to provide binding of impulses that had been free flowing. Natalie's example is a fascinating one to ponder. She provided a function for her patient of stopping, something the patient was unable to do at the time. We can see here how that function can serve a regulatory function as a prelude to the interpretive work that Natalie was able to engage in subsequently.

If you think about it, you can see that something else that Freud considers beyond the pleasure principle involves the operation of both the death instinct and the life instincts, as a system. The influx of massive overstimulation may be said to represent the rise in stimulation associated with the life instincts, but the life instincts in a completely unregulated form.

The death instincts are a manifestation of the effort to put the curb on that excessive stimulation, to join with the life instincts in ways that ultimately can stop the tension in its prelude to the pleasure principle's resuming its capacity to discharge it. However, when unregulated by Eros, the death instincts can lead to an excessive plummeting of stimulation. Together, both instincts work toward providing a binding so that they may cooperate toward a state of constancy. Note the dialectic here.

Ernest: I keep thinking about how the idea that humans fundamentally want to die seems to be a quite depressing image of human beings.

Eli: It leads me to think of the kinds of fear I experience when working with suicidal patients.

Natalie: I'm aware of a desire in myself to focus on more humanistic motives, like a drive toward growth. For me, that's important to think about especially given that we are trying to help patients to grow.

Ernest: It feels difficult to think about how we might work with the death drive clinically.

Instructor: We might find it more useful to think about the operation of the death drive in relationship with the life drive, but I see how there's a tendency to think of them at times in isolated ways.

Natalie: I sometimes feel worried that patients are repeating something dangerous, and I try to show the patient that what they are doing is a way of trying to bring reflection to something that seems driven and compulsive. I often reinterpret the repetition that is frightening to the patient as a communication.

Instructor: This reminds me of what Freud said about trying to keep the transference neurosis as much as possible within the psychic realm, even trying to help the patient maintain some reflective aloofness. The way you described it, Natalie, led me to think metaphorically it's kind of like trying to understand what a ghost is trying to communicate.

Reyna: We talked about a tension we feel in our work between inviting patients to give free expression to their feelings and impulses, while also trying to make sense of them psychologically. The feelings and impulses are like ghosts and they scare us at first until we learn to listen for what they are trying to say.

Instructor: We can hear in your comments a tension between opposing elements of the analytic encounter when these opposite poles of experience, danger, and potential growth seem to go hand in hand.

Ernest: For me the death drive feels like a violent metaphor for growth. I wonder if the death drive is a slanted view, one that leaves out something more loving. I think of developmental growth as having aspects to it that are pleasurable like learning new things can be a source of joy. The suffering and pain are not the only forces that propel development and growth.

Reyna: There is something about the idea of the death drive that feels ominous, like a danger lurking out there, but it's inside us, an enemy within us that we have to struggle against.

Natalie: It's important to think about what the concept is provoking in us. I do feel a recoiling from this idea, like I don't like thinking of having a part of me that is pulled toward death.

Instructor: Ernest, I think what you were speaking of what Freud thought of as the life drives. What Natalie's underscoring here is an important difficulty we seem to be having emotionally with the idea of a drive toward death, even when we know intellectually that Freud counterbalanced this with the life drives, as well as the forces of external reality, that no one side of this tension of opposites exists without their being in relation with the other. There nevertheless seems to be something repellent about this idea.

Midge: This way of thinking is embedded in Freud's writings and I think it's something we have struggled with since we started reading Freud.

Instructor: Can you say more about your own take on this struggle?

Midge: We talked about this before. Freud will start out describing one way of thinking about things and then he will bring in a completely opposing view and he may next undermine that view with something else entirely different. He creates a tension of opposing ideas in the process of writing which stimulates his thinking and seems very fruitful for him.

Instructor: How is it for you?

Midge: I'm appreciating it much more than in the beginning, but at first it was difficult to follow and at times frustrating.

Instructor: I wonder if anyone else has ideas on your own struggles in reading Freud, particularly in terms of this issue we're discussing?

Ernest: I still get attached to one way that Freud describes something and then I feel disappointed when he shifts to something else. It's like I start to settle into and feel comfortable and then it gets undone again and again.

Natalie: For me it's not so much a feeling of disappointment, but I do feel a sense of being derailed from a line of thinking I was beginning to see more clearly.

Reyna: The disturbance I feel is associated with what can seem like contradictions or opposing views wrestling it out.

Ernest: I often feel a desire for Freud to just cut to the chase and give me the answer so I can be done with it.

Eli: I'm reminded of watching especially foreign movies when it's not clear who is good and who is bad, and how that can feel frustrating. In my work I have a feeling, a desire to just be shown what the good is so that we can strive for that, like wanting a clear goal to aim for. It seems like maybe we're trained to be drawn to narratives that are more clear and less contradictory. I can see that this is problematic because it's a reductionistic way of thinking which doesn't do justice to how life really is.

Instructor: Eli's comment reminded me of how I felt as a candidate in training, particularly when he said the tendency to listen for what the good thing to do is so that he could focus on that and have a clear direction to aim for.

There are so many different ways of thinking about psychoanalysis and we can, especially early on, when we are beginning to acquire experience, desire something that feels more clear, simplified, and fixed.

Midge: What Eli was saying about aiming for the good and trying to avoid the bad does strike me as related to our reactions to the death drive, but something does seem kind of muddled here. It's not so clear cut that the life drives represent the good and the death drive the bad.

Ezra: That reminds me of what Freud said about the drives,

> It seems, then, that an instinct is an urge inherent in organic life to restore an earlier state of things which the living entity has been obliged to abandon under the pressure of external disturbing forces; that is, it is a kind of organic elasticity, or, to put it another way, the expression of the inertial inherent in organic life.
>
> (Freud, 1920, p. 36)

Here, he locates the disturbing forces as external. We seem to be thinking of the disturbance to look out for as internal, as the doings of the death drive.

Instructor: That's a great point. He also sees the life drives as causing disturbance. What you said, Ezra, raises questions about our own relationship to the experience of disturbance in our work.

Midge: The work we do is disturbing. Our patients come to see us because they feel troubled and they bring those experiences to us. There is also a great deal of pressure and tension that we have to deal with. That quote from Freud on the drives reminds me that disturbance and tension are not at all in opposition of what we are aiming for therapeutically. Just the opposite, they can actually help us in our efforts toward change and growth.

Bethany: There is something about the struggle and disturbance that Freud takes us into, a sense of holding a state of dividedness without rushing to unify things in a neat, clear, packaged way that we are sadly having a very hard time with.

Instructor: Why sadly?

Bethany: Hearing myself describe the difficulty reminded me of the position that we try to hold as analysts. Freud might be trying to demonstrate a cultivated state of mind in his writing that is crucial also for the practice of psychoanalysis itself, something we need to work on in our own training to become analysts.

Midge: This may be something that comes in part from acquiring more experience, gradually learning not to be so afraid of experiences that feel disturbing, learning to recognize the value of those experiences that at first feel like something bad is happening.

Instructor: I agree. I would also like to add that I do think that you are engaging in a dialogue here with one another that is analogous to the internal dialogue Freud illustrates in his writing. You're bringing in many ideas and holding them in tension with one another in ways that are generating new strategies for thinking that become more layered and complex over time. The death drive has been a source of contention among psychoanalysts since its birth. For me, I find it helpful to think of the death drive as existing in a dialectical relationship with the life drives.

Midge: In my case, I was having trouble locating it within the frame of the death drive, as a tendency toward something self-destructive. I can see how it was the interpretive process that helped her to work through the repetition. I was also thinking about how the repetition involved her seeking a lost object.

Instructor: This is an important reminder that the repetition compulsion, when associated exclusively with the death drive, can be mis-construed into blinding us to the fact that there are compulsions to repeat that do involve fantasies of efforts to get something from the object, as in this case, namely that are, in part, libidi-nally driven.

I was also thinking back to Ernest's comment about Freud's view of the repetition compulsion seeming slanted, leaving out something more loving. The notion that the repetition compul-sion is only driven by the death instinct and its resulting destruc-tiveness does not do justice to many experiences of the repetition compulsion, wherein something that might seem destructive on the surface is also driven by a striving for the love of an object, a libidinal trend associated with the life drive.

Reyna: I think that it's not only the interpretive work that assists the patient to work through her repetition. It's also being able to transfer the sought object to the analyst. In some ways that's similar to what Bethany described about her daughter looking at the framed picture of her. That gave her a substitute for an object she was seeking who was not available. It wasn't literally her mother, but a representation of her mother. The analyst offers that in facilitating the patient being able to use them in that way. That must be part of what makes the repetition less painful and then more workable psychologically.

Ezra: I really like that way of describing it. It reminds me of how important it is to be thinking about multiple streams of motives when we try to think about a manifest repetition and aspects of our treatment as well. We have to be careful not to reduce the meaning or the determinants to one dimension, but it is some-thing we can trend toward.

Instructor: An excellent point. When you say, trend toward, that does make think of the death instinct. Maybe we could see our trending

	toward reductionistic thinking as a similar conservative tendency, one that leans toward an inert state that feels safe in some way. We think of experiences of disturbance as the trouble, not realizing that these conservative tendencies can inhibit processes of change and growth.
Ezra:	That reminds me of the cognitive miser theory in social psychology. It's a tendency toward simpler forms of thought that require less energy expenditure, like the use of stereotypes. That is a conservative trend.
Midge:	Now, I can see another problem. We just shifted from viewing the tendency toward inertia associated with the death drive as a problem and the disturbances as serving our aims. This feels like a reversal that again takes us out of the dialectic between the life and death drives. Both of these trends serve important functions in relationship with one another, but it is hard to hold them in relationship. We keep breaking them apart and trying to assign value to one over the other in terms of our treatment aims.
Instructor:	That's a great point and very clarifying in terms of describing the kinds of struggles we are encountering in reading this text.
Reyna:	All of this makes sense clinically. I also wonder if it's really possible to repeat a painful, traumatic experience without in some way doing something different, even if by random chance.
Instructor:	Could you say more about why you think this is important clinically?
Reyna:	I'm thinking about patients who repeat painful experiences with me and it often seems like, each time, it's a little different, and that noticing those differences out loud gradually can help the patient see that they are involved, that they are actors in the recreation of whatever is being repeated, even if they are not consciously aware of it. They then can move from feeling like they are passive victims of a terrible fate toward feeling like active agents, playing more of a role in their troubles than they were previously aware of.
Midge:	Being able to see that might begin to slowly allow the patient to feel their way into how they are in fact making choices, even if not intentional or conscious. It might be a way of gradually making contact with a part of themselves that has unconscious agency, that acts independently of their own conscious intentions.
Instructor:	Any other thoughts about why that would be helpful?
Bethany:	Becoming conscious of this could help someone to get in touch with some of the deeper motives involved and then grapple with the resistance to give up on the previously unknown pleasures involved in the repetition.
Instructor:	I thought of an example of a comment my analyst made to me when I was engaging in an intense bout of self-criticism. He said

that I was really having quite a binge. That really woke me up at the time, into realizing that there was something pleasurable about what I was doing in that moment that I had previously not been aware of. I felt embarrassed at first, but it ended up being useful for me.

Ezra: Could you give a clinical example where thinking of it that way was useful for you?

Instructor: With the 6-year-old girl that I presented, she seemed compelled to repeat a painful experience of being abandoned. The interpretive work began to provide a stimulus for a restitutive function of her ego in its gradual expression and working over of these experiences, and consistent with the example Midge gave, making meaningful links to her past and its present manifestation in a gradual movement to bind a previously intolerable experience. That binding does provide a kind of stopping or attenuating of the tension similar to what Natalie described doing with her patent.

We could think of the life drives as the accelerator pushing to increase tension and growth, while the death drive pumps the brakes tending toward quiescence (personal communication, P. Gendrault, 2021). When the system that they are part of is functioning well, we have a steady rate of growth. Imbalances between these two poles can result in the kinds of disturbances Freud observed in the compulsion to repeat. Note that Freud here has increased the complexity of what occurs within the pleasure principle.

There is a kind of balance that we strive to maintain in our interpretive efforts, namely that we try to speak to what we infer is going on unconsciously, for example, in the transference, but we are also concerned with tact, timing, what someone is able to hear in any particular moment. We are employing a similar dialectic of opposing forces, one progressive and the other conservative. We can think of the economic metapsychological principle here.

Freud (1940) said,

> The aim of the first of these basic instincts (eros or life instincts), is to establish greater unities and to preserve them thus—in short to bind together; the aim of the second (death instinct) is, on the contrary, to undo connections and so to destroy things.
>
> (p. 148)

Ultimately, Freud was able to reconstruct a fundamental instinctual dualism on the heels of having temporarily lost that with the introduction of narcissism.

Note here, from your reading of Freud's paper on narcissism in 1914 that Freud had come to understand that the narcissism of the ego is libidinal in nature, that it is constituted by the sexual drives and so he could no longer maintain the instinctual dualism between the sex drives and the ego, a dialectical tension of instincts that Freud thought was necessary for his model of the mind. The new dualism here between the life drive and the death drive reconstitutes this important dialectic in his theory.

We can consider this dialectic between the life and death drives itself as beyond the pleasure principle, at least beyond the pleasure principle as Freud had initially defined it. Here Freud has moved his thinking in the direction of a more complex systemic view of pleasure and pain. He has moved beyond the old model of the pleasure principle without discarding it. Interestingly, Ernest Jones (1957) said that Freud's reframing of these matters was "a remarkable anticipation of the modern science of cybernetics" (p. 268), especially the kind of systemic thinking that I have been suggesting.

Thinking about how these two instincts may work together also reminded me of a quote from Ogden (1977), when he said, "In the absence of the deintegrative pressure of the paranoid-schizoid pole of the dialectic generating experience, the integration associated with the depressive position would reach", citing Bion, "closure, stagnation, and arrogance" (Ogden, p. 41). The negation of closure represented by the paranoid-schizoid pole of the dialectic has the effect of destabilizing that which would otherwise become static.

As Ogden (1977) said, "In this way, the negating de-integrating effects of the paranoid-schizoid position continually generate the potential for new psychological possibilities" (p. 41). This negation of closure, attacks on linking, reminds me of the way Freud talked about the trend of the death instinct toward disorganization and the undoing of connections. In Ogden's account, this trend is a crucial part of psychic change and growth.

What do you think are the advantages and disadvantages of Freud's way of conceptualizing these phenomena?

EZRA: It is fascinating to see the expansiveness of Freud's thought in this paper, but it feels very different than his clinical papers. The clinical papers feel more grounded in experience and resonate more than when Freud attempts to apply these concepts to all life, for example. I was thinking about some of the problems of applying ideas that we talked about being associated with excessive zeal.

BETHANY: I can see what you're saying Ezra, but to me Freud is demonstrating a transparent questioning of his speculations throughout. He also says explicitly that he is engaging in wild speculation to carry out a line of thought. I wonder about that itself as providing some tempering of the wide range of speculation that he engages in within this paper. Freud's curiosity and method of questioning his assumptions seems like the best approach to take clinically with our patients.

INSTRUCTOR: Ezra's comments about the different experience when Freud's scope goes beyond the consulting room led me to wonder about the increasing focus on larger social issues in psychoanalysis. Your critique of Freud here is one that touches on certain vulnerabilities we face when we take psychoanalysis on the road, so to speak.

MIDGE: The ideas feel more true when Freud is talking about actual clinical experiences he has had, but in this paper, at times, some things feel like a stretch, as if he has left the ground of his experience. We might think of it as a thought experiment, one that can lead back to shed new light on the clinical realm, but if we put too much stock in ideas applied to these more macro, extra-clinical matters, we could find ourselves far afield from the testing ground that enables us to differentiate a useful idea from one that is misguided.

INSTRUCTOR: You are making me wonder about a difference in praxis between knowledge gleaned from our clinical work and attempts to apply that knowledge outside of that grounding context. I wonder if your experience of a difference between these two realms may help us to think about our current efforts to bring psychoanalytic knowledge to bear on larger societal issues. We might problematize that in light of what you are saying here about the epistemological risks involved in applying psychoanalysis to realms outside of the clinical context.

In the clinical papers that we have read, especially his technique papers, Freud was working to do justice to the clinical experiences he was having. The concepts were born from that particular field of struggle. That context permeates his writings. When we try to apply these ideas to situations outside of the context in which they originate, it seems to me, as Midge was getting at, that we have to take that into account in some way. Midge's comment on how we would distinguish a useful idea from one that is misguided is an interesting one to ponder.

We can easily apply psychoanalytic concepts to anything. Outside the consultation room, we do not have constraints afforded by our interactions with the patient to help us know when we are wrong. That is an important epistemological loss. It also exposes psychoanalysis to the criticism that we can apply any idea to anything without restraint.

Reyna: I was thinking about a conference that I attended looking at a psychoanalytic understanding of social events. I thought that there were interesting ideas that came up there. I found it inspiring, like finally psychoanalysis is addressing social issues that it should have been addressing long ago.

Earnest: I really want psychoanalysis to address social issues. I want to be able to do something about social injustice. I agree with Reyna. I think we should be trying to address and redress these injustices. It feels more important now than it ever has, given everything that's going on politically.

Midge: I think the issue isn't about whether to do something about social justice or not, but more about the form that action takes. I too would like it if psychoanalysis could do something useful in this regard, but I think it's worth questioning the ground we stand on when we generalize knowledge gleaned from the consulting room to broader systemic political phenomena or any other discipline for that matter.

Instructor: This is an important discussion for all of us to continue to think about. It's clear to me that we and many analysts do care deeply about issues of social justice. I think that is important. At the same time, we need to be able to think critically, as we are doing in this discussion, about our limits. As Midge was saying that does not mean that one has to give up on taking actions to address social injustice, far from it. It may mean expanding one's actions beyond what may be a limiting model for addressing these larger social, systemic issues. All of these issues remain an open question for us.

Bethany: Thank you for saying that. That gives me a lot to think about.

Ezra: Doesn't Freud apply psychoanalytic ideas to social issues? It seems like he does that in other books.

Instructor: In Freud's Beyond the Pleasure Principle, he does say that he is allowing himself to engage freely in speculation, or as Midge said, in a kind of thought experiment. What follows that imaginative exploration is a return to the clinical realm. He seems to use his imaginative wanderings across other fields of knowledge, e.g., biology, mythology, philosophy, and civilization in order to expand his thinking, to freely associate, and later returns to the clinical ground of psychoanalysis with a fresh new perspective. Freud did something similar when he took a break from writing Beyond the Pleasure Principle to explore uncanny experiences.

                On a different note, a question that I will pose for you is this: How can it be the case that development appears to move in the direction of increasingly complex growth, some might say perfection?

Midge:	Well, I think that there are external forces that are at play which may lead to changes in the direction of progressive adaptive change. I'm thinking about evolution, for example.
Eli:	But those changes are not part of some pre-existing trend, not something innate that, in and of itself, aims in the direction of change.
Instructor:	Consistent with what you're saying, Freud appears to be advocating a position with regard to life and development that is deterministic and dialectical, that is, that there are natural laws and forces involved which leave living organisms with no alternative but to advance in the direction of growth. In this way, he's saying that growth occurs within a dialectic of opposing forces.
Ernest:	This is another way in which it feels like Freud is taking us far afield from the clinical realm. I'm not sure how this connects to our work.
Natalie:	He is talking about growth, the kinds of forces that contribute to movement and change.
Instructor:	We might think of this clinically in terms of what we have been discussing about the dialectic between the unconscious compulsion to repeat the past in relation to the constraints imposed by the analytic situation, like the constancy of the analytic frame, the analyst's consistently, doggedly gathering enactments into the boundaries of verbal, reflective narration as providing a gradient of forces, a torque that forces growth and change. Here, it is the external environment facilitated by the analyst that make it possible to disturb the internal conservatism of the instincts, ultimately resulting in movement and change.
Midge:	There are aspects of development that are painful, like toilet training, when we experienced pleasures associated with being free to shit at will whenever and wherever we wanted to, to even enjoy smearing our feces, and then suddenly we have to abide by all these rules and restrictions. There is an inevitable tension that arises from these opposing pulls. It's painful, but it does seem crucial in terms of growth and development.
Reyna:	The process of toilet training is a good example of the many kinds of pleasures, during childhood development, that have to be given up or replaced, but it's also important to notice that there are other pleasures involved in this too. It's not just painful. There are moments of pleasure and release of tension too.
Instructor:	Could you name some of those other pleasures?
Reyna:	The pride and mastery children experience when they are successful. The feeling of love and validation when you see how pleased your parents are when you are successful in defecating in the toilet. The first time my 2-year-old daughter was able to

defecate in the toilet, she called us all to the bathroom to see what she was able to do on her own. She was so excited. It was like she was showing us a gold medal she won in the Olympics.

Instructor: This is a good point. There are compensations for what is given up that make the pain associated with those losses more bearable. Similarly, in analysis, the experience of struggle is inevitable and put in the service of change, but it does have to be made tolerable for both patient and analyst. As Reyna illustrated, it's not just tolerable, there are even moments of triumph and pride involved.

I also want to underline the way we appear to be struggling with the painful aspects of growth, development, and the kind of learning from experience that occurs in analysis. We find it helps us in terms of our own emotional experience as analysts to emphasize the pleasures and mastery associated with growth and change, but we can find it difficult to include the suffering and losses of pleasure within our narrative. I wonder if you have any thoughts about that.

Eli: It doesn't feel good to think of ourselves as putting the patient in a situation that will cause them pain.

Instructor: What does it feel like?

Eli: Similar to what Ernest said about aggression, it makes me feel like I am doing something cruel to the patient.

Midge: I think we're losing the dialectic again and talking in an either/or way. It's not a Pepsi versus Coke or pleasure versus pain scenario, as if the pain of the compulsion to repeat wasn't also associated or in relationship with the life drives, the transference, and the interpretive work of the analyst.

Ezra: We tend not only to think about it one dimensionally but also in one direction.

Instructor: Say more about that.

Ezra: I think that we tend to think of the process moving in the direction of increasing insight and sense of agency and mastery, as if the patient will reach some stage of finally achieving these things and all regressions will come to an end. I think I do have that fantasy about the trajectory of my own analysis.

Instructor: Do you all agree with Ezra and, if so, why might we be inclined to look at our work in this way?

Bethany: It does give us a sense of things moving in a positive direction, onward and upward, in the direction of the patient becoming more mentally free.

Reyna: This way of looking at things makes me feel like there is hope of breaking free of worrying about my patients.

Midge: I wonder if it's possible that looking at it in this way might blind us to a broader view of the process. I wonder if the constant, repeated oscillation between more concrete, painful repetitions and reflective insight might be obscured as a result.

Instructor: We might be encountering a limitation in what we are able to perceive about our work that is associated with an image of our work that we find emotionally helpful for us.

Natalie: It could be okay and useful to look at the work in this way but maybe not hold to it rigidly.

Ezra: I wonder if some form of unconscious repetition, even over the course of a successful treatment, say late in treatment or even in termination or even throughout one's life at any age might serve the interests of growth in alternation with reflection and insight. I'm thinking again now about what Freud said about analysts preferring the patient to do something other than repeat their repressed experiences. We may prefer something else, but this is how it is, and crucial in terms of the growth we are all saying we desire.

Instructor: That reminds me of times when working with a patient for quite some time, something that appeared to be adverse occurred in the patient. Earlier in my career I felt quite anxious about this, and sometimes I still do, but I have seen how often these experiences have led to a deepening of the work, to further growth and development.

Eli: The image coming up for me is one of acceleration and then being stopped over and over again.

Instructor: What's the feeling associated with that image?

Eli: It feels kind of jerky.

Midge: That reminds me of what Freud said in the paper about how the trend toward dissolution is followed by being jerked back by the self-preservative instincts and reality. At least some of what we do as analysts may be imitating nature, the kinds of forces Freud is conceptualizing in this paper. The moral of the story is that life itself is a bumpy ride, and that doesn't stop until we die, unless we're in a kind of living death.

Instructor: This discussion reminds me again of the quote that Ezra drew our attention to earlier. Freud (1920) said, "It seems, then, that an instinct is an urge inherent in organic life to restore an earlier state of things which the living entity has been obliged to abandon under the pressure of external disturbing forces..."(p. 36).

Freud is thinking about the very inception of life itself and how the first instinct was a compulsion to return to the inanimate form from which life emerged, that is, the first, primary instinct and the aim of all life would be death. This tendency exists in a dialectical relationship with other disturbing forces which Freud would later embody within the concept of the life drives and external reality.

The picture that coalesces here is that life itself, as Midge summed up so well, development and growth are the result of an ongoing mutual, dialectical disturbance of conflicting, disturbing forces. To put it as Jung (1981) did, "It is the old game of the hammer and anvil: between them the patient iron is forged into an indestructible whole, an 'individual'" (p. 288). We can keep in mind here, that this development of the self, at least while one is alive, remains in operation or movement without resolution.

Ernest: I still feel that we seem to be overemphasizing the painful struggle in a way that feels one-sided at times. I realize that the struggle and suffering that come out of these dialectical tensions are crucial to growth and development. But I've been thinking about what Reyna said about the role of the patient's transference to the analyst that may make the struggle and pain tolerable.

Instructor: Does anyone else have any thoughts about this important idea?

Bethany: This is interesting. Notions like the positive transference, the treatment alliance, and transference love are all concepts that bring in a striving to win the analyst's love and alliance, so in the midst of the hardship, the struggle, and suffering, there is also love and affirmation or at least the hope of attaining it that make it bearable. These are substitutions that make the losses bearable. I do think that analysts hold a position of hope that what feels so bad now is on a path toward understanding something more fully in ways that will ultimately provide relief.

Ezra: I want to reflect back on an earlier quote from a letter Freud wrote during the time of World War I and the Spanish flu, "... knowledge of the truth can compensate us for much we are deprived of and also for much suffering" (Jones, 1957, p. 7).

Instructor: This compensatory quest for truth may begin with a transferential quest for the love of the analyst and develop into a love of this search for truth.

Reyna: This leads me to wonder if we might think of the compulsion to repeat, particularly given the push toward a perceptual identity with a traumatic experience, may on some level be seen as a tendency toward truth.

Instructor: Can you say more about this?

Reyna: The repetition of a trauma gives concrete representation, something to point to in external reality, like a monument to something that actually happened. It may ultimately, depending on being able with outside help to perceive it, affirm a truth of one's experience that would otherwise remain obscurely haunting.

Instructor: That's a fascinating example of the compensatory, validating, and delimiting functions involved in such a repetition. We might think of the relief experienced when this obscurely haunting and perhaps crazy making experience of feeling something without a referent finds an external form to attach itself to in the repetition. Freud's paper "Criminals From a Sense of Guilt" (1916) comes to mind here.

Midge: I wonder if we are thinking enough about how neurosis can disguise itself in ways that go unquestioned. I was thinking about neuroses being disguised in ways that take on the garb of things that are so popular, so in vogue that we wouldn't think to question it. We might even be criticized for questioning it.

Instructor: An excellent point and reminiscent of what Freud (1905) said in his paper on Dora. Something you drew our attention to earlier about how the patient uses thoughts that are seemingly incontestable, ideas that are least likely to come under scrutiny in order to hide other ideas that are meant to remain hidden from consciousness.

We explored feelings of subjective disturbance in contemplating this text. The notion of a fundamental, instinctual wish for dissolution was mentioned. When Freud speaks of the aim of all life being death because inanimate things existed before living ones, given our tendency to return to previous states of being, one might think of a profound human wish to self-destruct or to externalize that wish and destroy others.

Ezra: I want to re-emphasize that we are speaking to parts of the mind here. It doesn't make sense to isolate them and yet I think we have an overpowering pull to do so.

Instructor: It does feel necessary to make an effort to remind ourselves of that. Freud is saying that there is a tendency within the psyche toward reducing tension to the lowest possible level, toward annihilating the intrinsic tension of life, but that tendency does not exist in a vacuum. It is always in a dialectical tension with the life drives, that is, the sex drives and self-preservative instincts, as well as external reality, which continuously jerks us back into the tensions of life, and there is no final resolution to it, at least while we are alive.

Ernest: I keep feeling like it would be great to just have a still shot image of what psychoanalysis is so I could memorize it and just know it and be able to apply it, to just put a stop of what feels like a fast-moving river of concepts that I cannot keep up with.

Instructor: I think that Ernest's image is one we can all resonate with. I love the way you put it, Ernest, the wish to put a stop to what feels like a fast moving river of concepts that cannot be kept up with.

Over time, with the grounding provided by accumulated experience, I think we do learn to not concern ourselves so much with trying to keep up with it, but rather to appreciate the continuous movement, even to acquire the skills to transiently capture fascinating and unexpected moments of interactive motion within our work. Of course those will unravel too, but that keeps the road open for further, novel developments. Over time it is possible to give up trying to get that ceaseless flow to adapt to us and instead adapt to it, i.e., to move with it.

Midge: The image Freud is giving us of human nature is one that often goes against how we would prefer to see ourselves.

Eli: There may be cultural aspects to this. I'm thinking about how Americans in particular seem to need to think of themselves as exceptional, as standing for what's good, fighting for what's good, often as rescuers.

Bethany: This image serves to obscure and excuse so much disavowed aggression that we have committed and continue to perpetuate as a nation.

Ezra: This reminds me that Freud himself struggled for a long time before he could attend to the phenomenon of human aggression in his theory. Maybe that's part of what we are struggling with in the text, that humans aren't only good and aren't only striving for good, that we also have tremendous capacity for evil doings, but it's very painful to face that and so terribly dangerous not to.

Instructor: It's also important to note what many contemporary Freudians have done with the death drive. Given that the death drive was viewed as manifesting in the form of aggression, they decided to dismiss the death drive and focus instead on the aggressive drive.

Bethany: Thinking about the way Freud ignored aggression for a long time leads me to think about other issues that psychoanalysis have ignored. I'm thinking of larger social issues, issues of race, gender, oppression within the broader social context which have often been ignored in written clinical case reports and in psychoanalysis as a whole.

Instructor: There is an author who speaks to these matters in a recent book. The book is called, *A People's History of Psychoanalysis* (2019) written by Daniel Jose Gaztambide, professor at the New School for Social Research in New York.

In the book, Gaztambide looks at Freud's papers on social phenomena, including *Civilization and Its Discontents*. He poses many fascinating questions for us to ponder, related to the ubiquity of social oppression. Gaztambide makes use of psychoanalytic ideas to try to understand the nature of the forces involved in sustaining oppression, including racism.

Gaztambide is raising some interesting ideas, much of which I found fascinating to think about. Given our previous discussion, however, we do have to be careful and consider the difference in praxis between knowledge gleaned from our clinical work and attempts to apply that knowledge outside of that grounding context. The application of psychoanalytic concepts, derived from the clinical realm to larger societal issues does require careful scrutiny. The risk of forcing meaning that we see on the individual level can likewise be a big problem on the macro level of social issues as well. Midge's question earlier about how we are to distinguish a useful idea from a misguided one, without the constraints of the clinical situation, is an important one to grapple with. There is the ever present risk in such applications of psychoanalytic knowledge of serving a role of hiding the true forces and social powers behind these social injustices.

A Note on What Happened

Students talked about their experience of Freud's paper as a repetition, in a new form, of his earlier studies of trauma. This led to a discussion of how Freud's writing itself contains hidden subtexts wherein he may be unwittingly enacting something analogous to what he is writing about. A number of comments were made expressing a difficulty with Freud's concept of a drive toward death, finding that there was something that felt repellent about it.

The exploration of the tension between the life and death drives led to a recognition of similar tensions in Freud's writing and thinking. The discussion of opposing elements of the analytic encounter led to a consideration of how these opposite poles seem to go hand and hand.

The feeling of something repellent about the death drive was repeated in our discussion, which provoked curiosity and deeper thought about the group experience.

There was a detailed description of the experience of Freud's dialectical way of holding opposing trends in relationship with one another. Students were able to express their experience of difficulties doing that themselves. This moved into a recognition of variability with regard to being able to hold these tensions, noticing that there are times when we seem to be able to do that and other times when it feels distressing. The discussion moved further into the sense of difficulty in struggling with Freud's way of thinking as manifest in his writing, in particular his use of tension in juxtaposing opposing ideas. There was a description of the experience of beginning to settle into one way of looking at things and then experiencing it becoming undone, again and again. Some spoke of feeling derailed from a line of thought that had felt comfortable. Others observed themselves, at times, thinking in a reductionistic way. There was an expression of desire for clear, simple, fixed, and settled answers. These comments morphed into a more clear description of Freud making use of a particular kind of struggle in his writing and in his clinical work, one that we at times appeared to be making use of ourselves in our own dialogue.

I noted a tension in our discourse between a longing for a neat, clear, packaged way of understanding Freud in tension with a more creative process of discovery. An important link was made between this tension and the position we try to hold as analysts within our clinical work. A comment was made that our dialogue here seemed at times similar to the internal dialogue Freud illustrates in his writing. This was described as bringing in ideas, holding them in tension with one another in ways that generate new ways of thinking that become layered and complex over time. There was a clear recognition of a parallel between this process, our own process of learning psychoanalysis through our engagement with Freud's text, and the process of psychoanalysis itself.

Students speculated about there being something productive about holding tensions associated with opposing ideas in mind. These ideas were linked to similar experiences within the clinical realm of psychoanalysis. There was an expressed desire for psychoanalysis to address broader social issues and a critique of Freud's apparent application of concepts born within the consulting room to broader phenomena, with what I thought were implications for contemporary trends in applications of psychoanalysis.)

References

Freud, S. (1905). Fragment of an Analysis of a Case of Hysteria. SE 7: 3–122.

Freud, S. (1914). Remembering, Repeating and Working-through. SE 12: 145–156.

Freud, S. (1916). Some Character-Types Met with in Psycho-Analytic Work. SE 14: 309–333.

Freud, S. (1917). General Theory of the Neuroses. SE: 16: 243–463.

Freud, S. (1920). Beyond the Pleasure Principle. SE 18: 3–64.

Freud, S. (1940). An Outline of Psycho-Analysis. SE: 138–207.

Gaztambide, D.J. (2019). *A People's History of Psychoanalysis: From Freud to Liberation Psychology*. Lexington Books.

Gendrault, P. (2021). Personal Communication.

Jones, E. (1957). *The Life and Work of Sigmund Freud: The Last Phase, 1919–1939* (Vol. 3). Basic Books, p. 268.

Jung, C.G. (1981). *The Archetypes and the Collective Unconscious*. Routledge.

Ogden, T.H. (1977). *Subjects of Analysis*. Jason Aronson, 1994.

7   The Ego and the Id

A Note on My Intentions

I intended to try to facilitate an open exploration of our own resistances in our clinical work as a corollary to fleshing out Freud's writings on unconscious defenses and unconscious resistances. I hoped that students would be able to share their own experiences of resistance, either within their own analysis or in their reactions to their own patients. I wanted us to explore the way in which we as analysts are struggling with unconscious phenomena within ourselves in ways that are quite similar to what our patients contend with in the analytic relationship.

Instructor: I thought we might check in and see where you are at in your reflections on this paper so far.

Ernest: I'm thinking of something that came up for me in reading this text, but it feels broader than that too. I've been thinking about the inherent power differential within the analytic relationship, and, in particular, the dangers involved in losing track of this and even abusing that power for our own narcissistic gratification.

Ezra: I think that the sense of power attributed to us in the role of the analyst can feel gratifying, but, to Ernest's point, there is also something frightening about it.

Natalie: It can be disappointing and frustrating in that we are destined ultimately not to live up to the fantasies attributed to us in the transference.

Bethany: I feel kind of fraudulent when the patient sees me as powerful and wise. I feel like it's just a matter of time before they see me as just a regular person, nothing special.

Instructor: That reminds me of the idea of being a tantalizing and disappointing object. One tension I'm hearing in this discussion so far is the expression of opposing feelings of both an overwhelming sense of power and also a feeling of insignificance.

I am reminded of comments Freud has made regarding the transference. It seems to me that ideally we are making use of

DOI: 10.4324/9781003610977-9

this power, invested in us by way of the transference, in order to help the patient to become conscious of many things that are holding them hostage, keeping them from living their lives more fully and freely due to their repressed unconscious conflicts and phantasies.

Ernest: This reminds me of our conversation last week about the positive transference. In this case, the striving to win the love of the analyst would provide motivation to engage in the psychical work of analysis, to try to reflect on painful experiences, and join the analyst in the struggle to put these experiences into thought and words.

Midge: It is very difficult in analysis, when you are in the grip of intensely passionate feelings to rip yourself from that stronghold of those feelings and look at it from a more reflective place. One's feelings of love for the analyst do provide something of a substitute object of passion, maybe making it more tolerable to do that reflective work.

Ezra: This piece of the work does bring in an additional competing force.

Instructor: What kind of force are you thinking of?

Ezra: It's like there are two competing passions, whatever it is the patient is in the grip of internally, something that preceded the analysis, and then there's the analyst offering herself as an external point of contact, a place for those passions to attach to, and if they do attach to the analyst, they can be put in the service of looking at oneself in interaction.

Bethany: I'm thinking of a regressive pull inward, something pulls the patient inside themselves and takes them away from the present reality. The transference to the analyst directs the patient's emotional struggle back into the present moment and back to reality.

Instructor: That's a good link.

Reyna: In the last two case presentations, Louis does act like a kind of transitional object that allows the patient some room to think about themselves in ways that they would not otherwise be capable of.

Midge: A transitional object is still not the original object or even necessarily the original aim. It's a substitute for the object and aim of one's passions and so there would likely be an experience of something unsatisfying in that.

Instructor: Does anyone have any reactions to this?

Bethany: It sounds to me like an example of the reality principle in that the erotic longings are not able to reach satisfaction in an immediate and identical way, and so there's postponement of that pleasure in order to achieve something that would ultimately be more beneficial for the patient in the long run, like the freedom from the compulsion to repeat some unconscious scene, but I think there would be some unpleasure initially on some level, maybe in the form of frustration.

Ezra: It's frustrating on one level and then there is the substitutive solution that allows for some compensation and potential sublimation into the analytic work.

Reyna: When the patient is experiencing the erotic transference to the analyst and the analyst guides the patient to reflect on the meaning of what is happening, like recognizing and reflecting on a past pattern that is repeating, there is likely a transforming of a libidinal cathexis to the object into a narcissistic one wherein the ego can use that energy for such creative purposes.

Instructor: I think what Freud is highlighting here is important to ponder in light of our discussion. Our patients, including ourselves, can go through life driven by unconscious conflicts and their related fantasies. We relive these within the transference enactments and repetition compulsions in the analysis.

Our task as analysts is to use these passionate, illusory powers attributed to us through the transference in order to help our patients to see and hear what their unconscious is communicating, ultimately to expand their field of vision and mental freedom to move forward in their lives. They/we do that painful work, as you've described, for the love of the analyst, driven by the transference.

Paradoxically, in a way this can feel impersonal for the analyst, as some of you have spoken of earlier, as if we are an insignificant vehicle for this task and that any importance attributed to us is only fantasy. We can come to feel quite literally that we are nothing but a tool and there is a great deal of truth in that. However, as we have also explored, the patient's reliving through the transference will also evoke our own transference, and so the work of speaking the unspeakable will involve something very personal within our own inner world. We are neither as significant nor as insignificant as we may think we are.

Midge: That idea of being like a tool, of allowing ourselves to be made use of, within the transference, does involve a kind of non-self-ness. We sort of empty ourselves in order to go along with the current of the patient's transference needs. So in that odd way, we are kind of like a sort of cipher, lying in wait to be given shape to. On the other hand, that's only part of the story, because we do emerge from that place to speak to what we have become for the patient, the quality of the interaction, and how it repeats experiences from the patient's past.

Ezra: I love the way you put that Midge. You captured something impor-
            tant about the dual nature of our role. On the one hand, we let
            ourselves be drawn into a field of forces that have a life of their
            own and so there's a letting go of our own ego, a kind of emptying
            ourselves out to be able to do that. But then we come back, and
            regain our critical judgement about what is playing out.

Eli: I think the path to coming back or resurfacing after being taken
            over by the patient's transference is where things get very per-
            sonal for the analyst. I see that as requiring of us that we have to
            navigate through our own transference to get there.

Midge: What would that look like for you?

Eli: I was thinking about a patient who can become quite hopeless
            and attacking of my efforts to help him. There are moments when
            I do lose hope of being able to have any positive impact on him
            and I get overtaken by those feelings. Coming out of that dark
            cloud always requires of me that I connect the feelings I'm hav-
            ing to earlier experiences in my own life and the things that led
            me to feel that way early on.

Ernest: That's all well and good, poetic the way you both describe it, but
            don't you ever worry that you'll lose yourself in the first part of
            that duality?

Bethany: I can relate to that. Sometimes I'm afraid that I will be com-
            pletely swallowed up by the intensity of feelings that get stirred
            up in me, like I won't be able to come back up to the surface and
            speak in a coherent and clear way about what's going on.

Reyna: When I experience that fear of losing myself, of getting flooded
            and taken over by feelings, I pull back in ways that feel safe
            but there's also a loss there. I'm not engaged with the patient
            anymore.

Instructor: We are dealing with very powerful forces in our work. As we
            have been talking about, the patient's transference will stir up
            our own transference reactions and this will often affect our
            thinking in ways that can feel frightening at times. Eli's example
            is one that I think we are all familiar with. Note the private work
            that Eli described himself engaged in. He returns to his past in
            the context of his transference to his patient which enables him
            to regain clarity on what is happening with his patient. The expe-
            rience of immersion or being swallowed up by our own trans-
            ference reactions is likely to intensify when we lose the past/
            present relationship.

            What you said, Reyna, in light of our earlier discussion about
            the risks of abusing power, I want to highlight an abuse of power
            within our role as analysts that I think is underestimated. That
            is, when analyses become excessively comfortable, when much
            of what is interpreted is of the patient's life outside the analysis,

namely when the heat of the transference relationship is avoided or diluted. There is a loss of dialectical tension here. It may feel safe, which is important, and may even be accompanied by some improvement in the patient's life, but it does sacrifice the depth of internal change that is possible within the emotional intensity of the transference within an analysis.

In James Strachey's paper, "The Nature of the Therapeutic Action of Psychoanalysis" (1934), he spoke about the analyst's sense of danger in making these types of interpretations, "Such a moment must above all others put to the test his relations with his own unconscious impulses" (p. 159). It's important that we cultivate our capacity to listen to how we speak to our patients, to be able to detect the often subtle ways that we use language that can be distancing from the heat of the moment.

Can you could think of any examples of these types of struggles in your own work? .

Natalie: I often struggle to speak to what is happening between myself and a particular patient in moments of conflict. I can see it more and more clearly with the help of supervision, but I keep failing to bring it up. I'm left feeling like I'm chickening out every time, even though I go into the hour with the intention of speaking to it.

Ernest: I've had similar feelings in my work, especially with one case.

Instructor: How do you think about the nature of this difficulty that we are hearing about here?

Midge: It sounds similar to the way Freud is talking about resistance in this paper, but in this case we're talking about resistance in the analyst.

Instructor: Could you describe the similarity that struck you?

Midge: Freud is emphasizing unconscious ego functioning, for example, unconscious defenses and unconscious resistances. The discussion so far seems to be about unconscious resistances in the analyst.

Instructor: So, you're saying that Natalie has more going on that is stopping her from speaking than she is consciously aware of.

Ezra: Also, I'm hearing something that sounds like the influence of the superego. The comments about failing and chickening out stood out as harsh and self-condemning.

Instructor: We might say that the operation of the superego is also occurring on an unconscious level. Do you have any thoughts about the function this self-condemnation might serve?

Midge: That could be another form of resistance in that attacking oneself as a chicken or a failure would likely diminish one's curiosity and openness to exploring our motives for keeping quiet. While painful on the surface, this may actually relieve pain in the sense that it can help to keep our minds off of our own transference.

Instructor: You are all speaking to a ubiquitous struggle in our work, namely to grapple with our own conscious and especially unconscious resistances to speaking. It's particularly difficult when we are in training and feel the scrutiny of our work being evaluated, but crucial to strive to maintain an open curiosity about our own internal obstacles to speaking in our work.

Reyna: It feels to me that the process of evaluation itself, like the progressions committee focusing on whether we are moving forward in our training, looking for evidence of our success or lack of success, and focusing our attention on that, can not only lead to self-condemnation, but it also deflects our attention from learning for its own sake.

Instructor: How do you picture learning for its own sake? What does that look like for you?

Reyna: For me, it's a process of intensely involving myself in a curious way about what's unfolding. It's more of a learning from experience which is intrinsically motivating. The focus on indicators of success creates a risk of deflecting and derailing that process.

Instructor: You're making an important and quite reasonable point here. The focus on achievement, successful outcomes, even indices of progress can interfere with the process of learning in the way Reyna described. I think we also have to question whether bringing in such a reasonable and sound external reality of the progression committee might serve as a resistance to thinking about more personal motivations underlying our inhibitions to speak, in the sense that Freud described of how that which we wish to keep hidden will often be couched in something reasonable and even seemingly unquestionable.

Natalie: When we condemn ourselves harshly, we are often shutting down that exploration, which is also something to be curious about.

Midge: I think that the guiding light in all this might be to stay curious and passionately interested in everything that happens and try to hear the siren call of self-condemnation as the resistance that it most often is.

Instructor: That sounds like an excellent beacon in our night sea journey, one very much in the spirit of Freud's attitude toward the work of analysis.

Ernest: Sometimes I feel frustration alongside, a wish for a simple, clear outline of exactly what Freud means about everything he says. The ambiguity though does open up space to think together about what we think Freud is getting at, how it relates to our own struggles, and that can sometimes feel more interesting.

Eli: There is a lot of ambiguity in Freud's writings and I wonder why that is?

Ezra:	It makes me wonder if much of the ambiguity reflects the nature of what Freud is trying to talk about, namely unconscious phenomena. I wonder if part of the frustration may have something to do with our feelings about the unconscious itself.
Instructor:	Could you say more about that?
Ezra:	The experience of encountering and trying to make sense of unconscious experience is a nebulous one. It throws us into doubt, confusion, feeling like we're grappling in the dark and we have no idea what's going on or where it's going. It shakes us out of a more clear, confident position within ourselves.
Instructor:	I wonder if this discussion may be touching upon the ways that we may at times wish to compensate for the feelings you described in the manner that we try use of our theoretical knowledge.
Ernest:	The idea of having a theory that explains everything, that gives us the answers and defines everything for us is very comforting. It does feel scary and uncomfortable when I don't know what's going on and I feel that the patient is looking to me for answers, expecting me to know what's happening.
Natalie:	The way you just described that reminded me of a child's experience of a parent who has all the answers. But having the answers, knowing what's going on is treated as if it's there in mind to be applied. I don't think that's how it works in analysis. I think the interpretations that help are formed right there in the moment, mostly by the tensions that we're struggling with.
Midge:	I really like that way of putting it. It has to be created in the actual struggle of the moment and that's going to be very particular to that patient's experience.
Natalie:	And the way it interacts with the analyst's experience.
Instructor:	And as you're saying, we can't know what we will say in any pre-scripted way. Whatever knowledge we have is going to have to be reconfigured to give form to the unique singularity of that experience in that particular moment with that particular patient. So we have to forge what we say from scratch within the emotional force field we find ourselves in.
Reyna:	It reminded me of how frustrated and angry a lot of people felt toward the World Health Organization and CDC in the information they were giving about the pandemic. I wonder if there were similar fears and frustrations involved.
Instructor:	The pandemic, at the time, was quite confusing and there was so much that was not yet known. It was very scary and people angrily wanted answers from those in authority, also showing a lot of mistrust in those authorities. Perhaps we wanted more from science than it could give us, as Freud has spoken of.
Midge:	People also wanted contradictory things, which is also something you see when we are in the grip of our transference.

Instructor: Let's keep these important ideas in mind as we continue to explore what Freud had to say in *The Ego and the Id*.

Prior to the writing of the *The Ego and the Id* (1923), Freud spoke of the central conflict involved in neurosis as one between repressed unconscious impulses pressing toward consciousness and a repressing force aiming to keep those impulses from becoming conscious. He pictured this internal battle as occurring between the repressed unconscious and the preconscious/conscious ego.

Clinically, Freud learned from his experience, much as you have in terms of discussing your own resistances, that a great deal of the ego itself can be described as unconscious. As Strachey put it in the Editor's Introduction, "the criterion of consciousness was no longer helpful in building up a structural picture of the mind" (Freud, 1923, p. 7). This puts Freud in a position of having to reframe his map of these agencies of the mind to more accurately represent the nature of neurotic conflict. He is trying to find a way to help us envision the psychic processes involved in the types of conflict that give rise to neurotic pathology.

Keep in mind here that a neurosis is constituted by an intrapsychic conflict whose resolution involved repression, but that repression has not been completely successful. Hence, we have the return of the repressed in the form of ongoing struggle between the repressed and the repressing forces, that is, the defenses. This struggle was vividly illustrated in the 6-year-old patient that I presented.

Eli: It was helpful to think about what Freud was trying to accomplish in creating this tripartite structure. He was trying to provide a representation that gives structure and form to the idea of a conflict between competing forces in the mind, some way for us to represent that.

Instructor: Does anyone have any ideas about how this might be helpful?

Ezra: Having a clear image of what kind of conflict we are listening for can help us be more primed to listen and look for it.

Ernest: The image of opposing forces in the mind reminds me of listening to a patient and having the feeling and image of the patient in a fight within himself, a fight that he is often unconscious of. The idea of intrapsychic conflict is useful especially in situations when I feel pulled to oppose the patient. It orients me to remind myself where the fight is stemming from.

Midge: That idea of being unconscious of one's own inner conflict, of being in a fight with oneself, one that is unknown to oneself is interesting to think about. I can see how that could incline someone to feel pulled to get into an external fight. It can be hard to resist. Being in a fight with oneself can make you feel crazy, and so you might exert a lot of pressure on someone else to take a side. I imagine that would be a relief from having to face one's own inner division.

Natalie: That made me think about times when I have gotten into unnecessary arguments when I felt bad about something that I'm trying not to think of. I've pushed away the content of what it was I didn't want to think about but the feelings were still there.

Midge: That's a good example of what I was thinking. Something you feel bad about might be driven out of your consciousness but the feelings might still be there and so you may have feelings associated with being in a conflict, in a fight with yourself without a context for it.

Ezra: As Midge was saying, the situation you're both describing can feel crazy making, to have intense feelings and then have no clarifying context for why you're feeling that can be super disorienting. Getting into a fight then would provide some relief from that. It does give you a place to locate an experience that otherwise would feel very confusing.

Instructor: And, as Midge also said, an analyst may experience a lot of pressure to jump in the ring of that fight. These are very important reflections and quite relevant for our work. There are times when we may feel strongly pulled to fight with patients. The perspectives that you are sharing on these dynamics and their link to unconscious conflict are quite valuable to keep in mind. When we think about neurosis as involving conflict, we can expect that conflict will inevitably be part of the transference.

Freud (1923) describes the clinical experiences that gave rise to his creation of the structural theory of the mind:

> We have come upon something in the ego itself which is also unconscious, which behaves exactly like the repressed—that is, which produces powerful effects without itself being conscious and which requires special work before it can be made conscious.
>
> (p. 17)

Ernest: My mind is going back to what we were talking about earlier in terms of the analyst's resistance. I wonder whether the example given of chickening out, of failing to make an interpretation that one feels they should make, is really an unconscious resistance. Natalie was aware of having a resistance. Doesn't that make it conscious?

Natalie: I can say that I was aware that there was something that stopped me from speaking. I know what I want to say, but still I don't know what stops me. I have ideas about what might be stopping me, but so far those ideas don't seem to be reaching me in a place where I can overcome the resistance or even fully feel myself into it. The ideas about what might be stopping me are like guesses or inferences. I don't know for sure what they are and I don't have a sense of conviction about my guesses. Whatever it is that I am trying to uncover is still very much in the dark. I just can't see it yet, certainly not with any real emotional conviction.

Midge: It sounds like Natalie, in this situation, has a conscious, intellectual knowledge that resistance was taking place, but she doesn't yet know it in the way of actually being emotionally aware of what's so terrifying that it shuts her up and in that sense it is unconscious.

Instructor: So, consistent with what Freud wrote in this paper, you're saying that for the resistance to become conscious, the analyst or patient has to be in a place of becoming more acquainted with their experience of terror and continue to struggle to speak in the midst of this terror.

Bethany: Part of what I think gets in our way is that on some level we may not believe that we have an unconscious. If you have a conscious inference about what's going on, it's easy to convince oneself that you are conscious of it.

Instructor: Our shared laughter once again seems to imply that there is some resonant truth in your comment.

Ernest: This doesn't make sense to me because we of course know that we have an unconscious, given what we know about psychoanalysis and our theories of the unconscious.

Instructor: I think you are both speaking to different levels of knowing.

Bethany: We may think we believe that we are affected by unconscious forces but maybe secretly, on a deeper level not really believe it in the same way that we may now that we will die, but on a hidden level not really believe it.

Instructor: We may "know" it, but with fingers crossed behind our backs, maybe hoping that we might be an exception to the rule.

Ezra: I'm thinking about the way the analyst's self-directed anger, when they fail to say what they feel they must say, implies the idea that they shouldn't be stopped by unconscious forces, as if they should be exempt, should have been able to say it, as if unconscious resistance shouldn't affect them in the way it affects our patients.

Instructor: That's a great point.

In this paper, note what Freud is saying about aspects of the ego and superego that he had thought of as latent but readily accessible to conscious awareness if pointed out. He's saying that these resistances are actually unconscious in the same way that repressed material is unconscious and therefore not easily reached, as Natalie's experience illustrates.

Relatedly, the defense mechanisms themselves are often inaccessible to consciousness. Clinically, this is very important for our work and linked to Freud's experience that the resistance is occurring unconsciously, that the patient is often quite unaware that they are trying to avoid saying something or to avoid thinking about something, for example engaged in repressing a sexual wish. Pointing out the resistance does not readily lead to the patient becoming conscious of their defenses or the impulses behind them in the same way that Natalie's guesses do not bring her unconscious motives to consciousness.

Midge: I'm thinking again about resistance in the analyst. Given what Freud is saying here, it makes absolutely no sense at all that we condemn ourselves for "failing" to say something that needed to be said to the patient, given that it is likely due to unconscious resistance. It makes much more sense to try to be curious about it, to learn more about what's going on within ourselves, to listen for our own unconscious. The condemnation in that scenario really does seem like a rejection of one's unconscious experience.

Instructor: That is very well said and a valuable reminder for us. It also touches on our earlier discussion about questioning whether we really believe that we are susceptible to unconscious influences, even though we may intellectually, consciously subscribe to the notion. We can know something and yet, on a deeper level, not believe it.

The two major ideas in this paper are the structural division of the mind between the id, ego, and superego and the introduction of the superego itself.

Freud will speak of the ego along two dimensions, the perceptual and the libidinal drives. For example, Freud (1923) says,

> Moreover, the ego seeks to bring the influence of the external world to bear upon the id and its tendencies, and endeavors to substitute the reality principle for the pleasure principle which reigns unrestrictedly in the id. For the ego, perception plays the part which in the id falls to instinct.
> (p. 25)

Here Freud is bringing in the version of the ego that forms out of our perceptions and relations with the external world; in the next paragraph, he says,

> Thus in its relation to the id, it (the ego) is like a man on horseback, who has to hold in check the superior strength of the horse; with this difference, that the rider tries to do so with his own strength while the ego uses borrowed

> forces. This analogy may be carried a little further. Often the rider, if he is not to be parted from his horse, is obliged to guide it where it wants to go; so in the same way the ego is in the habit of transforming the id's will into action as if it were its own.
>
> (Freud, 1923, p. 25)

Ezra: What does Freud mean when he says on page 40, "...perceptions may be said to have the same significance for the ego as the instincts have for the id."?

Instructor: Could you first say more about what drew you to this quote?

Ezra: It seemed to be an odd statement or a strange analogy. I don't think of perception as comparable to the instincts in that the instincts have energy and force, a power that has to be reckoned with, but it's hard to imagine perception having any comparable force or power.

Instructor: Ezra's point makes a great deal of sense. One might say that there seems to be a contradiction here. Can anyone think of a way in which Freud's statement about perception and instinct could be true?

Bethany: I wonder if perception maybe has a kind of power for the ego that is on a different level than the power of the instincts.

Instructor: Can you say more about this different level?

Bethany: What comes to my mind is the story of David and Goliath and how Goliath represented the instincts, a kind of brute physical power, whereas David represented the power of a higher level, a power associated with intelligence and ingenuity.

Midge: That's very interesting. The power of perception reminds me of Freud's comments on signal anxiety. The early perception of a small dose of anxiety was depicted as a kind of power, not brute instinctual power, but the power of an early warning system that could afford the opportunity to prepare for impending trouble.

Instructor: These are fascinating ideas and they emerged from an initial observation of something that seemed like an odd analogy as Ezra put it.

Eli: I've been noticing this kind of thing happening in reading Freud. I will encounter ideas that initially caused me confusion and I try to grapple with it, start to question Freud in my mind, read more, study, feel confused again, write about it, something starts to feel a little more clear, then gets blocked again, I step away from it, then come back, read it again, some other thoughts emerge, and then it starts to turn into a conversation like the one we just had and some unexpected clarity presents itself in a new idea that comes to mind.

Instructor:	I think what you're saying here is very important. You're learning about your own process of working to learn about Freud's ideas in dialogue. I would add too that Bethany allowing herself to engage in her association to the story of David and Goliath was a kind of speculation, analogous to Freud's self-referred wild speculation, that served as a bridge for Midge to make an important theoretical hypothesis about what Freud might have meant. The process of reading Freud that Eli just described, particularly the oscillation between experiences of confusion, self-questioning, moments of clarity and insight, becoming blocked again, stepping back to reflect again with greater scrutiny on what we thought we knew, as well as moments of insight that seem to come from nowhere is also very much akin to the experience of practicing clinical psychoanalysis.
	The piece about the ego making use of borrowed forces from the id has precursors in Freud's earlier writings. He spoke about how the energies associated with infantile sexuality provide motive power for other aims.
Reyna:	This whole idea of borrowed forces and what we talked about earlier with the analyst channeling the patient's passions in the direction of reflection made me think of the role of creativity and art in psychoanalysis.
Instructor:	How do you see that?
Reyna:	The patient is struggling with passionate internal conflicts and we can't really get rid of that suffering, but we can use it to create something else, in this case, a creative reflective process that puts those experiences into a narrative and practice that makes it meaningful and even fascinating.
Eli:	I think of analysis as creating a sketch of one's own mind and the way it works.
Ezra:	We might choose to become analysts as a way of doing something creative with our own suffering, putting it into a form that makes sense of dynamics that have caused us much personal confusion and suffering.
Instructor:	I think that is quite true. And I imagine that each of you will create your own version of that portrait over time, as well as remaking it as you acquire more experience. Freud (1923) returns to the perceptual view of ego formation, saying,

> A person's own body, above all its surface, is a place from which both external and internal perceptions may spring. It is seen like any other object, but to touch it yields two kinds of sensations, one of which may be equivalent to internal perception.

(p. 25)

Natalie: The handling of the infant must play a role in the ultimate, grad-
             ual creation of an inner body image of self.
Instructor: Could you say more about what you have in mind?
Natalie: I imagine that the bodily care-taking of the infant, alongside of
             the parents gazing and speaking to the infant might gradually
             allow the infant to feel a sense of wholeness, of his parts being
             sort of brought together, maybe like the idea that Ezra just talked
             about. With the sketch idea, the analyst does that, helps to bring
             pieces of the patient's experience together into a coherent and
             cohesive image, a more felt held together image of oneself.
Midge: The analyst's observations over time, from different vantage
             points, might gradually build up a narrative about the patient's
             self that can be integrating, like a way that an ego can become
             less fragmented over time, especially if the analyst's vision is
             built on an accurate perception of the patient based on their
             experiences of them over time.
Eli: I am thinking about Freud's (1923) idea that "the ego is first and
             foremost a bodily ego" (p. 26). I wonder if Freud is speaking to
             how the mind and body work together in ways that lead to the
             development of self-consciousness.
Reyna: I'm imagining a sense of self-consciousness emerging gradually
             out of the early undifferentiated bond with the mother, if there is
             a very early proto-self-consciousness that arises from the shared
             bodily experiences with the mother which organize the infant's
             image of itself.
Ezra: I question whether or not there really is a coherent, integrated
             self. The self or identity could be thought of as a fixed or reified
             structure that can work against growth and development.
Instructor: Your comment reminded me of how repression closes things
             down and can lead to a rigidity that in combination with the
             superego works against the flexibility associated with change
             and growth. In our work in analysis, we strive to loosen the
             repression, allowing for a more free flow of previously repressed
             fantasies. That loosening can feel, at first, quite disorienting to
             the patient. It also reminds me of an earlier discussion we had
             about different views of interpretation, one involving the integra-
             tion of bringing experiences together in an organizing way ver-
             sus another involving the breaking up of established meanings.
Midge: I think that there's both a need for a flexible self, but also a
             coherent self that can synthesize novel experiences. We need to
             be able to synthesize our experiences into a life story, but also
             be open to having those integrations undone in order to move
             into new ways of being. I remember when I started analysis, I felt
             initially quite confident in the narrative I had built of myself over
             the course of years in psychotherapy. The problem was not about

that narrative being untrue. The problem was that it became a kind of frozen image in my mind, like a script for who I was. It was part of who I am, but not all of it. It became limiting. In my analysis, a lot of that unraveled and it was very unsettling at first, but that led to new ways of thinking about myself and it opened up new possibilities. Once again, it seems important to think about some kind of dialectic between stasis and movement, as we discussed in Beyond the Pleasure Principle.

Instructor: If the child's early experiences go reasonably well, the self becomes relatively cohesive. The child learns that stress is followed by relief, due to consistent care, attunement, and a healthy balance between stimulation and quietude. Many things can interfere with the early development of the body ego, such as having a psychotic or absent parent, chaotic and neglectful early experiences, and severe misattunement, for example.

Natalie: The mind of the early caregiver seems so important for the development of a cohesive and coherent body ego. I could imagine a mother who is unable to hold a whole object relation of the child in mind and how she might reflect split off bits of her experience of the child leaving the infant with a very fragmented self-representation.

Midge: It seems that our early self-image is formed in the mirror of the parents' vision of us and that the way their minds work will impact the deepest ways that we see ourselves.

Bethany: I was thinking about Freud's (1917) description of the superego and its role in melancholia. This quote from Freud (1923) stood out for me,

> How is it that the superego manifests itself essentially as a sense of guilt (or rather, as criticism—for the sense of guilt is the perception in the ego answering to this criticism) and moreover develops such extraordinary harshness and severity towards the ego.
>
> (p. 53)

I wonder about the way externally directed aggression gets shut down and how the excessive control of aggression can lead to it being directed against the self.

Reyna: This may be my own bias here, but it seems to me that girls might suffer more than boys in having their aggression suppressed. Culturally, men are often valorized for expressions of aggression, whereas women are viewed more pejoratively even when not being aggressive, but merely assertive. I think it is associated with oppression that women experience.

Instructor: We can think here about how that kind of oppression can give rise to internalized aggression in the form of a harsh superego. That is one possible path, for example, an identification with the aggressor, one wherein the aggression is directed at one's own ego.

Reyna: This brings to my mind my experience of how unsatisfying Freud's account of the female's oedipal complex was. His discussion of the complete Oedipus complex was much more interesting and I wonder why the discussions of the Oedipus complex are often reduced to a very simplified and normative version that leaves out the bisexual dimension of the complex.

Instructor: In Chapter 3, beginning on page 28, Freud (1923) begins to speak about the Oedipus complex. He directs us to the fundamental bisexuality of the child and how we cathect both parents. Here, as Reyna drew our attention to, he is saying that the ego develops through the identification and internalization of both parental positions. The idea is that we convert these object relationships into an internal identification. He first identified this in melancholia but later viewed it as a much more ubiquitous process, one that actually results in superego formation and the building up of the ego. So the ego is here considered to be built up through successive identifications with love objects that have been given up.

I want to say a few things here that I think will be a helpful context for the clinical case that I am going to present which I think will also touch on your comment, Reyna.

Freud describes the oedipal age boy as experiencing an intense and frightening situation. He wants his mother to be his exclusive position and wants to kill off his rival father, but he also loves his father and is terrified of him. The image of his fear of his father is manifested in his fear of castration. He solves the problem under the terror and pressure of castration anxiety. He gives up his erotic love for his mother, identifies with his father, and his ego then takes on qualities of his father that he has internalized. Now, we can think about how this process plays out with each parent in both ways, as lover and rival.

Reyna: These ideas are useful to me, and I was especially interested in what Freud was saying about the complete Oedipus complex. That did feel to me to be a more complex and potentially fascinating expansion of thinking, but then I felt dismayed when Freud goes back to focus exclusively on the male Oedipus complex.

Ezra: That's interesting. When I first read that piece, I was excited by it and then waiting for what Freud was going to say next, hoping he would flesh that out, but he just left it there.

Instructor:	He just left it there.
Midge:	That caught my ear too. Just left it there, makes me think of leaving something touched upon but open for others to do something more with it.
Bethany:	So maybe Freud is leaving hints for future analysts to do something, to take things a little further.
Ezra:	Now I am thinking about how I felt excited about what Freud said, and then I was waiting for him to flesh it out, but I wasn't curious about my own excitement, about trying to articulate what excited me about it.
Instructor:	That's a good insight. It reminds me of a kind of passivity. We're expecting someone else, in this case Freud, will do something about a problem that interests us.
Reyna:	I was sort of doing that too because I did have some ideas come to mind when I read Freud's piece on the Oedipus complex. It actually reminded me of going to an event and I saw my analyst, a man, hugging my supervisor, a woman. It was an intense moment for me emotionally. I felt a simultaneous jealousy in both directions. That is what I think of when I think of the complete Oedipus complex. When each parent is both an object of lust and a hated rival, I know these weren't my actual parents, but they were symbolically acting in loco parentis.
Bethany:	Thinking about that example you just gave, Reyna, makes my head want to explode.
Instructor:	Yes, and you can imagine what that would be like for an oedipal age child. Let's hold this loosely in mind as we get into the clinical hour.

Clinical Presentation of an Hour with Latency Age Boy Highlighting Some of the Oedipal Themes We Have Been Discussing

When I go to the waiting room, I see the patient sitting on the couch looking quite relaxed and confident. He is talking to an attractive adult woman about how many girls at school are attracted to him.

Patient:	Do you know that girl? Dude! Did you see her?! (he sounds and looks very excited) The girl in the waiting room.
Analyst:	Yes, I did. You're excited about her.
Patient:	Did you see me talking to her?
Analyst:	I noticed that.
Patient:	I'm just saying that I don't like her but she is the kind of girl that I could really like. She's beautiful and really nice and friendly and has a really nice smile. Don't you think she's pretty? But doc, I want you to really understand this. What I'm saying is that she's

	like the kind of girl I could really like. But I don't really like her okay?
Analyst:	You want to make sure I don't think that you like her.
Patient:	Yes, that's right.
Patient:	(he claps his hands and starts jumping up and down excitedly)

Okay, here's what we're going to do. How about we have a block fight. (he pulls out the container of soft, sponge blocks and begins to put them down on the chair next to him) Okay, wait. Let's do something different. Let's make it like dodgeball. Let's start with you trying to hit me with the blocks and I'll try to dodge them. (we proceeded to do this. I threw blocks at him while he tried to avoid being hit by them. He was actually quite fast and only got hit a few times. He was quite excited about that and spoke about how quick he was and how I couldn't hit him. He started to dance around in a celebratory, victorious way.

Then he suggested that we each take a pile of blocks and set up forts to shield us from being hit. He said that we were to engage in battle. In the midst of the battle, he asked for a momentary ceasefire.

Patient: This is like a war and usually when there's a war, each side is fighting for something, like land. Hmm. Let's make this interesting shall we gentlemen?

Analyst: What do you have in mind?

Patient: Well, let's say the winner of this here war gets to go out on a date with that girl. Okay, let's go. (He quickly threw the first block pretty hard and it hit me in the face. Then he jumped behind his chair/fort and yelled, "yes, got you!" He then threw two blocks and missed widely and his performance continued to steadily plummet.)

Analyst: You're throwing more sloppily now, like you're holding back.

Patient: (he ran over to pick up some blocks, but then slowed down and made himself an easy target. I threw a block and hit him.)

Analyst: You're starting to slow down now and make it easy for me to hit you. You were moving very fast at first and now you're slowing down.

(He threw three more blocks. One of them hit my foot. The others were way off. By the way, whenever we have played this before, his speed, marksmanship, and very high energy destroyed me every time. Something unusual was happening in this oft-repeated play.)

Analyst: Your aim was so much better before. I've never seen you play this badly. You're missing a lot. I'm beginning to have the feeling that you might have mixed feelings about winning this war.

Patient: What?! You think I don't want to win. Okay, that's it. No more Mr. Nice Guy. Okay let's make this a new battle. Let's use the giant pillows.

(He showed me that he wanted to use these very large heavy pillows, with each of us holding one and pushing against each other, the way football linebackers practice for a game.)

Analyst: I don't think that's a fair battle given my size and strength.

Patient: No, let's try.

(While playing, he fell a few times, and again seemed to be approaching the battle in a half-hearted way.)

Analyst: I think you're only half fighting. I think you want me to win. If I win, you might feel some relief and not feel scared about winning a date with a grown woman. It would be natural and understandable for you to be afraid of that because you're not ready for a relationship like that yet.

Patient: Hey, I'm almost ten!

Analyst: Yes, ten.

Patient: (starts laughing) It sounds younger when you say it. I do want you to go out on a date with that girl.

Analyst: How come?

Patient: I want you to take her out to a really nice restaurant for dinner and then you can tell me everything that happened and how it was. Then I'll know how to go out on a date someday. Can you do that? Then you can tell me about it next time we meet.

Analyst: It feels like a better idea not to compete with me to win the girl, but instead to watch me and try to do things the way I do so that someday you can have your own girl.

Class Discussion

Ernest: The patient appeared to be setting up an oedipal situation, one where a new, more adaptive solution could be fashioned. That might allow him to identify with you and internalize regulatory structures.

Instructor: That's a good point. One important piece of this involved his creation of an oedipal rival within his play. All of this raises many questions for us, related to the increasing complexity of Freud's conceptualization of the ego, that we read in *The Ego and the Id* and what we will read more about in Inhibitions, Symptoms, and Anxiety.

If we think of the ego having unconscious agency, we might wonder, to what extent one can unconsciously aim toward constructing potentially growth-promoting scenes. Joseph Weiss (1993) developed this line of thinking, stating that "A person suffers from pathogenic beliefs and is highly motivated to disprove them" (p. 9).

Ezra: I feel uncomfortable with this way of thinking about it. It seems to give the ego too much control over orchestrating the direction of what gets enacted.

Instructor: What is your discomfort about that?

Ezra: It leads me to feel suspicious that this way of putting it down-plays the unconscious libidinal and aggressive forces pushing to enact something that isn't in the control of the ego, even unconsciously.

Natalie: I'm thinking about the role of the analyst as interpreting the enactment in a direction that helped the patient to get in contact with his need for such a father figure and his fear of being alone with a woman without the mediating protection of the father.

Instructor: Could you say more about the connection between what you're saying and what Ezra was talking about?

Natalie: It might look like there's an unconscious ego agency moving toward a progressive development of identifying with the ana-lyst, but it may actually be that the interpretations are serving the function of helping him to become more conscious of his need for that. The role of interpretation in bringing his wishes to consciousness may be an important force here and not so much the ego's control over orchestrating the scene, at least not exclusively. The interpretations of his unconscious resistance, for example, clue him into that underlying fear of the very thing he's consciously so excited about.

Bethany: Yes and that we might be fooled into thinking that there is some unconscious plan as a prime inner mover and ignore the role that the patient's transference and the analyst's interpretations together play in shepherding the outcome that we might other-wise over-attribute to some internal, unconscious plan.

Instructor: You are thinking about the clash of forces between the patient's transference to an oedipal rival and the analyst's channeling of that passionate conglomeration of forces into a form of reflection that distinguishes his wishes from reality. This kind of interaction also provides some containment or binding for what might oth-erwise be experienced as overstimulating.

Midge: This clash of forces reminds me of the way we talked about the tensions between the life instincts and the death instincts, how the life drives, especially the sexual impulses may have driven him in his excitement to wish to actualize an oedipal scene, but the death drive, as manifested by the analyst as a superego or limiting force put the brakes on it, and may be said to have tamed these impulses, allowing for more reality testing and regu-lation of what may have felt otherwise overwhelming. In many ways, you were performing the superego functions that his father seemed to abdicate.

Instructor: Midge just answered a question posed some time ago about a clinical example for working with the death drive. I also want to highlight here the movement in our dialogue from initially focusing on an unconscious plan coming exclusively from an inner force within the patient to a dialectic of opposed forces, both within the patient and in the interaction with the analyst. This, I think is an important shift toward a more expansive and inter-active way of conceptualizing the situation. In fairness, though, I do think it's worth reading more about control mastery theory. A careful reading may help us to ascertain whether or not this model would rule out the way you're thinking about it.

Reyna: I was wondering about the patient's pent up arousal emerging in the session. He was remarkably excited, like in a way that wasn't containable at times. He was so excited, jumping up and down, and then creating a game where he was able to put that excite-ment into the physical exertion of the battle with you.

Instructor: This brings up the issue of overstimulation associated with the patient's experience of a relative absence of limits and bounda-ries in his family. I will say he did have excessive access to his mother's bodily complaints and there was a complete absence of paternal prohibition. We might think of the economic model here when thinking about the intensity of his excitement.

Midge: The energy and intensity may have to do with the way the ana-lyst experiences it, that to be on the receiving end of the patient's desires and passions may feel very intense for the analyst, but maybe we need a more inclusive language.

Instructor: More inclusive of what?

Midge: I was thinking of inclusive in terms of a concept that holds both patient and analyst experiences together in some way, in a more holistic way as both interacting in ways that are a part of a bigger picture, a shared interpersonal context.

Ezra: Midge's comment helped me to realize one reason why I don't like the concept of energy. It's often used in a way that feels cut off from the relationship, like imagining that this energy resides in the patient then gets projected onto the analyst. This feels too neatly divided than what's actually going on. It seems to me that the energy that the patient manifests is always in relation to an object.

Instructor: That's an important point. It reminds me of the patient's over-stimulation in the context of excessive access to his mother's complaints about a litany of things.

Eli: That does make me wonder what the father was doing, where he was when the boy was hearing all this.

Instructor: Do you have any hypotheses about that?

Eli: What I imagine is a father that either isn't around or is relieved that his son is taking on this role. It feels very sad to me, that he's left alone to care for his mother, and without a father to have in mind how this is impacted him.

Midge: It does feel that way to me. I'm thinking about the Oedipus complex and how the boy really needs the father as a protection from what can become an emotionally overwhelming situation. The father could provide a limit for him in the way that you seemed to be able to provide him in his play.

Bethany: This case focuses exclusively on the boy's Oedipus complex, his rivalry with the father and his sexual longings for his mother. Here, I do wonder about the complete Oedipus complex.

Instructor: You have your own ideas about it?

Bethany: I do wonder about his longings for his father. Are these limited to longings for a father's protection or is there more to it, like some sexual longings?

Reyna: So now I'm thinking about something else in this case that we haven't talked about and it surprises me that we haven't talked about it because we were just talking about the complete Oedipus complex and I think it's right there in this material under our noses. The focus has been primarily on the boy's attraction, desire for the woman, his mother and the woman in the waiting room, but his excitement as enacted in the room is primarily directed at Louis, in a quite physical way.

Instructor: That's an excellent observation. Any other thoughts about that?

Ezra: The image that just came to my mind is of men sitting next to one another in a strip club, feeling excited without any real awareness that, in addition to the erotic feelings toward the women, they are also sharing erotic feelings with one another.

Midge: This does bring us back to the complexity of what goes on for the oedipal child, contending with erotic and murderous feelings for each parent. What comes to mind for me is how confusing that must be for the child. It's a lot to deal with at such a young age.

Eli: And even Reyna's example earlier of an adult version of that when she saw her analyst hugging her supervisor led me to imagine a kind of short-circuiting of my brain in such a situation.

Natalie: Maybe those kinds of feelings are involved in missing this piece at first and focusing on something simpler, something more manageable. Although I do think that the focus on the boy, and how little Freud wrote about the oedipal situation for girls is troubling.

Instructor: That takes me back to some of the critical reactions you have had on Freud's views on women, I want to mention another analytic writer who has made significant strides in expanding our views on gender is Patricia Gherovici, from Philadelphia. I've been impressed with her very well-integrated knowledge of Freud. So, what stands out about her work is that it is actually very consistent with Freud's writings and she seems to tune into the more expansive, radical implications of Freud's writings. She's written two books that I am aware of:

1 Transgender Psychoanalysis (2017)
2 Please Select Your Gender: from the invention of hysteria to the democratization of transgenderism. (2010)

Our speculations about the way cultural misogyny could have insinuated itself in Freud's views on women are an important issue worth serious and devoted reflection and study. One book I would recommend is Elizabeth Young-Bruehl's book, *Freud on Women* (1990). She has gathered all of Freud's writing about women. While she does offer some interesting reflections of her own, she also writes in such a way facilitates the reader coming to their own conclusions.

When we spoke about the Oedipus complex earlier, Reyna expressed frustration in reaction to Freud's views on girls/women. Some of what Freud spoke of regarding women can, at times, feel like a narrow frame and there are ways that Freud puts things that can be off-putting at times. This brought to mind thoughts about the misogynistic culture of Freud's time as well as our own.

Another angle, without disputing these experiences, is the sense, also in Freud's writings, sometimes explicit, sometimes implicit, of the potential for a whole new way of seeing things, that is, for an expanded view of the Oedipus complex. For example, as you drew our attention to, when Freud speaks about our essential, fundamental bisexuality, and how what he says about the Oedipus complex occurs with each parent. Each parent is both the object of our erotic longings and a rival for the affections of the other parent.

These potentially more complex and inclusive ways of thinking about the Oedipus complex are lying there quietly waiting in Freud's text or as Ezra said, "he just left it there." In thinking more about this in the context of our discussion, I was struck by the, at times, paradoxical tensions in reading Freud that many of you have spoken of. It's interesting to think about our experience of disappointment and feeling put-off by Freud in relation to other experiences of feeling amazed at what he has allowed us to see.

I was reminded of something that Jonathan Lear said about Hans Loewald's reading of Freud. He said, "Loewald will typically find a variant strain in Freud's thought, enhance it, and thus give back to us a Freud who is unfamiliar and original, yet genuinely Freud" (1994, p. 679). It's interesting to think about this way of reading Freud.

In some ways it reminds me of a sort of developmental model of reading that we have been engaged in, wherein we read what is actually being said, the literality of the text, but also begin to use our own experiences, both clinical and personal, and our imagination to tune into unstated, implicit potentialities within the writing itself, the variant strain that Lear mentioned, a potential for more that has yet to be actualized. We can read Freud and listen to Freud not only for what he says, but also for hints of what he seemed to be leaning toward, but wasn't quite able to fully say. I think that's not a bad way to listen to each other, to our patients, and to ourselves, wherein we try to listen for the seeds of potentiality, the possibility for more within what we and others are trying to say.

The way you have been discussing Freud in this class often will respond to something that feels one-sided, something left out, something that feels odd or strange, something that feels frustrating, too comfortable, suspicious. All of these reactions help us to maintain a useful tension which contributes to round out the picture and broaden our thinking about what Freud is grappling with and trying to conceptualize. Something will come together, but over time, new tensions arise and that coherent image will unravel and lead to something new.

Reyna: This way of listening is linked to a comment Natalie made earlier about the analyst's interpretations as having a shaping influence on the patient material, at times in the direction of a movement toward something more inclusive and expansive.

Ezra: I wonder though about the dangers of misreading our own projections and imposing something onto the patient under a well-rationalized guise of hearing an imagined potentiality in what we are hearing from the patient.

Instructor: This is an excellent point and precisely the kind of self-critical thinking that is so crucial for analysts to engage in. This is why it's so important to cultivate an atmosphere wherein we can step back from our associations to are patients and the text and subject them to more critical scrutiny, as you are doing here.

Are there any other thoughts about this concern?

Bethany: I'm thinking about the context of Ezra's expressed concern. The comment itself reminded me of what you were saying about how we often respond to something that feels one-sided, something left out or something frustrating or concerning. These kinds of comments are more likely to occur when that kind of tension and open expression of criticism is part of the group's ideals or culture, something that is cultivated and welcomed. I wonder if it might be possible to cultivate something like that in the clinical relationship and if that could serve as some kind of safeguard or corrective for the risk of imposing our projections on the patient.

A Note on What Happened

Our open exploration of our own resistances in our clinical work felt quite fruitful in terms of experientially fleshing out Freud's writings on unconscious defenses and unconscious resistances. Students talked about their own experience of trying to speak to what felt like important points of urgency and being held back from doing so in spite of their conscious intentions. Moments of harsh superego attacks were noted and explored, manifesting as a tendency toward self-condemnation in the face one's own resistance. We returned to discuss a tension between a wish to know the exact meaning of everything Freud said versus an appreciation for the way ambiguity opens up a space to think together, collaboratively about what Freud is getting at, how it relates to our own struggles, and how that can feel more fascinating, albeit less certain. This led to a recognition that the ambiguity we struggle with in learning Freud and in our collective efforts to think together appears more and more relevant to our psychoanalytic work of encountering and exploring unconscious phenomena. This moved into a discussion of our own relationship with encounters with our own unconscious experience. The experience of feeling unseated from a more clear, confident, and certain position was raised. The sense of reassuring comfort associated with the notion of a theory that explains everything, that gives us all the answers, was expressed, albeit with greater skepticism. The idea that we may have difficulty believing that we are driven by unconscious processes, in spite of an intellectual acknowledgment that we are so driven, was discussed and related to our struggles in reading Freud. An important question was posed regarding safeguards against imposing meaning on patients via projection under the guise of hearing potentiality in their comments.

References

Freud, S. (1917). Mourning and Melancholia. SE 14: 236–258.

Freud, S. (1923). The Ego and the Id. SE 19: 2–66.

Gherovici, P. (2010). *Please Select Your Gender: From the Invention of Hysteria to the Democratization of Transgenderism*. Routledge.

Gherovici, P. (2017). *Transgender Psychoanalysis: A Lacanian Perspective on Sexual Difference*. Routledge.

Lear, J. (1994). The Introduction of Eros: Reflections on the Work of Hans Loewald. *JAPA*, 44 (3), 673–698.

Wiess, J. (1993). *How Psychotherapy Works: Process and Technique*. Guilford Press.

Young-Bruehl, E. (1990). *Freud on Women: A Reader*. Norton and Co.

8 Inhibitions, Symptoms, and Anxiety

A Note on My Intentions

In this reading, *Inhibitions, Symptoms and Anxiety* (1926), in addition to wanting to cover some of the central ideas from the paper, I also aimed to have us make links between these concepts and our own personal struggles in practicing psychoanalytic clinical work. I hoped that we would be able, in that way, to recognize the important connection between Freud's concepts and his clinical struggles, e.g., how those ideas came out of his struggles. I also wanted to make space for us to re-visit areas of tension, difficulty, and important themes that have come up in previous classes.

Instructor: Up until this paper, Freud's notion of repression was that once the sexual impulses are repressed, they are transformed into anxiety. So, essentially, anxiety was, for a long time, viewed as a transformation of the repressed sexual wishes. The energy associated with the repressed libidinal impulses was thought to have been transformed so that it wasn't experienced as sexual anymore, but instead as an unpleasant feeling of anxiety.

    In the Inhibitions paper, Freud says he was wrong about that. He recognized that his first theory of anxiety was a problematic view for a number of reasons. It didn't fully clarify what causes repression. It didn't take into account the fact that anxiety can occur in response to external stimuli, e.g., traumatic events. With the introduction of the structural theory in 1923, *The Ego and the Id*, it became possible to think of an agency that could unconsciously respond with anxiety to both internal and external dangers. These reactions of the ego may not reach consciousness. So, here he is saying that anxiety causes repression, not the other way around, as he had earlier conceived of it.

Ezra: The transformation of sexual energy into something different reminds me of the way Freud talked about the defusion that occurs during the transformation of object libido into

DOI: 10.4324/9781003610977-10

narcissism, although narcissism is still sexual energy but a different form of it.

Natalie: I can see why Freud thought that anxiety was associated with and seemed to follow repression. We can see it manifesting when repression fails and triggers other defensive maneuvers.

Instructor: For a long time, prior to this book, Freud often referred to repression as signifying defense in general. In this paper, he replaces that with repression as a specific type of defense. Repression is viewed here as the withholding or exclusion of an idea from the ego. Repression is forgetting something that would be painful to know, and it requires an ongoing expenditure of psychic energy to maintain it.

Going forward, Freud will use the term defense in a general way covering the many types of defenses that the ego employs to protect itself from psychic pain. In this paper, he articulates a variety of techniques for defending against the anxieties that are associated with various danger situations.

It is important to think about Freud's description of two different types of anxiety-provoking situations. The first involves the excessive stimulation and rapid accumulation of instinctual energy, particularly in situations of unexpected fright when the protective barriers of the ego are overrun and a state of panic and trauma results. This he refers to as automatic anxiety. He had spoken of this in *Beyond the Pleasure Principle* when he talked about trauma.

The other type of anxiety is the major new idea of the paper, signal anxiety. This typically occurs after the structural organization of the psyche has developed. Here anxiety arises in anticipation of danger, rather than as a result of repression. The anxiety may be induced by a scenario that is similar to a danger that has already occurred.

The affect of anxiety serves a protective function signaling the person of the approach of danger. It may arise because a person has learned, at a preconscious or unconscious level, to recognize aspects of a scenario that had once proven to be traumatic. This function of the ego allows us to make use of an array of defenses to escape real or imagined internal and external dangers.

Eli: This brings to my mind Freud's discussion of the binding that has to happen before the pleasure principle can be put into operation. The ego is able to bind the rising tension in the form of a tolerable anxiety that can be used to then allow the pleasure principle to operate in a way that provides relief.

Bethany: It seems like a previously experienced anxiety state can be repeated when a similar situation occurs, but this time the anxiety is kept within some kind of containment or titration, giving the person something of a taste of a more severe anxiety experienced at some earlier time.

Ernest: It's like a smaller dosage of what may have been a traumatic anxiety and this allows the person to use that anxiety to marshal one's forces to deal with it. This strikes me as a very adaptive way to deal with one's fears, kind of like turning your fears into something you can have some control over. It makes me wonder about how this develops.

Natalie: When we talked about ways of managing erotic transference, one idea that came up was that the analyst could allow themselves to feel their own reaction to the patient's transference but within limits. That is similar to the way signal anxiety involves a more limited quantity of anxiety, one that makes it more adaptively useable.

Instructor: That's a good link and overall you're getting at signal anxiety as an important developmental achievement that has potential for a more adaptive response to experiences involving danger, a way of putting one's anxiety in the service of a potentially healthier response. Ernest's question about how this might develop is important to think about.

Midge: I'm thinking of biofeedback, a way of learning to have some control over processes that one had been helpless to do anything about. I do wonder about possible clinical implications.

Instructor: It sounds like you have some ideas about that.

Midge: I was thinking about repetitions that occur in analysis and I wonder if it might be possible to develop signal anxiety as a result of the analytic work. I'm not sure how that would play out though.

Instructor: I wonder if anyone else has any ideas about how that might happen?

Ezra: I was wondering if maybe the way signal anxiety develops is in some way similar to the way infants gradually make use of previous responses to distress.

Instructor: Could you say more about what you're picturing here?

Ezra: First, I'm imagining an infant in distress, experiencing some dysregulation, flailing about in response to it, crying. I think of the infant having an automatic response to a potentially traumatic situation, so like automatic anxiety. But, maybe over time, the infant develops some nascent control, and that allows them to make use of what had been an automatic anxiety associated with crying and to actually use crying as a signal aimed to trigger a response.

Instructor: That's a fascinating idea and maybe one we can play with.

Bethany: In that example, the infant gradually learns to use what was an automatic response to a rise in tension in order to signal the

	caretaker to respond. So the signal was meant to trigger relief coming from an object. What or who is being signaled in Freud's signal anxiety?
Midge:	Freud said that the signal anxiety triggers the pleasure principle to respond, to do something that decreases tension. I'm still curious about how signal anxiety could develop in analytic work.
Reyna:	I imagine a repeated enactment with your analyst that gets processed a little each time it happens, adding to your sense of what it's about, like you describe the pattern in a little more detail each time you rebuild the alliance that had been disrupted and then maybe you start to notice more about it and over time you're able to gradually diminish the anxiety and you can start to reflect on the beginnings of it, sooner in the cycle in ways that both prevent the experience of overwhelming anxiety and allow you to use the smaller amount of anxiety to begin reflecting on it in the service of developing some insight about it.
Midge:	I think that a very similar process could occur in the analyst. I kept getting overwhelmed with anxiety during a repeated struggle with my patient. I was gradually able to notice the beginnings of that cycle and be curious about it earlier on in the process in a way that prevented the overwhelm. It helped me to speak to it earlier than later.
Eli:	I can relate to that. I was getting angry with a patient, but I gradually learned that I could speak earlier, before my anger reached a high level of intensity. That allowed me to get a better handle on the what was playing out between the patient and myself.
Instructor:	Those are great examples. One theme from your comments for us to keep in mind is the way in which experiences that we initially had no control over, e.g., automatic anxiety, are made use of in a way that becomes useful, almost like turning the anxiety into something like a psychic tool that we can utilize.

Freud spoke of four fundamental dangers, each associated with a different stage of development. The first of these dangers that Freud wrote about is the loss of the primary object. The second one is the fear of losing the object's love. One might think of the toddler's experience of being scolded or of receiving some other type of disapproval. The separation/individuation process subjects the child to both threats of loss of the object and loss of the object's love.

The third fundamental danger is castration anxiety, the fear of loss of or damage to one's genital. This appears within the oedipal phase when the genitals become the site of intensive focus and sexual stimulation.

In latency, the major fear is that the parental representatives, in the form of the superego, will be angry, punish, or cease to love the child. This fourth fear can be described as the fear of the loss of the love of the superego. Often it manifests in the form of unconscious guilt or conscious anxiety.

Ezra: It feels really important to me to be thinking about the dangers and anxieties associated with the experience and threat of loss. This sounds like a unifying thread linking all of the major developmental dangers.

Natalie: I agree. So much of what we are dealing with clinically has to do with losses that have occurred or threats of impending losses. This central theme of loss as a danger feels organizing for me in my thinking about patients' motivations in analysis. I could imagine moments when the patient is afraid of losing the analyst when anticipating a break in the treatment, or afraid of losing the analyst's love if they disclose something that could be offensive to the analyst, or unconsciously afraid of castration, losing or damaging one's genital associated with lustful feelings for the analyst, or fear of being condemned by the analyst in situations of perceived moral failings.

Instructor: In what ways do you imagine knowing about these motives being helpful clinically?

Midge: It could be helpful as an accompaniment to an interpretation, like if you interpret the patient's resistance to expressing their lust or anger, and then add the motivation of fear of loss. I think that may help the patient feel understood in a more complete way.

Ezra: The anxious anticipation of loss can also be something re-experienced in the present that has actually already happened in the past but has not yet been fully processed.

Instructor: You've raised important clinical considerations. The fears we've been discussing occur at particular stages of development and this also has implications for our thinking about the persistence of earlier forms of anxiety in our adult patients and how they might contribute to neurotic fixations at earlier stages of development, conflicts characteristic of those stages, and defenses particular to them as well. Obsessional neurosis, for example, is linked to Oedipal conflicts handled through a regression to the safety of the anal-sadistic way of relating and becomes associated with the use of particular defenses, for example, undoing, reaction formation, isolation, and intellectualization.

Natalie: I have a patient that often makes use of isolating threatening thoughts. I noticed a pattern where he would mention something he's upset about at the beginning of the session, but then talk in a very finely detailed way about something mechanistic for much of the session. I can see that it does fit with the kind of isolation that Freud talked about when the patient interposes an interval where nothing is meant to happen after some threatening idea or feeling emerges.

Eli: I've experienced that too. I have to listen very carefully for what thoughts are being kept separate by sometimes very long intervals. The content can be distracting from recognizing the use of isolation. Sometimes, I write it down. A particular patient I am thinking of will say that he is feeling upset about a fight with his wife, then shift to talking in great detail about some project he is engaged in. It gets so involved and distracting that if I don't write down the first thing he said, it's completely lost to me.

Bethany: I wonder about the potential benefit of interrupting an interval like that, like commenting on the observed pattern of the patient making use of this defense and describing it to the patient so they might become more conscious of it. Related to what we were talking about earlier, it seems possible that the more articulate we can be in describing the ways the patient defends against painful feelings, the more acquainted they will be with them, the more likely they will be able to see it happening earlier on in the process. In some ways, that's like making use of defenses that had been automatic in ways that allow us to learn more about our fears and conflicts.

Instructor: That makes a lot of sense to me, Bethany. Becoming more familiar with the varied defensive strategies is very important in this regard. As Freud learned about transference, these phenomena are not mere obstacles to be overcome, but important sources of insight.

It is important to think about neurosis and neurotic symptoms. As I mentioned previously, neurosis involves an intra-psychic conflict, a conflict between Freud's hypothesized agencies of the mind, the Id, Ego, and Superego. The patient's response to the conflict was to use repression, but ultimately repression was not successful. The global repression that occurs at the end of the Oedipal phase shuts things down and in a way freezes them in place. The good thing about it is that it allows the latency age child to be able to go to school and to learn, without being overwhelmed by sexual and aggressive feelings.

We see what the absence of repression looks like with kids who never really enter a true latency phase due to trauma or chronic overstimulation of various kinds. It's really hard to pay attention and learn when your mind is flooded with conscious thoughts and feelings associated with incestuous and murderous wishes and fantasies, especially given that during this stage of development your thinking still hasn't developed beyond the equation of thought and deed.

On the other hand, too much repression can hinder growth and development and lead to rigidity, inhibition, and restriction. What happens in analysis, among other things, is that we try to facilitate a situation where the patient can make projections and introjections, for example, the re-projection of the patient's superego, through regression, onto the analyst within the transference. These kinds of processes allow for a reworking of one's internal conflicts and neurotic symptoms.

Midge: The idea of repression closing things down reminds me of the idea we explored previously of Eros as a kind of accelerator and the death instinct as putting the brakes on. That made me think of the psychic equilibrium associated with the cooperative functioning of these different but related parts of the mind operating in interactive ways.

Eli: I'm thinking about how we previously discussed the way the ego does not replace the id in the same way that the reality principle does not replace the primary process, but that we find new forms of expression and compromises.

Instructor: So here, you are reminding us that the ego has to find a way to provide some satisfaction for each of these diverse psychic factions.

Ezra: Too much dominance of any one part or function, like excessive repression or excessive expression of sexual and aggressive impulses, would disturb this hypothetical equilibrium. Balance of these opposing tendencies seems to be associated with the idea of mental health.

Bethany: I wonder if we might think of this equilibrium as a kind of natural ecology within the psyche. We need the passion, pleasure, and joy connected with the energy associated with the drives. It's where life is, but it has to be channeled in ways that protect us from the kinds of potentially destructive repetitions that Freud talked about.

Reyna: There are few places in life other than analysis where we can give full expression to all of our fantasies, thoughts, urges without having to put the brakes on. It is so important to be able to bring that energy and passion into some outward form that is creative and fun.

Natalie: I've noticed that there are times when it's very difficult for me to be completely honest with myself about my own thoughts and feelings when listening to my patients. I can feel disturbed by the more crude and raw fantasies that come up, as if it's not what I should be feeling. I worry that my reaction to these experiences might be inhibiting my pleasure in the work.

Instructor: We often hear analysts talking and writing about analytic virtues, ideals, even beauty, that we are meant to aspire to in our work.

These can leave us feeling bad about the ways in which our feelings in the moment-to-moment process of our work deviate from those idealized images.

Ernest: I feel bad and like I should not, as an analyst, be feeling things like contempt, hatred, boredom, rage, and a host of other ugly human emotions in my work.

Instructor: I want to draw attention to the word human that Ernest just used. It reminds me of something that I mentioned before about an attitude that I believe Freud exemplified, that nothing that is human is alien to us. I think it's a helpful guide in our work. What we choose to say in our interpretations is one thing, and tact and timing is always important, but our work necessitates that we strive to have full access to all of our feelings and fantasies.

Ezra: When we discussed the transference love paper, we talked about how we experience moments of treating our thoughts and feelings as if they are actions.

That may be part of what leaves us feeling bad about these thoughts and feelings.

Instructor: Again, this is an important reminder that, in our work as therapists and analysts, we struggle with many of the same issues, including regressions, that our patients struggle with in their analytic work. Also, the nature of the unconscious itself, the particular currency of unconscious thought Freud talked about is relevant here, e.g., unconscious thought is equated with actualization. We can end up feeling bad for even thinking something, as if we have committed a terrible crime.

Bethany: This is feeling like a repeated experience for us. We keep rediscovering that we have an unconscious just like our patients, which we know intellectually, but seem on a deeper level stubbornly resistant to.

Instructor: We're laughing again, maybe a sign that we are approaching something that resonates as having truth for us, as well as it being anxiety provoking, I suspect.

A neurotic symptom is what forms when some of our repressions fail and previously forgotten impulses and fantasies push toward consciousness. For example, related to what we were just discussing, in the formation of a neurosis, when an Oedipal-related wish is perceived as dangerous even to think about, defenses are issued against that wish. The agencies of the mind we spoke of in the structural model are each in play, so the wishes from the Id, the defenses of the Ego, and punishment of the Superego will each be represented within the symptom.

Eli: I'm thinking about an experience with a patient who is very self-condemning, at times in ways that feel quite violent and self-abusive. I often find myself working really hard to combat the extreme harshness of the patient's superego. It is very frustrating.

Midge: I can relate to your discomfort witnessing this kind of attack in your patient, but I do wonder if there are problems with an analyst opposing the patient's superego in the way Eli described?

Instructor: Could you tell us any thoughts you have about it being potentially problematic?

Midge: Eli was taking a side in the conflict. He was trying to get the patient to stop doing something, in contrast to showing the patient what was going on dynamically, showing them the nature of the conflict they were having, by speaking to all sides of it, like the motives of the id, the ego, and the superego. I'm thinking about what Freud said about the importance of the patient becoming more acquainted with these experiences within themselves and how important that is in terms of developing a sense of conviction.

Instructor: This is an excellent point, and especially in the kind of situation described, it can be very difficult to navigate. There are also times when we might interpret some of these things that you are suggesting in ways that interrupt a repeated self-attack and that can be helpful.

          For example, you may have a patient who is engaged with you who suddenly starts bashing himself in a way that you've learned can grow into a binge of self-aggression that is re-traumatizing and makes it impossible for him to reflect meaningfully on what's going on. You might interpret the rage he feels toward you sooner than later, in part to interrupt that and draw the patient's attention to what is motivating the attack. It would be preferable if you could interrupt that in a way that speaks to the underlying dynamics involved.

          Are there any other thoughts, reactions, or questions about this paper?

Natalie: I'm wondering about the distinction between an inhibition that is the result of a conflict, for example, between a sexual urge and a superego prohibition, versus a function that has never developed, more like a deficit.

Ernest: I wonder about that too. How would we distinguish a conflict from a deficit?

Instructor: These questions remind me of Anne Alvarez' work with severely neglected children (2012). She talked about children who never developed the capacity to look up to someone. One could mistake this for an inhibition due to conflict, especially when the environmental context of the child is not taken into consideration.

This distinction has important clinical implications and we can make mistakes in either direction, for example, assuming we are dealing with an inhibition due to conflict when we are dealing with a deficit versus assuming we are dealing with a deficit when we are dealing with an underlying conflict.

In general, the former mistake will lead to a situation wherein there appears to be no change, for example, we would interpret inferred conflicts associated with the apparent inhibition and it would remain the same. That might clue us in that we are incorrect in our assumption. In the latter case, we may unwittingly invite a regression and participate in a strengthening of the resistance in the patient.

Bethany: One implication in this has to do with the analyst being able to notice when they're making a mistake.

Instructor: Great point. Do you have any ideas about what might get in the way of noticing that?

Bethany: Theoretical allegiance comes to mind. If you identify yourself as a conflict theorist or alternatively as a deficit model theorist, you may feel more wed to your approach in ways that lead you to keep going with it even when it's not working. I am thinking here about our sense of tribalism, how we can overidentify with what our tribe or group thinks, in ways that dissuade us from considering explanations that we perceive as outside of that.

Instructor: You raise an interesting problem here, one that we might think of as associated with our identifications, as you described. Interestingly, when we are fixated with particular ways of thinking about our work, we may find ourselves in a more rigid position, with less elasticity in terms of changing course when it is necessary.

Midge: That makes me wonder if the idea that we need to have an analytic identity might similarly contribute to this kind of rigidity.

Instructor: This is a fascinating idea. It reminds me that Freud once said that he did not consider himself a Freudian. Does anyone have any reactions to that? Do you think having an analytic identity could contribute to rigidity? Do you think it's necessary to have an analytic identity?

Ernest: That confuses me. Is it even possible to acquire analytic skills, to learn the practice of psychoanalysis without identifying as a psychoanalyst?

Instructor: Can anyone imagine what that would look like, assuming it's possible, just to play with the idea?

Midge: My father just came to mind. He's woodworker. I picture someone like him who practices a craft, someone who loves the craft and loves what he is doing when he's doing it, but doesn't wear it everywhere he goes. You could think of a woodworker, or a different kind of craftsman in that sense, but he doesn't necessarily relate everything back to his woodworking or craft, whereas sometimes it seems like analysts tend to do that in ways that feel narrow-minded.

Instructor: You're onto something very interesting here. If we think about what we do as a craft, we have ideas related to the craft of psychoanalysis, concepts derived from our efforts to practice analysis and these ideas help us do and achieve real things, like tools of our trade. When we identify excessively with the profession, as an identity as opposed to a craft, we run the risk of turning our tools into something more fetishistic or perhaps better said, something more reified and static.

Bethany: I'm curious about what you initially meant by fetishistic?

Instructor: I was thinking of it as a kind of inappropriate application of the ideas that are applicable to our craft, say, for example, a way we can turn these ideas into something that is meant less to achieve practical aims conducive to psychoanalytic work, the treatment of our patients' struggles in contrast to something that enhances our own narcissistic self-regard and security, a way that we dress ourselves, create an image that is meant to provide some status or something to hold onto.

Ernest: I'm still grappling with an earlier conversation we had about how repeated enactments in analysis might contribute to the development of signal anxiety. The repetition of a trauma in a mitigated form implies that something about the repetition has changed. It is not the same repetition if it's in a weakened form. This makes me wonder if there might be some gradual development of agency within the process of repeating the trauma in analysis.

Ezra: I am going to reference Freud's (1926) comment, "The ego, which experienced the trauma passively, now repeats it actively in a weakened version, in the hope of being able itself to direct its course" (p. 167). It's like a traumatic experience is somehow turned into a tool that one can make use of.

Midge: I'm thinking about Freud's comment about how this process involves an attempt to master a traumatic experience psychically in the way children do in their play.

Instructor: There seems to be something important about the struggle to think about this again, something we are both drawn to about these ideas and also something unsettled.

Natalie: The idea of mastering a trauma in the process of repeating it is very appealing to think about especially from the perspective of the analyst because these repetitions can feel so daunting. I like the idea we were considering earlier, about how we might be able to make use of traumatic anxiety, or any affect that we felt helplessly overwhelmed by, toward effecting some change in the repetition.

Reyna: There are also traumatic repetitions that can go on and on without much change or even change for the worse. I'm very much interested in what might contribute to a change.

Bethany: I wonder if there could be a gradual subjective sense of agency within the repetition, especially, like we talked about before, if the analyst and patient were able to notice small subtle differences from previous repetitions, some small evidence that the patient was actually doing something different in each repetition. Could the analyst noticing these new developments expand the patient's ability to see some movement when they otherwise might feel hopelessly and endlessly repeating the same self-destructive thing. And might that itself facilitate more movement in the direction of transforming a compulsive repetition into something aimed at growth.

Eli: I wonder if a repeated scene or enactment with the analyst might, in incremental ways, over time, become more and more recognized, remembered, elaborated, and finally expected. The patient and analyst might start to see it coming a mile away and then begin a reflective process sooner in ways that offset a more compulsive and destructive repetition.

Midge: The analyst's drawing the patient's attention to subtle changes in the repetition might also enable the patient to begin to make links to and ultimately own motives they have that had previously been unconscious.

Instructor: There is value in your returning to these unsettled conversations, particularly the ones like this one that you feel drawn to and perhaps troubled by. You're thinking about your attraction to this idea, questioning that itself, and also you've added some very compelling speculations about the role the analyst might play in transforming a repetition into a channeled version that can be profitably worked with.

Reyna: Freud said that in the repetition of trauma, there is an effort to experience the anxiety that failed to appear during the initial fright associated with the traumatic event.

Instructor: What are you thinking in relation to that?

Reyna: This kind of repetition with the analyst's help might assist the patient to sharpen their capacity to perceive the very subtle early signs of anxiety, as we have been talking about, so the analysis could heighten the patient's perception so that some kind of binding of otherwise overwhelming stimulation could occur.

Eli: The analyst's ability to reconnect with the patient after each enactment especially if it's one that disrupts the alliance might also increase the patient's expectation that the repetition is one that can be tolerated, lived through, repaired, thought about, and learned from. For example, it might be relieving for a patient who feels and believes the repetition will destroy his relationship

	to experience the connection with the analyst surviving such enactments.

Ezra: The notion of working through became an important addition to Freud's idea of therapeutic action. We might think of the work as still about making the unconscious conscious, but in a way that has meaning and conviction for the patient.

Midge: I'm thinking again about the issue of the analyst taking sides in a patient's conflicts, for example, trying to oppose the patient's harsh superego attacks. It seems, in light of the idea of working through, that it would be preferable for the analyst to bring the patient into closer contact with their own inner division, to help them face the opposing workings of their inner factions and to then be in a better position to see it and grapple with it.

Instructor: Does anyone have any thoughts on why this might be a better approach, given our understanding of working through?

Midge: It would afford the patient an opportunity to experience the conflict for themselves, as opposed to the analyst telling him or worse of the analyst trying to get him to do something different.

Ernest: Why would it be better for the patient to experience the conflict for themselves instead of being shown that he's in conflict? The latter is still a form of insight.

Midge: It would likely result in a greater sense of conviction of both their own inner resistance and more importantly of the power of these unconscious conflicts. It's much more convincing when you feel it for yourself.

Ernest: This feels like a shift in the conversation, but I feel it's also related in a way. What were the advantages of Hans' horse phobia?

Eli: I think it allowed him to locate his own aggression outside of himself, in the horse, which would be a relief to not experience himself as murderous especially toward someone he loves.

Ezra: The last comment implies another advantage, namely that his trouble with his father would be located somewhere else. If he was aware that it was about his father, being that his father is much more difficult to avoid than horses, then he'd be much more anxious in a continuous way.

Instructor: Consistent with what you are saying, Freud (1926) speaks to the advantages that Hans' phobic symptom provided,

> This substitutive formation has two obvious advantages. In the first place it avoids a conflict due to ambivalence (for the father was a loved object too), and in the second place it enables the ego to cease generating anxiety. For the anxiety belonging to the phobia is conditional.

(p. 125)

And a little later Freud (1926) said, "… symptoms are created so as to avoid a danger-situation whose presence has been signaled by the generation of anxiety" (p. 129).

This is important to remember. The neurotic symptoms are produced in part to bind potentially overwhelming, unmanageable affect. They serve the function of the pleasure principle, to delimit unpleasurable stimulation caused by previously repressed urges and their representatives coming into consciousness. As you have described, we can see how Han's phobia removes the conflict of ambivalent feelings toward his loved father away from their relationship. As you also said, it takes those feelings out of himself. It's the horse that harbors cruel intentions, not him. It limits the anxiety to a specific and bounded situation, providing borders to what might otherwise be experienced as a ceaseless influx of interminable, traumatic excitation.

Bethany: The increasing centering of the patient's transference upon the analyst and the consulting frame itself create a similar border or boundary around the patient's affliction. Increasingly, over time, it's as if all of the trouble is located in that relationship and that itself is a kind of binding that may make the patient's suffering more tolerable.

Reyna: My relationship with my husband improved dramatically coincident with the increasing negative transference to my analyst.

Instructor: We can think here of the transference neurosis, the way the symptoms become transferred and located within the boundaries of the analytic relationship where they can be worked through psychically, but also in a way that has a binding analogous to the function the original symptoms provided. The neurotic symptoms have shifted onto the relationship with the analyst which is where we can have some traction to deal with these dynamics more directly and experientially. And as you just described, the conflicts in one's everyday life can abate given that they are more securely located in the analytic setting.

Midge: As analysts we have to respect the functions that are being served by the symptoms.

Instructor: What do you have in mind here?

Midge: It seems to me that if we move too quickly in an analysis to interpret and remove the patient's symptoms, we may be taking away the binding function of it that is desperately needed. We have to respect the symptoms and treat them carefully.

Instructor: Yes, before the transference neurosis has had time to develop and provide the kind of substitute binding that you've been speaking of.

Ernest: It makes sense to me for the transference to grow and build over time before interpreting symptoms. It can then be interpreted more within the transference.

Instructor: That's a good point. I also want to draw your attention to Freud's (1926) comment, "…anxiety arose originally as a reaction to a state of danger and it is reproduced whenever a state of that kind recurs" (p. 134). A little later Freud said (1926), "We cannot find that anxiety has any function other than that of being a signal for the avoidance of a danger situation" (p. 138).

Here, and much of the paper is about this central issue, I think that Freud is speaking to how the ego can acquire a certain amount of control over awareness of unconscious processes, a kind of unconscious decision-making process about when it is safe to feel and become aware of something versus when it is too threatening.

This also touches on the point made earlier about the importance of the function of perception. One has to be able to detect a change, some difference that clues us into anxiety in order to achieve this form of control and, as mentioned, this can be subtle and not easy to notice. This is related to the conceptualization of an unconscious ego that Freud described in *The Ego and the ID* (1923). He is speaking to the concept of an unconscious mind capable of determining what gains access to consciousness.

Your reflections clarify what goes on in analysis that facilitates making the unconscious conscious in ways that promote ego growth as opposed to traumatic anxiety. It seems to me that when analysis is going well, there is an increasing expansion of new material, previously blocked off, threatening experiences are, bit by bit, integrated into one's ego.

While there certainly is struggle and courage in this process, I think there is also an increasing sense of safety as well. It is not the illusory safety of avoiding dangers and risks. If the ego is monitoring unconsciously for when it is safe versus unsafe to become aware of an internal impulse, I would imagine that the interactions with the analyst would having a bearing on that. What do you think?

Eli: I'm thinking about my struggles to deal with intense negative transference, specifically trying to deal with my own feelings of failure and hopelessness. It seems to get in the way of facilitating a sense of safety in the patient, when I react in this way.

Natalie: I find it very difficult to not take the patient's attacks literally. When a patient tells me that the treatment isn't doing anything to help, and that nothing is changing, and that I'm just watching him suffer and doing nothing about it, it makes me feel helpless and very guilty.

Instructor: What do you do when you feel that way?

Natalie: I get quiet. I withdraw for a time until I can muster the courage to speak. When I can differentiate myself from the comments, take it less personally, I can see how what the patient is saying is so important and meaningful within their own developmental history.

Reyna: I can resonate with Natalie's experience. I wonder about a parallel process of sorts, like if we are unconsciously identifying with the patient's helplessness and traumatic anxiety in those moments. Being able to say something about it does provide the patient with a vicarious experience of it being possible to do something with that experience.

Ezra: This type of questioning of our own feelings of helplessness, being curious about it, reflecting on what it might mean is exactly what the patient isn't able to do in those moments of traumatic repetition. It just feels literally true, no question about it.

Instructor: That feels important. Can you say why you thought that was important to emphasize?

Ezra: I wonder if those feelings in the analyst might be inevitable and even necessary, that maybe the analyst has to go first in a way, begin to serve as a proxy for the patient to gradually connect to the analyst's reflective capacity in moments of hopelessness before he can do it himself.

Midge: I wonder if there is value not only for the patient to begin to connect with the analyst's ego functioning in itself, but also to connect with that very functioning in particular when s/he is under fire.

Instructor: Can you say more about what you're thinking here? This does feel like another moment of returning to an earlier conversation and taking another look at it, which is something we do in the practice of analysis itself.

Midge: It might be important for the patient to be able to experience their analyst feeling something similar to the helplessness or hopelessness that they feel, like a weaker version of it or a smaller dose of it, and then be able to do something reflective with it, after having struggled and suffered with it, but suffered with it only up to a certain point.

I've experienced this in my own analysis. I would feel utterly hopeless and convinced that I would never have the kind of life I wanted. I felt that my analyst would be somewhat taken aback by the intensity of my despair and hopelessness, something I normally keep under wraps. At first, he would seem speechless and somewhat overwhelmed for a time, and then would say something that felt very moving to me.

Instructor: What felt moving about it?

Midge: It felt like the words were reflecting a suffering that was like mine, even though it wasn't exactly the same as mine and the words weren't exactly a correct reading of what I was conflicted about. It seemed like he was talking from a place of having felt something a lot like what I had been feeling and he didn't collapse into the kind of hopelessness that I do. It was, like signal anxiety, like a smaller dose of what I was dealing with and it gave me a picture of it that seemed more manageable, less overwhelming for me.

Natalie: I wonder about the idea of conviction here, that if the patient can experience the analyst being able to think creatively when they appear to be in the grip of some state that's like the patient's hopelessness, that might have more resonance for the patient, more of a sense of conviction that this is thinkable.

Instructor: Yes. I noticed, Midge, that your analyst's intervention conveyed to you that he was feeling something similar to your felt experience, but you said that the words were not exactly correct. And, Natalie, you focused on the analyst being able to think creatively. I'm marking these comments because they speak to a form of action in the analyst's interpretation that has to do with doing something with the emotional experience they are in the grip of. The content of what the analyst is saying may not always match up with the patient's reading of what's going on with her, but it may still be helpful.

Reyna: That felt relieving for me. I am so often paralyzed by my own doubts about whether what I'm thinking is going on with a patient is right or not and I don't feel I can say anything to the patient unless I'm sure that I'm right about it. It's particularly painful when the patient is in a lot of pain and needs me to say something. What's relieving is that maybe trying to do something with the emotional experience is more important than getting it right.

Ezra: It also does potentially provide the patient with a more bridgeable gap between himself and the analyst.

Instructor: Say more about that.

Ezra: If the analyst is actively struggling with intense feelings and musters the capacity to reflect within that struggle, the patient may experience his comments as closer to where he is at emotionally, as something that he might be actually able to do himself in the future. If the analyst is too calm about it, untouched by it, and speaks calmly in a totally unruffled way from the start it may feel like a kind of thinking that is more out of reach for a patient in the grip of utter hopelessness.

Instructor: This reminds me of Vygotsky's idea of a zone of proximal development (Yasnitsky, 2018). This has to do with a gap between the learner and the teacher that was not too wide, where the teacher,

	or in this case the analyst would be able to do something the patient isn't yet able to do, but the patient could still recognize something of his struggle in the analyst as he's doing it.
Reyna:	I think whether or not this is helpful depends on the quantity of distress the analyst feels and unwittingly exudes. If the analyst is able to experience a relatively modulated version of painful feelings, like what Midge described, that may be useful. But if the analyst experiences excessive upset, like being taken over by negative feelings, that could leave the patient in a place of feeling hopeless about being able to fully express their suffering.
Instructor:	That's a great point.
Natalie:	What Reyna said about the analyst responding with a modulated version of what the patient is feeling shows the patient in action how to bind an overwhelming experience. In that way, they may be helping the patient learn how to develop signal anxiety.
Instructor:	Interesting idea. Are there any other thoughts before we come to a close today?
Bethany:	Freud's (1926) comments about Weltanschauung on page 96 really struck a chord with me. The wish for a handbook of life seems related to some struggles that have come up in the class.
	It reminds me of some of the frustrations when we talked about the ambiguities in our experience reading Freud, like wanting to have more definitive answers, a feeling of wanting to be told what it means and what to do with it, a wish for that all-knowing guidance.
Ernest:	I have felt frustrated when I have to work so hard to grasp what Freud is saying. Sometimes I have even used AI on my computer to try to get more clarity on it.
Reyna:	It reminds me of how angry I sometimes feel with my supervisor for not just telling me what to say to my patient. I feel like I'm not getting enough feedback, but now I'm wondering if it's about this wish for an all-knowing guidebook, wanting to be sure I get it right.
Midge:	I feel that way sometimes when I go to meetings and listen to presenters or lecturers. I get excited and hopeful that we will finally be given the answers, like something regressive happens where I want to be told what to do and what it all means and then I stop thinking for myself. That can get scary because I then notice moments when I can't access my own ideas.
Instructor:	It seems meaningful that this comment occurred on the heels of our earlier conversation about the idea of the value of the analyst's reflections coming out of an experience of a place of emotional struggle, and as Reyna clarified, a mitigated form of it.
Ezra:	I think there is value in having to go through our own struggle in our own way through our personal analysis, reading, studying, learning, and practicing analysis, but there is also something very

compelling about the fantasy of bypassing that, like someone could just tell us the answers. If we can just know the answers, we can solve these problems without getting so embroiled in the painful feelings.

Ernest: I think a lot of our patients come into therapy and analysis with that fantasy in mind. I say that, in part, because that's what I expected when I went into analysis. There is something very alluring about someone who has all the answers in a way that seems so divorced from any messy struggle and ambiguity, like someone who just has it in a seemingly effortless way, adding that maybe there is a wish to acquire experience and knowledge without having to go through the struggle to get it. It's like going to see the Wizard of Oz.

Natalie: It did feel amazing when I presented a case to a senior analyst who seemed to know what was going on with my case after just hearing an hour of material. I imagine that comes from many years of experience, although it can seem a little too easy from another perspective. I think the idea of effortlessness that we see in more senior analysts in meetings is an illusion. It looks that way because we don't see firsthand all the strain and effort that went into building the competence that we do see.

Midge: I wonder if we are looking for an analytic version of a god or messiah and if so why?

Instructor: You're expressing important tensions here. On the one hand, we have the sense that we do need to have our own personal experience of striving, of tussling with the ambiguity of our work and study, to do that at times painful work for ourselves and perhaps the scariest of all, to speak from our own personal experience, our own voice, which can feel like quite a risk. These are the efforts that lead to a felt sense of conviction and making what we know our own. On the other hand, the idea of someone who can stand above the fray, who can know these things without having to go through that arduous process of working in the dirt of life can be very attractive and compelling to us.

Bethany: I'm thinking about our mixed motives for embarking upon this career. We may on the one hand want to face our unconscious and engage in that work of encountering and contending with our own demons, but maybe we also want to be masters of our unconscious and then we see those who seem to have all the answers, those who we imagine as so above all the suffering as exemplifying that, like they have finally made it to the finish line of what we are seeking in training, the place of nirvana, the transcendence of psychic suffering once and for all. A kind of Shangi-La.

Instructor: One thing I'm noticing here is that we are emphasizing the struggle and pain pole of the process of following our own passionate curiosities in learning about psychoanalysis. That is certainly there and a vitally important part of our experience, but I wonder what we might be leaving out.

Bethany: You saying that reminds me of something else that is really appealing about speakers at conferences. I love it when they seem so unabashed about openly enjoying their work and talking about it. Like when they can laugh about their mistakes and have fun in their work.

Instructor: The word unabashed implies some conflict about allowing oneself to do that.

Reyna: Is it safer to enjoy someone else's unabashed excitement and pleasure in the work?

Ezra: I think it's the unabashed excitement yes, the joy in one's work, and also it's very relieving to hear someone speak openly about the parts of our work that feel ugly in an accepting way, acknowledging vulnerability, in contrast to the images we espouse that are so idealized about psychoanalysis.

Instructor: Could you say more about the parts of our work that feel ugly?

Ezra: For me, it comes back to what Freud (1930) wrote about in both early and later sexual development, and in much of his writing in Civilization and its Discontents. His comment, "homo homini lupus" (p. 111), man is a wolf to man, and that includes the analyst. We are confronted in our work with coming into more intimate contact with so much about ourselves that go against the ideals of what we are led to believe is human and some of the ideals of what it means to be an analyst only increase our guilt about these realizations.

A Note on What Happened

Our dialogue led to ideas about the transformation of automatic anxiety into signal anxiety with a number of clinical and personal examples shared. A repeated thread was drawn of how we are finding that there is much of our own struggles as analysts that overlap with what our patients face in analysis. The students articulated the experience of repeatedly encountering such tension and difficulty with their own unconscious in the process of the reading and studying Freud and relating his concepts to their personal lives and clinical work.

An interesting problem was raised, one that we might think of as associated with our identifications. Interestingly, when we are overidentified with particular ways of thinking about our work, we may find ourselves in a more rigid position, less flexible in terms of changing course when it is necessary.

This led to considerations about the experience of frustration with Freud's way of thinking where it can feel difficult to settle into one comfortable way of viewing the work. We explored how Freud's writings keep us unsettled, unraveling previous meanings. He doesn't let us get too comfortably attached to one way of looking at things. We could begin to see how this uncomfortable experience mirrors the nature of our psychoanalytic work.

An important tension became clear in our dialogue. On the one hand, we seem to have the sense that we do need to have our own unique experience of striving and contending with the ambiguity of our work and study, to do that at times painful work for ourselves and perhaps the scariest of all, to speak from our own core. On the other hand, the idea of someone who can stand above the fray, who can know these things without having to go through that arduous process of working it out for themselves is very attractive and compelling to us.

I thought that the students were increasingly open to expressing personal battles in practicing psychoanalytic clinical work. There was recognition of signs that, while we know that we are as affected by unconscious processes as our patients, we appear to be quite resistant to acknowledging it in the moments when that appears to be playing a role in impeding our work. Recognition of feelings of frustration with the way in which our reading of Freud keeps us unsettled, in a process within which there appears to be continuous movement and change. There was much of this experience of frustration in reading Freud that appeared to mirror the kinds of frustrations experienced within clinical psychoanalysis. A core theme emerged of experiencing a continuous tension between a wish for a comfortable stasis, a kind of safe harbor wherein one can feel solid in one's understanding versus the continuous unraveling of previously established meanings which move into novel ideas. Again, this led to another recognition of the parallel between the experience of reading Freud and feelings about the psychoanalytic process itself.

What felt very compelling to me were the students' comments about facing the emotions we experience in our work that we experience as ugly in contrast to ideals that we hold of what we should be. It led me to think more about how an open-minded approach to the work of analysis will inevitably lead us to face our own demons, what can feel like the parts of ourselves that we hate. Turning away from that, an ever present temptation, is self-alienating, which is only a hairsbreadth away from dehumanizing others.)

References

Alvarez, A. (2012). *The Thinking Heart: Three Levels of Psychoanalytic Therapy with Disturbed Children*. Routledge.

Freud, S. (1926). Inhibitions, Symptoms and Anxiety. SE 20: 75–174.

Freud, S. (1930). Civilization and Its Discontents. SE 21:57–145.

Yanitsky, A. (2018). *Vygotsky: An Intellectual Biography*. Routledge.

Part III
Reflections

9 Reflections on a Dialectical Approach for Teaching Freud

How Students Engaged with Freud's Ideas

At the beginning of the class, the students were candid about their prior struggles with Freud. They found it difficult to feel a sense of mastery of Freud's ideas. Some took it a step further and talked about feelings of shame associated with difficulties encountered in trying to understand Freud. But when invited the students would often flesh out their readings of Freud with their own imaginings and experiences within which they could see and feel the dynamics Freud wrote about in ways that felt tangible for them. They would actively relate Freud's concepts to their material realities in ways that brought Freud back to life.

For example, students would speak about how they felt transference themselves and considered what was clinically useful about the concept. This included the particular ways of conceptualizing transference and the language they preferred to use when describing it. These novel constructions fed their passion and curiosity for the study of Freud and analytic work itself.

In their efforts to engage with Freud and his concepts, they translated what he had written into a language of their own everyday lives, in that way, joining him across time. Their comments were a conversation with Freud, a dialogue between his ideas and their own experiences.

They often thought about the clinical value of Freud's concepts before considering their truth. This gave them room to think about the place of theory in clinical work, i.e., they appreciated the idea of theory emerging from clinical experience.

They also began to see a connection between what they described clinically and what they felt reading Freud. Freud's thought was a creative disturbance to one-sided ways of thinking. The struggle with reading Freud sparked a movement in their own thinking and stimulated new and more nuanced conceptualizations in their classroom dialogue. Bit by bit, they made Freud's ideas their own.

Over time they became more observant of Freud's thinking. They described how he would begin with one position and then bring in a completely opposing view.

DOI: 10.4324/9781003610977-12

They noticed that Freud created a tension of opposing ideas in the process of writing which stimulated his thinking and led to new but always tentative syntheses in search of new tensions. They also noticed the same thing happening in the class dialogue.

Reflections on My Process and Approach to Teaching Freud with Core Psychoanalytic Principles

Defining My Approach

In the following attempts to think about my experiences in teaching, I use words like *aim, aspire, try, struggle, cultivate,* etc. – all terms that emphasize conscious, deliberate intentions. While I do experience those strivings, especially when I am speaking at this level with students, i.e., letting them know explicitly what my frame for teaching Freud consists of, they are also convenient, heuristic ways of describing part of my experience. While I trust that these positions in my mind are there, I am not usually aware of them while I am teaching.

Over the years, I have learned to set a frame for students at the beginning of each course, laying out very clearly what it is I would like us to strive for in this approach to learning Freud. I have found this very helpful in terms of defining ideals that have been conducive to learning. Students have told me they appreciated knowing what kind of process I was aiming for, as well as what I expected of them.

As I define my objectives for the class, I emphasize the ideals of attending to aspects of our work that are most challenging for us, that we feel bad about, that seem impossible, and that we wish to hide. I see these aspects of our work as extremely important, and I normalize their presence as an expected part of the work we are striving to learn to do. By marking these objectives as group ideals to aim for, I hope to cultivate a collaborative group atmosphere in which we are all working together to speak as honestly as we can, and to associate such candor with feelings of respect.

I ask students to write papers in response to each week's readings, focusing on anything that resonated with them, disturbed them, particularly struck them, or stirred their curiosity. I ask them to relate their readings to their own experiences as clinicians and as patients in psychoanalysis. My focus here is on what students are able to find in their interaction with Freud's writings. The depth of their personal engagement with his text facilitates a process of discovery that becomes energizing and that contributes to a greater sense of agency in the learning process.

I try to establish an atmosphere within which participants accept and value collaborative work and are not afraid to bring in tensions that generate movement in the thinking process. We welcome listening for gaps in the conversation, and we notice what's missing. Repeatedly, students encounter tensions in their efforts to understand Freudian concepts, typically followed by a momentary relief associated with an organizing idea. Then a new tension arises, associated with something left out of the narrative, followed by a new idea that is more inclusive, only to be problematized later on, leading to more struggle and more complexity. Our dialogue typically evolves into more refined and broader ways of thinking, often leaving us with more questions than answers.

Looking back at my development as a teacher, I see the same oscillation between playful association and reflection that I aim to generate among my students – the same dialogue that defines psychoanalytic work. For me it began when I was in the grip of an internal struggle that led to seeing myself as a student among students. That helped me shed the demand to be the one who knows, and instead to relearn Freud within the ever-novel contexts of my shared interaction with students around their own clinical experiences.

This position is one that I have come to think of as a Zen-mind/beginner's-mind approach to engaging with Freud. It is one that relates very much to how an analyst best works with patients in psychoanalysis. Such a stance primes us to approach Freud with an open mind, with a focus on discovering him for ourselves within the context of our shared and individual interactions with his writings. This involves an active effort to forget what we know and/or think we know about Freud, our preconceptions, and instead imagine encountering his text for the first time, engaging in a shared exploration. We keep in mind that we are all starting at the beginning with Freud, in that we do not yet know how our engagement with him will manifest, or what novel illuminations of his ideas will come out of our dialogue. We learn together to approach Freud's text without a priori assumptions, with an increasing acceptance that there is no outside authority holding the golden key to understanding Freud. We have to think for ourselves and be open to being surprised by what we discover.

This is very relevant to the practice of psychoanalysis itself. We can acquire much knowledge from our readings and study of psychoanalysis, and yet in order to make meaningful contact with our patients, we have to strive to approach each of them with an open mind. We must learn and relearn everything within the context of the interactions that unfold in that singular treatment. Each analysis and each reading of Freud is unique.

Just as we track the subtle tensions in our patients that allude to the unsaid, the parts left out, and any contradictions or notable absences, so do I draw attention in our didactic discussions to points of tension between seemingly opposing ideas. For example, I once presented a patient whom some viewed as operating in a "high-functioning neurotic" structure, while others expressed concern and surprise by how much the patient was consciously aware of.

I often suggest that students try to pretend they have never read Freud before, that they act like a tourist in a foreign land and retain an openness to discovery. I contend that in order for us to understand the context of Freud's ideas in depth, it is necessary to experience the particular forms these ideas take on within the context of our interactions and dialogues with the text.

A Personal Engagement with Freud's Text

I have seen that students engage with Freud's text in very personal ways, thinking about their own struggles to practice psychoanalysis and psychotherapy – what is at the forefront of their concerns, interest, and, more broadly, the time and space within which they live. I have found that when students are able to link what they are reading to what is most present for them, the learning process comes to life. What they are learning is no longer something from the past that they were not involved in, but instead it is alive in the interaction.

This component of my approach involves an emphasis on personal engagement with the text. When invited to do so, students often flesh out their readings of Freud with their own experiences of relationship, within which they can see and feel the dynamics Freud wrote about in ways that feel personal for them. They actively bring these concepts into relation with their experiences in ways that are consonant with the fluidity with which Freud held them. We can see this clearly, for example, in how students brought the concept of transference to life as described in part A of this chapter.

I aim to focus on the centrality of savoring each moment with its own unique, ever-shifting contexts. I emphasize the notion of constant movement and interactions involved in these concepts and note that our process is not about pinning these ideas down to achieve an illusory feeling of mastery. I call attention to the importance of each student's living interaction with these ideas – trying them on, showing how their own flesh-and-blood struggles bring Freud's concepts to life and allow his ideas to taste the blood of the students' present-day, alive experiences and reciprocal interactions.

Relatedly, I find the idea of looking at Freud's concepts through a pragmatic lens quite useful and relevant. In teaching Freud, it is helpful to think about his concepts in the context of his struggles to create an analytic process. This pragmatic vantage point allows the students and me to get a feel for the tangibility and clinical use of these ideas in practicing psychoanalysis.

I have also recommended that students allow themselves to riff off of Freud's writings and our shared dialogue, keeping especially their own experiences as clinicians and as patients themselves present in their minds. This part of the process involves letting ourselves respond spontaneously to the text and our dialogue, without concern for whether our thoughts are right or wrong. It is analogous to a playful, creative process of brainstorming. This allows Freud's ideas to take on new shades of meaning. For example, I sometimes reflect back to the class how our discussion has moved from an initially one-sided view of what the patient does to the analyst, to one that has become much more complex and interactive.

It is from a place embodying these tenets that I can serve more as an experienced guide in the process of struggling in dialogue with Freud. This position involves reimagining quite vividly that this is my first time encountering Freud, as I noted I sometimes encourage my students to do, and resisting pressure to be the authority who thinks he "knows." This state of mind has allowed me to sink into a deeper, more open appreciation of the complexity and ambiguities inherent in the text and in the dialogue with students.

Appreciating Freud's Theory-Building

Something I emphasize early on is for students to reflect upon the clinical struggles that led Freud to develop the concepts we are reading about. For example, when thinking about Freud's recommendations regarding the frame, such as neutrality and evenly suspended attention, they initially suspended thinking about whether these are achievable or not, but instead focused on what effect these positions might have in terms of either facilitating or interfering with analytic aims.

I have emphasized our thinking about the similar struggles that led Freud to create his concepts, bringing our shared work into relationship with Freud's. This has allowed us to see the ways in which Freud's struggles, my struggles, their struggles, and our shared struggles all have parallels to the kinds of processes that are part and parcel of the work of clinical psychoanalysis.

I wish to engage with Freud's ideas as a living presence while also engaging with his thinking in a critical way, posing questions to him and wondering imaginatively what his answers might be, in addition to considering our own answers and questions. I try to join my students in thinking about the very real clinical struggles that led Freud to constantly change and develop new concepts – to appreciate the history of those ideas, the actual struggles from which they were born. The attitude that I convey is one that sees potential value across a wide range of Freud's diverse ideas, because each can help us accomplish real goals in our clinical work.

Rather than beginning with Freud's conclusions, I try to have students engage in a problem-solving experience alongside Freud. I note certain areas in the discussion, including tensions, pressures, difficulties, ambiguities, and areas, that could benefit from expansion and elaboration. I highlight the ideas we seem to be drawn to, as well as those we appear to be averse to.

For example, I sometimes suggest to the students that we try to imagine the Freud of the technique papers in contradistinction to the Freud who treated Dora. I focus on our observation of his apparent tensions and evolving viewpoints, juxtaposing them, past and present, and invited students to try to relate them to similar changes and contradictions in themselves and in our ongoing dialogue.

When a particular way of thinking seems to coalesce in the dialogue, I pose questions in order to bring in opposing ideas, drawing on these tensions in the service of critical thinking. For example, when students remarked on aspects of Freud's work with Dora that they appreciated, I asked if there was anything in the paper that raised concerns or seemed problematic, in an effort to bring in aspects of the treatment that weren't being addressed. This provided a bridge, similarly to my presentation of my own early-career clinical work, which helped demystify the process of a psychoanalyst's evolution.

Responses to my question about the Dora case brought in contrasting reactions that we could play with together. Explicating the generative tension sharpened our thinking and allowed us to establish a form of rhetoric not unlike Freud's own thinking process. I aimed for us to think about Freud's limitations, mistakes he made early on, and to contrast them with things he later learned as manifested in subsequent writings. I related these to our own limitations and experiences of making mistakes and missing things, in an effort to learn from them. This led to an interaction with ourselves and Freud's writing very much akin to Freud's capacity to engage in critical self-examination, a crucial skill for psychoanalysts. The spirit of this dialogue was one of curiosity in the face of disappointments and even failure. We contended with these experiences together in an open, nondefensive and noncondemning way, again quite similar to Freud's own processes.

"De-Authoritizing" Freud – and the Instructor

It is not uncommon for students to idealize Freud, nor is it uncommon for students to idealize senior analysts as able to know all the answers and to have conducted analytic treatments as finished achievements. At times, students may even feel that they themselves will never reach this level of knowledge and competence. But my position is one of deconstructing the tendency among students to idealize Freud's as well as the instructor's position as an authority, in ways that can unfortunately lead to passivity and disconnection from the actual work and struggle. Instead, I invoke the eventual progression to real, pragmatic analytic competence. This is a process that leads toward increased ownership for students in terms of taking greater responsibility for their own analytic formation.

Treating students – and patients – as partners in creating dialogue brings with it a fresh sense of wonder and curiosity. I have learned that I hold an array of lenses that have become part of my clinical and theoretical repertoire. These are ways of looking at things that, over time, have provided me with a useful frame for teaching Freud. They work together to create what feels like depth and richness to my experience. These vantage points enable me to feel a sense of fascination with the subject matter as it comes to life in discussion with students. They help me see and experience what the students are saying with a sense of fascination.

I have noticed that when I have spoken from a position of knowing and clarifying the meaning of the text in a more definitive way, a kind of bystander apathy ensues, wherein questions are posed for me to answer in ways that bypass the students' struggles with Freudian concepts. I have learned that this denies them the precious opportunity to collaborate in ways that will result in ownership of their knowledge of the material, a knowledge that bears the stamp of their own interactions with the text and with one another.

It has been important to me to work within myself to contact a genuine interest in the thoughts the students choose to share, to be open and receptive to learning from them. I want to listen for their originality, creativity, and the unique experience that each one of them brings to the material. When I am not immediately clear on what they are saying, I strive to listen for where their thoughts might be trying to go. I listen for the potential for deeper, more complex reflections that the student's contributions implicitly hold. I know from my own experience that being listened to in this way can lead to an increased sense of freedom to speak, as well as to an increased excitement about making new discoveries. I think this has been an important experience, in large part because the particular transference involved in the student-teacher relationship can stimulate both parties to continue trying to learn amidst the inevitable frustrations that arise in the process.

These interventions are grounded in lessons learned in the practice of psychoanalysis. They are related to Freud's ideas about the unobjectionable positive transference and the therapeutic alliance. Freud believed, that is, that the positive transference involved in the treatment alliance provides compensation for the painful aspects of analytic work, allowing patients to continue to associate freely and to speak in the face of emotional pain, in part because they have a bond of trust – even one of affection – with the analyst; patients come to feel that they are embarking on a shared exploration and experience of the unknown. The collaborative bond provides a compensating sense of safety vis-à-vis the ever-present threat of superego condemnation.

In the teaching context, I provide a similar compensation by making use of teacher/student/group transferences to promote analytic ideals and the development of a group ethos valorizing open dialogue and shared exploration. Anything that may have been an experience of shame, something to hide, can gradually become an object of study and fascination from which new, valuable discoveries can be gleaned. Analogous to the clinical function of the therapeutic alliance, the established sense of safety lends itself to the creation of a pedagogical alliance, one that facilitates freer self-expression, learning, and a more sublimated version of constructive self-criticism.

I have wanted us to listen to one another with the assumption that there is something potentially important and useful in whatever is being said. In listening from a place of trying to see what resonates in what we hear, I attempt to ferret out the direction in which these ideas might be headed. This requires using the imagination. My hope is that we can create an atmosphere within which we can play with the ideas expressed.

I sometimes observe out loud that the students have moved from feeling intimidated by Freud and ashamed about their difficulty in grasping his concepts, to being able to master a considerable amount about how he thought. They have progressed from feeling cowed by Freud's brilliance (quite an understandable experience) to asking themselves how he was able to do what he did.

Drawing on Multiple Perspectives

I aim to demonstrate that studying Freud is a lifetime process of encountering him repeatedly from various perspectives and at different experiential phases of life. I seek to convey an attitude toward his ideas that celebrates the spirit within which he himself held them, as unfinished and continuously evolving. I hope our discussions will have the quality of joining Freud in conversation, imaginatively associating with him, just as we do with one another, while remaining open to being carried along into unexpected places. I try to embody an openness to learning new, fresh ways of experiencing Freud through the students' ideas and spontaneous reactions.

I want us to feel the movement of Freud's ideas, both in the text itself and in our ongoing, shared reflections on these ideas. Toward this end, I try to create a culture within which we continuously reexamine our thoughts in light of new struggles that emerge in our discussion, cultivating an oscillation between past and present thinking, with an openness to finding new connections.

I suggest to students that we relate to Freud's text as a living presence that can be engaged with not as a finished product from the past, but as a present-day, unfinished, actively evolving, and unsettled dialogue to which we can make meaningful contributions. In some ways, I see this as analogous to the transference neurosis, a reenactment of the past within the analytic relationship. Past objects come to life within the interpersonal enactments that ensue within the analysis. I tell the students that they will each have their own transference to Freud, and that this will give rise to something unique and original for each of them. They will each give birth to their own version of Freud. I invite them to speak openly about their reactions to reading him, thereby illuminating the unique version of Freud that they have been in dialogue with. I draw attention to the way this manifests in the novel comments they make, with each of them participating in a separate and distinct dialogue with Freud, in addition to our participation in a shared dialogue with him.

Playing and Free Association

The free-association component of my approach is analogous to play. It grew out of my experiences working with children, where the child is invited to engage in free play. The free flow of this play leads to an unfolding of material that would otherwise feel too dangerous to speak of. Similarly, a sense of safety develops here in the student group when there is shared agreement that part of our process will be making use of this psychoanalytic tool in order to see where our thoughts go as we read and discuss Freud's writings. There is an explicit suspension of criticism in this dimension of our work.

I ask students to allow themselves to associate freely to the readings and the dialogue in our class meetings, to engage in an imaginative exercise wherein we are brainstorming with Freud, permitting ourselves to freely follow the train of our spontaneous associations. Our task is to suspend critical judgment of ourselves and each other during these moments of association. We react to one another's comments in the spirit of finding something of value and letting ourselves respond with spontaneous associations of our own.

At the outset, I have in mind the notion of holding a tension between inviting a free-flowing associative process, on the one hand, while also trying to anchor it with clinical material and written summaries, on the other – added information, that is, that synthesizes the concepts with core themes from our discussion. I like to emphasize these as in-process ideas, noticing their movement and sequence from multiple angles, while tailoring the material to what feels most relevant to the students.

After we have shared playful associations with the text, I then invite reflection on the ideas that were generated. I emphasize a process of discovery through dialogue; that is, I notice and reflect back to students how they appear to be working with Freud's ideas, highlighting the movement and themes in their dialogue. We repeatedly return to ideas previously shared, but often from a new vantage point.

It has been striking to note how often graduate students and analytic candidates, in their course evaluations, have described their experience of a class taught in this way as fun, stimulating, alive, and playful. Those descriptions resonate with me as well; I feel those same things in my experience of teaching, and I find that positive and meaningful memories of my earlier experiences as a student are rekindled.

Supporting Students' Learning

As noted, I encourage an approach to learning Freud through dialogue, including posing questions, sharing reactions, associations, and reflections upon associations. I valorize open sharing of challenges as inherent to the learning process. This includes the students' own personal experiences of resistance in their clinical work, as well as in response to reading Freud. In order to further cultivate a sense of safety in speaking freely, I suggest a way of listening that holds the attitude of not treating any human experience as foreign to ourselves – a stance that I believe Freud himself endorsed.

At the beginning of the class, when invited, the students are often able to be quite candid about their prior battles with Freud. Many comment on how difficult they have found their experience of learning Freud's ideas; they feel they are being asked to master a dead language. I then invite students to openly share the details of their difficulties, especially the things they have felt bad about in their interactions with the text and in our dialogue, as well as in their clinical work. I emphasize the value in creating an attitude within the group of openness to these experiences. As mentioned earlier, by making this an explicit ideal to aspire to, my hope has been to counteract a tendency toward self-condemnation that I have observed in many students over the years. I note how important it is for us to have a space in which we can shed our pretenses and get real with each other about the anguish associated with our internal obstacles to doing this incredibly difficult work.

Our open exploration of our own resistances in doing clinical work has felt quite fruitful in terms of experientially fleshing out Freud's writings on unconscious defenses and unconscious resistances. For example, students have talked about their experience of trying to speak to what feels like important points of urgency, yet being held back from doing so in spite of their conscious intentions. Moments of punitive thinking were noted and explored, manifesting as a tendency toward self-blame in the face of one's own resistance. Eventually, there was an increasing acceptance of resistance as inherent to the process of learning and practicing psychoanalysis, as well as a new-found appreciation for the clinical value of this concept.

This ethic has allowed us to more clearly see the significant role that our own resistances to unconscious processes play in our difficulties with Freud and the practice of psychoanalysis. It also serves to remind us of the very important fact that we are struggling with the same kinds of unconscious dynamics that we try to help our patients with. This reminder aims to help students appreciate that our respectful attention to our own resistances to the learning and practice of psychoanalysis is a crucial lifelong practice, essential for our ongoing development as psychoanalysts.

Many students experience the difficulty and struggle to learn as a threat to their self-esteem – leading, at times, to feelings of shame and self-condemnation. I try to reframe the experience of difficulty, hard work, confusion, and even suffering as an expected part of this particular learning process and as a valuable sign of deep engagement in that process. In addition, I strive to find something in the students' efforts, particularly during times of heightened frustration, to genuinely value and hold on to. This helps cultivate a sense of safety in the class, in large part by counteracting the kinds of harsh superego attacks that can inhibit open expression in dialogue.

I am invested in students' ability to begin to gain comfort with concepts that may have earlier seemed confusing, ambiguous, or difficult to grasp – but this is not emphasized in an over-zealous, fixed, or simplified manner. Instead, I try to convey my conviction that struggle, tension, and uncertainty are inherent to the process of learning psychoanalysis and to emphasize the solidarity of our efforts in tension with Freud and with one another as we grapple with these complex ideas.

This valorization of active personal effort and hard work as a crucial dimension of learning involves an added component. It is one thing to advocate for the importance of difficulty, intense effort, ambiguity, confusion, and suffering, but quite another to join students in the process of such grappling with the text. As I began to describe in my introduction to this book, I have found myself increasingly joining students in such struggles to actively dialogue with the concepts that we are learning, to show my own tensions in the process of learning and exploring the material in fresh new ways. As much as I am able, I try to be transparent about tensions that come up for me in our dialogue, while simultaneously conveying my conviction that these tensions are valuable and to be accepted as inherent to our work.

I demonstrate parallels between students' efforts to read Freud and our efforts as clinicians to practice psychoanalysis – that is, how the dialectical nature of our interaction with Freud's writings parallels the dialectical relationship in the practice of psychoanalysis. Increasingly, I have come to view the experience of grappling with Freud's writings as a flight simulator for the practice of clinical psychoanalysis.

Students have commented on the difficulties they encounter in digesting the reading material. I attempt to slow things down, to create an atmosphere wherein studying Freud is viewed as an ongoing process, one in continuous movement that is not meant to be fixed as a form of dogma. Taking into account the culture of our pressured, fast-paced, rushed lives in today's world, and how this can manifest in an oppressive feeling that we must rapidly master new ideas, getting them "nailed down" as quickly as possible, I try to embody instead an unhurried approach to learning. I emphasize the value of taking our learning slowly, of experiencing the encounter with these ideas within the frame of lifelong learning. The image of returning to the river of Freud many times throughout life, and of it being different every time, has been a guiding light in my mind.

This is a respectful approach in that it embodies an empathic way of learning, keeping in mind the personal struggles behind these concepts, giving us permission to try them on and see what they can do for us and our work. In a way, this reminds us that these theories are maps, or lenses, that we employ as useful tools, but we should take care not to overidentify with them. We can draw upon them in our efforts to approximate truth and insight, but ultimately they do not completely capture the truth of our experiences. There will always be something new to discover.

We have therefore been better able, I think, to engage in questions such as: "Do these ideas help me in my work as an analyst?" "What do these ideas do for me and the patient in the consulting room?" "What do they help me achieve?" "Do these ideas help me with the most pressing struggles I face in my work?" "If they do not help me, might they be helpful for another analyst, perhaps one of a character type different from mine?" "Do these ideas enable me to experience a sense of fascination and wonderment as I listen to my patients?"

This aspect of my approach further counteracts the tendency to feel shame around one's experience of difficulty and struggle, lending itself to an atmosphere of safety and openness in the group. One example of this came up in our discussion of Freud's Dora case. Here, by showing Freud's early struggles and falterings in relation to his evolution as an analyst and relating these to our own analogous efforts – e.g., showing the tension and movement between Freud's early work and later understandings – we were able to facilitate the experience of a microprocess of psychoanalytic development.

When students inevitably return to earlier unsettling conversations, at times repeatedly, I remind them that earlier views can change. For example, on one occasion, I underscored how the discussion of an idea from control mastery theory demonstrated an important development – that is, from initially focusing on an unconscious plan coming exclusively from the patient, to a dialectic of opposing forces, both within the patient and interpersonally in interaction with the analyst. I view this as an important shift toward a more expansive and interactive way of conceptualizing the clinical situation.

Two Sides to Approaching New Material

I am reminded of something I noticed in my early studies of Freud. In discussions with other students, there was a tension between competing trends. On one side, I would experience a childlike curiosity, an openness to exploring, wondering about, and playing with these ideas. On the other side was something else: i.e., moments of a grasping feeling of trying to acquire knowledge, to have it, to hoard it, a feeling of tightness, perhaps a tight-sphincter feeling of mastery and pride.

I would notice that in those latter moments, I would lose the depth and play of what I was pursuing, and my fascination would die. Other students also seemed to lose the joy of learning at such times. The feeling of escaping from such narrow confines of "knowing" to a new opening, a jump to a higher level from which I could see a more complex image of life, coincided with the feeling of being freer to think spontaneously. Everything would become interesting and joyous again, reinvoking a state of wonder.

I've been wondering about that grasping side, with its tendency to firmly grip what we have gleaned, to put a flag on it. It's a wonderful feeling, after a period of struggle, frustration, and hard work, to suddenly grasp something that has felt so elusive. There can be an inclination to turn that new knowledge into a shrine, an emblem of our success. That for me is where the movement stops, at least for a time. That's where the move to a complex, freer view tends to degrade into something one-dimensional, wherein deeper interconnections and wider perspectives are foreclosed. Perhaps that's an inevitable part of being human; maybe it's one pole of a dialectical process of learning. It may serve to provoke us in ways that keep us striving to be free, to fight, to struggle for that fleeting experience of mental freedom, which is not a thing but a process that keeps us in a reciprocal, systemic state of movement – i.e., the student-teacher dialogue.

Learning from My Own Learning

It is personally meaningful for me to have students know that I am taking their ideas seriously, that these ideas are important enough to include as crucial to our evolving thinking as a collective in working together, building on the ideas that each student contributes to the discussion. As a student myself, it was my great good fortune to find two teachers in particular, one in college and one in psychoanalytic training, who thought I might have something meaningful to contribute to the collective discussion. The origin of a spark of life was ignited in me, one that would grow into a lifetime of joyful learning. The perpetual reenactment of those memories through teaching keeps the flame of those experiences alive for me.

I remember with much affection the psychoanalytic teachers I had who seemed not only to truly enjoy and love their subject, but also love the life of the dialogue itself. Those teachers appeared to be in it primarily for the love of a particular kind of unfolding process. Another way of putting it would be to say that some teachers appeared to reach a point at which they really lost themselves, i.e., their self-conscious sense of self, their conscious egos, and became as if one with the learning process, incarnating a love of shared discovery in pursuit of the unknown.

My teachers who taught from a place of love of exploring the unknown were those who gave me images of future possibilities for myself, for my own potential to participate in something that felt meaningful and joyful. They created conditions in which we students could experience a series of vantage points from which to view our world, trying on the different views to see what happened, and over time creating our own kaleidoscopic view. These teachers also made the learning process fun. That was a life-saving revelation for me. I began to see a future life to aspire toward, one that I wanted to pursue, conveyed by these teachers who really loved what they did and felt fascinated by it. A richer, more variegated lens for looking at my own world emerged and made everything light up in living color.

Conclusion

Psychoanalysis is grounded in a dialectical framework. Clinical psychoanalysis is a dynamic, evolving dialogue. Learning Freud's concepts requires finding them within oneself, akin to how a patient discovers previously unknown parts of themselves in analysis. Teaching Freud from a position of knowing asphyxiates interaction. It is no more helpful than telling a patient of your formulation without allowing them the time and space to become acquainted with their own ideas and experiences over time through reciprocal dialogue.

Along the way, I've come to some general conclusions:

1 Students and patients learn best when they feel safe enough to show their thoughts, feelings, and vulnerabilities openly.
2 The aim I've found most conducive to teaching Freud is to approach every class as an opportunity to discover something new.
3 Poor clinical work treats the patient as a theoretical type, already known; ineffectual teaching treats Freud as a fixed text.
4 The teacher's acceptance of the role of being a fellow learner builds a climate instilled with the openness and trust necessary for learning Freud's concepts through collaborative dialogue.
5 The teacher who is able to lose themselves and follow the current of the classroom dialogue cultivates an experience wherein ideas come to life.
6 The teacher who listens not only to what students are saying but also to where their ideas are trying to go plants seeds for novel ideas.
7 The most important authority the analyst and teacher have to offer involves having learned through experience how to guide and facilitate a particular kind of process, one which stimulates an atmosphere of discovery.

There is a striking parallel between students learning Freud and patients learning about themselves in psychoanalysis. Both engage with ideas that are felt to be foreign or threatening to them, whether due to defensive processes or because of the age of the text, it's language, translation, contradictions, and ambiguities. In both cases, it is the living, dynamic, fluid dialogue with a trusted other that bridges the chasm. The role of being a student among students is a vital part of building that trust. It is one wherein the teacher, rather than imposing certainty, creates space for the student's own understanding to emerge.

In retrospect, I've realized that teaching, just as one's analysis, plays an important role in furthering the process of becoming one's own kind of analyst. It's not only about learning Freud's concepts – it's about finding them within oneself in such a way that they can be reconfigured to the contours of our own being and subsequently integrated into one's life and practice. Freud himself said that his way of practicing psychoanalysis reflected his own singular experience and character, adding that others may be driven to approach patients in different ways (Freud, 1912). Psychoanalysis can take on a vast range of possible shapes across individual psychoanalysts. The transmission in teaching Freud involves making space for the content and knowledge to materialize in the form of an active praxis through dialogue.

Reference

Freud, S. (1912). Recommendations to Physicians Practicing Psychoanalysis. SE 12: 109–120.

Index

For Product Safety Concerns and Information please contact our EU
representative GPSR@taylorandfrancis.com
Taylor & Francis Verlag GmbH, Kaufingerstraße 24, 80331 München, Germany

www.ingramcontent.com/pod-product-compliance
Lightning Source LLC
Chambersburg PA
CBHW052006270326
41929CB00015B/2803